Marketing Research for M

Sunny Crouch became Chief Marketing (
Before that, she was course manager for th
studies at Portsmouth Polytechnic and sen
market research and advertising. She spent seven years as director for short
courses in marketing research at the Institute of Marketing and, from
1978–1982, was a member of the Market Research Society's academic
standards committee.

Sunny Crouch is the co-author of a book on mass media research. She has
worked in product and export management and is a consultant for
consumer, industrial and service organizations.

Marketing Research for Managers

Sunny Crouch

Pan Books
in association with Heinemann

First published 1984 by William Heinemann Ltd
This edition published 1985 by Pan Books Ltd,
Cavaye Place, London SW10 9PG
in association with William Heinemann Ltd
© Sunny Crouch 1984   9 8 7 6 5 4 3 2 1
ISBN 0 330 28699 4
Printed and bound in Great Britain by
Cox & Wyman Ltd, Reading

Preface

Many books on marketing research are aimed at developing the technical expertise of the intending or actual research practitioner. This book is aimed at those who are intending or actual managers with a need to *use* research rather than practise it. It owes its existence to managers from many different areas of industry who have attended courses run by the author. They demonstrated the need for a book aimed squarely at the individual who wishes to use marketing research as an aid to better decision-making. Their feedback suggested that the material was both relevant and useful.

These managers attended courses to learn more about marketing research because they believed, as I do, that the more a manager knows about this management tool, then the more effective he or she can be in using it. The book therefore aims to develop a better-informed approach to the use of marketing research as an aid to decision-making, by giving an insight into how marketing research is carried out. No previous knowledge of the subject by the reader is assumed, and the areas which normally receive a statistical treatment are here explained without the use of statistics.

My warm good wishes to all readers for their success in improving their managerial ability through applying the techniques of marketing research described in the following pages.

Sunny Crouch

Acknowledgements

In presenting this book, my thanks are due to all those who have assisted in its preparation, and who will recognize their influence in these pages. The managers referred to in the preface provided both the impetus and many of the examples. Jackie Marrian suggested that I write the book in the first place and encouraged me in the early days of my doing so. She and Bob Maxwell (of Croydon College) were conscientious reviewers whose constructive criticisms led to many improvements as the manuscript developed. Dr Edgar Hibbert (of the Institute of Marketing) supported the book in its Heinemann edition.

Certain individuals have made major contributions in particular areas. Here I acknowledge my debt of gratitude to: Lionel Gordon (of Gordon Simmons Research Ltd) for Chapter 9, Nigel Spackman (of RSGB Research Surveys of Great Britain Ltd) for Chapter 11, Jim Basker (of Portsmouth Polytechnic library) for the secondary desk research section in Chapter 4, and Neil Botten (of Portsmouth Polytechnic Department of Mathematics and Statistics) for reviewing Chapter 10.

I have received help from many other people and would like to thank them all for their ready co-operation. Some are listed here, but I am no less grateful to those who are not. Tim Bowles (Audits of Great Britain Ltd), Peter Clark (The Market Research Society), Paddy Costigan (RSGB Research Surveys of Great Britain Ltd), Cliff Holmes (Business Decisions Ltd), Tony Lunn (Cooper Research and Marketing (CRAM) Ltd), Philip Mitchell (British Market

Research Bureau Ltd), Alan Morris (Communications and Information Technology (CIT) Ltd), Brenda Setchell (The Market Research Society), Alan Wolfe (Ogilvy and Mather Ltd). My thanks are due, too, to my competent and willing typists Joyce Moore and Margaret Khan.

Writing a book when you are also doing a full-time job is never easy and I am particularly grateful to the staff of Heinemann who undertook the final editing.

Most of all, I acknowledge with gratitude the constant support and encouragement from my husband, without whose willingness to forego so much of my time and his comfort this book would never have been possible. I dedicate it to him.

There will, of course, be omissions, errors and short-comings in the book and these are my sole responsibility. If any reader would care to write to me about them, then I would be happy to make improvements should the book be sufficiently welcomed to run to a second edition!

Contents

1 Introducing Marketing Research

1.1 INTRODUCTION

Politicians look anxiously at the results of political polls. They indicate the standing of the party in the country, and the standing of its leader. They show what issues are most significant to the electorate and which seats are most likely to be marginal at the next election. Politicians react to polls by putting extra effort into areas of the country which are 'marginal' i.e. where additional effort to 'market' the attractions of the party are more likely to pay off. When the polls say the leader is unpopular, pressure is put on the leader to change stance so as to become more 'popular'. When negative reaction to a leader is strong and sustained, the party thinks of appointing a new one. Which issues to push as the main planks of the party's electoral platform are also influenced by the polls. There is no point in strongly pursuing issues about which the electorate is unconcerned – that is not the most effective way to win votes.

> 'Cheap hand-tool imports from Taiwan and China, like hammers, spanners, pliers, planes and socket sets have grabbed a £60m share of Britain's £400m market. . . . With tools only being used a few times a year, the importers have spotted that not everyone in the do-it-yourself boom wants to pay £10 for, say, a Stanley Steelmaster hammer. Says the marketing director of a British DIY superstore chain, "British manufacturers have not geared themselves up to the new shopping habits of people in Britain". A buyer with another DIY group adds, "British manufacturers still have not woken up to the need for more tools in the middle price range".

It's not the first time that British manufacturers have failed to read the market right!'

(*The Sunday Times*, 5 December 1982)

'It is not just steel and cars. How about Britain's once-proud furniture industry? Output fell 40% from its pre-1979 peak as destocking retailers chased falling sales and imports from Eastern Europe took hold at the cheapest end of the market. Factories have closed like train doors in the rush hour and even the best names, like G-Plan, are registering alarming losses.'

'A marketing man has spent the past three years building his own cabinet business by buying ailing factories cheap, cutting over-heads to the bone and tailoring products strictly to the market. His secret for doubling sales is disarmingly simple. Instead of designing products and financing them to cover costs, he reverses the process, finding out from retailers and mail order houses what is wanted and at what price, and then engineering furniture to fit. Of the failed firms he has bought and turned into profitability he says, "Their products were over-engineered. They were building in value that people just aren't prepared to pay extra for." '

(*The Sunday Times*, 5 December 1982)

'What is the general attitude of the overseas buyer towards the purchase of products from Britain? A survey suggests that buyers are very willing to consider buying British. However, they do have reservations about the ability of UK companies to supply goods of the right quality, at the right price, and, most importantly, to provide the necessary delivery and aftersales service. And buyers say that no one from Britain comes to see them. When they do, they are often ill-equipped to speak the local language. Export organizations need to consider whether they are paying enough attention to the key organizations whose purchasing is vital to a product's success. Like their UK counterparts, foreign buyers are professionals who expect regular visits, comprehensive product information, attractive prices and a sense of commitment from the manufacturers seeking their business. However, research among senior buyers in major Continental European retail groups indicated that many are totally unaware of the size of the relevant market, of shares held by manufacturers, and of advertising and promotional spends. Where figures are quoted, they are often inaccurate or out of date. These views are then reflected in the stock being carried and the prominence given to certain brands.

'What, then, should UK manufacturers do to gain distribution through these important wholesale and retail outlets? First, they must study their market in sufficient depth to be able to measure the relative strengths of the various groups, the products which they stock, their pricing strategy and their overall merchandising policies. This has to be related to the known strengths of competitive manufacturers, so as to identify gaps in the market. Standards of packaging and presentation are much higher in Continental markets because consumers are willing to pay for quality appeal in a way which, it is often said, the UK consumer will not. One of the major benefits deriving from a determined effort to generate Continental business is the development of a marketing package which can tap new demand in the UK, so creating further profitable business.'

(*Marketing*, 18 November 1982)

'Mini-holidays are seen as one of the few growth markets left to the declining UK hotel industry. The bedrock customers of the business are professional or semi-professional people aged over 45, whose children are grown up. "There are stacks of people with all the right credentials who have not yet sampled a mini-holiday," says the marketing director of a hotel chain. "We estimate that only 10% of ABCI's (people of higher social grade) have bought the product so far. That is a measure of the potential".

'It is a business built on marketing skills, virtually from scratch, and it is still evolving. The weekend occupancy rate in London hotels in winter used to be 25% in the 1960s and there was massive scope for selling on marginal costings. Now, some hotels are busier at weekends than they are midweek, and mini-holidays have become a central part of their business, and no longer merely contribute to overheads. The "perceived price" is important to customers, "People can see they're paying less than the full tariff".'

(*Marketing*, 18 November 1982)

1.2   WHO NEEDS MARKETING RESEARCH?

What these stories have in common is that they illustrate the value of good, up-to-date and detailed market information in making marketing decisions vital to the success of an organization. This holds equally true whether the 'marketing' is concerned with national or local government, fast-moving or durable consumer goods, trade outlets, industrial organizations, services or non-profit-making bodies.

'Marketing' is defined by the Institute of Marketing as, 'the management process responsible for identifying, anticipating and satisfying customer requirements profitably'. This definition identifies the crucial part marketing research has to play in designing and implementing an effective marketing strategy. Marketing research provides the mechanism for identifying and anticipating customer requirements and for measuring whether customers are satisfied by these product offerings. For non-profit-making organizations the concept of 'profitability' used in the definition may be translated to 'using resources optimally, i.e. gaining maximum customer satisfaction through the most effective deployment of resources'. It is in this sense that marketing and marketing research have just as important a contribution to make in the public sector and in non-profit-making organizations as in the private sector.

That customer requirements must be paramount in the thinking of any organization providing goods or services is illustrated by the anecdotes with which this chapter begins, by the growth of imports to the UK, and by the demise or declining profitability of British companies whose goods do not meet current market requirements. The problem for many British organizations has been their lack of a mechanism for detecting change in the market-place. Markets have become more competitive, the pace of technology has accelerated change, and consumers are readier to make changes. Organizations can no longer afford to rely simply on making a good product for it to be successful in the long term. It now has to meet a real market need in a very precise way, and perhaps for a shorter period of time than in the past. This book is about the mechanisms available to managers to make organizations more responsive to their markets. This is the province of marketing research and hence the title of this book. It is properly termed 'marketing research' rather than the more colloquial 'market research' because it is research applied not only to measuring and identifying markets and market characteristics, but also to measuring the effectiveness of marketing decision-making. Research can be applied in deciding which products or services to offer, what their characteristics should be, the price at which they should be sold, the outlets through which they should be sold and the selling and advertising messages which are likely to have greatest appeal. Others would argue that there is a separate type of research called 'social research' which is used by those in local and national government in making decisions about the provision of social services. A further debate is concerned with whether research in industrial and service markets differs from research in consumer markets.

This book takes the view that the techniques developed for marketing research in the cause of more effective marketing of fast-moving consumer goods have proved themselves equally effective in contributing to decision making about resource allocation and market response in all consumer markets, in political and social policy decision making, in industrially based markets and in service-based markets. The techniques introduced here are generally applicable in all of these areas, although there may be differences of detail and emphasis in their application.

1.3 WHO SHOULD READ THIS BOOK?

The belief that the research techniques dealt with in this book can, and indeed should, be used by anyone with responsibility for resource allocation, whether they are in product-based, service-based or public-sector-based organizations, accounts for the fact that its main emphasis is to offer an outline of the process and techniques of research, which the reader can apply to his own management situation. The aim is to aid managers in generating reliable research-based information; to enable them to judge the reliability of research produced for them; and to give them a basis for knowing when, and when not, to use research.

It is assumed that managers who will find the book most useful are those who wish to use marketing research as one of the tools of a manager's trade and not those whose major responsibility is for the design or conduct of research. For this reason, the emphasis is on the manager's role in commissioning and controlling, rather than conducting, research.

Nevertheless, the manager who must do his own research should find considerable guidance to help in that task. It is not suggested that reading this book is all the preparation necessary for carrying out a 'do-it-yourself' research project. In fact, the reaction of most managers learning something about marketing research for the first time is, "I didn't realize this was such a technical area!" That is not to say, of course, that the manager who is interested will never be able to carry out all or some of the parts of a research project, but simply that the aims of this book are to offer an introduction to, and appreciation of the subject. For the majority of managers this is all they require. Those who wish to take their interest further after reading the book, should consider following the suggestions given at the end of the book in, "Where do you go from here?".

Although this book is aimed primarily at the practising manager with a need to use marketing research, it provides worthwhile reading for those studying business subjects. It is particularly appropriate as background reading on marketing research for those studying general management, or specific areas of it such as marketing or finance. Students following business or management degree courses, BEC courses or Diploma courses of the Institute of Marketing or the Communications, Advertising and Marketing Foundation, will also find the book useful as an introduction to their studies in this area.

1.4 WHAT DOES THE BOOK COVER?

Marketing research involves the analysis of marketing problems and techniques for the collection of data to assist in developing good solutions to them. It is concerned with identifying and anticipating customer requirements and measuring satisfaction with products and services made available. It also produces data used in assessing and controlling the performance of an organization.

This book aims to assist managers in any organization to become more informed, and therefore more effective, research users. It introduces marketing research by explaining:

	Chapter
What marketing research is	1
Why an organization needs it	2
What research can be carried out within an organization	3
What research data is already available	4
How research surveys are carried out	5–10
How research services are bought	11
How research is used	12–14
How to build on this introduction	15

Two features of the text will be particularly useful for new users of research. Chapter 4, on 'Off-the-peg' research, guides the reader to sources of readily available information. Two sources not readily identifiable by the new user are listed and indexed: syndicated research services and omnibus surveys. These listings form a helpful 'ready reference' for those unfamiliar with the research industry. Another highly practical feature of the book is the 'Research Users' Guides' and their accompanying 'Notes' which form the basis of Chapter 14. The objective here is for the new research user, having read the book, to be able to consult the Guides and say, 'With this problem, I have these research possibilities for finding an answer'. Any technical terms not already covered in the text are explained in the accompanying notes, and all research suggestions are referenced to sections of the text where explanations appear. Because this is an introductory text, it makes no assumptions of background knowledge. Chapter 7, which deals with sampling, and Chapter 10, which deals with statistical analysis of data, quite deliberately avoid the use of statistical formulae. The aim is to give the research user an understanding of what statistical approaches can do to data, and why they are useful and sometimes essential. Research users do not need to be statistically competent themselves, but they should appreciate the contribution statisticians can make in the design and analysis of research surveys. It is not the aim of this book to teach basic statistics, so those wishing to carry out the statistical manipulations described will need to have, or to acquire, the appropriate statistical expertise. Chapter 15 suggests some books which will assist in this. It also suggests other ways in which those wishing to develop further their interest and expertise in marketing research after reading this introductory text, can do so.

1.5   USING THIS BOOK

Each chapter is prefaced by a detailed listing of contents, and ends with a summary. The summary should be consulted for an overview of chapter content, and the chapter contents pages will identify where particular topics are dealt with. This format will help those who wish to consult the book on particular topics. For those who want to introduce themselves to marketing research by reading the book right through, it will probably be helpful to read the summary of each chapter before reading the chapter. This will prepare the reader with a framework for what is to be found in the chapter itself and learning will be further reinforced when the summary is read again at the conclusion of the chapter.

Throughout the book the word 'product' can be taken as meaning 'product or service'. Services are amenable to research in the same way that products are, and can be considered the 'products' of the companies which provide them. Also, the words 'him' or 'he' have been used when talking about managers, and 'her' or 'she' when talking about interviewers. This reflects the fact that in practice most managers are men and most interviewers are women. It is not meant to suggest that there are not many highly competent and successful women managers or men interviewers, and readers are asked to take the words 'him' or 'he' as also meaning 'her' or 'she', and vice versa.

2 Getting Started

2.1 INTRODUCTION

All kinds of organizations use, and need to use, marketing research techniques. The traditional, and still the biggest users, are the large fast-moving consumer goods companies. Increasingly marketing research is being applied by smaller organizations, by manufacturers of consumer durable products, of industrial products, and by suppliers of services. In recent years it has been employed by non-profit making organizations like charities, churches, official bodies and by Government departments at both local and national levels. Despite diversity in the aims and objectives of these widely differing organizations, what they have in common is the need to make decisions about the allocation of resources so as to be as effective and efficient as possible in achieving their goals. Resource allocation decisions can be improved by the acquisition of accurate, relevant and timely data and it is this which market research seeks to produce.

Getting started as a research user begins by answering three questions:

What does the organization need research for?
What type of research data are there?
How can the organization obtain the research it needs?

2.2 WHAT DOES THE ORGANIZATION NEED RESEARCH FOR?

Being able to define precisely what marketing research can and should be doing for the organization is the first step in achieving it. One way of doing this is to reflect on the organization as a whole and decide what are its most pressing problems.

The answers below were given by delegates to the Institute of Marketing's introductory course on market research:

From an insurance company: 'We are a relatively small company in a growing but fiercely competitive business. We need research information to decide how to increase business from out existing customers and attract business from new customers.'

From a whisky manufacturer: 'Whisky sales generally are in decline. We need research to evaluate the potential of new whisky-based drink products. We also need research to select the most effective packaging to maximize product sales in an increasingly self-service market.'

For an advertising agency: 'Our clients look to us for advice on advertising strategy. How can research help in providing more effective advertising?'

From a carpet manufacturer: 'The floor-coverings market is in decline and over-supplied. We know that design is an important factor in the market. We need research to help us maintain and improve market share by identifying appealing designs and appropriate target markets for them.'

From an office equipment supplier: 'Technically we are able to produce a range of new electronic information transfer products. We need research to discover whether a market exists for these possible products, who our potential customers might be, and whether they know our name and would buy from us.'

From a manufacturer of industrial machinery: 'We have never done market research and have no way of evaluating our performance in the market. We need research to establish our market size and indicate the type of machinery we should be selling and to whom we should be selling it.'

Another approach to defining why a particular organization needs marketing research is to consider the range of uses to which it is already put by other organizations. Six main areas are listed here.

2.2.1   CORPORATE PLANNING

Research is used in corporate planning in order to make decisions about what goals the organization as a whole should have in both the short and long term.

Forecasting the size of future demand and trends for the organization's products;
Identifying markets to be served;
Assessing the strengths and weaknesses of the organization both absolutely and relatively to competitors;
Measuring dissatisfaction and needs in relevant market segments;
Industry/market structure and composition;
Competitors;
Market share and profitability analysis;
Highlighting significant marketing problems;
Stimulating research for new or exploitation of existing products and markets by planned policies;
Evaluating corporate identity and image;
Selecting companies for acquisition or divestment.

2.2.2   MARKET PLANNING

Research is used in market planning to keep the firm in touch with its markets.

Identifying, measuring and describing key market segments' behaviour and attitudes;
Assessing relative profitability of markets;
Analysis and interpretation of general market data;
Analysing business potential of new market areas;
Identifying and evaluating markets for products, and products for markets;
Measuring consumer preferences;
Identifying changes in competitive activity;
Sales forecasting.

2.2.3   PRODUCT PLANNING (including packaging)

Research is used in making and adapting products to fulfil

customer wants more accurately and profitably.

Generating and screening new product ideas and modifications;
Concept testing;
Product testing and re-testing for acceptance and improvement;
Testing formulation and presentation preferences;
Packaging tests;
Product name tests;
Test marketing;
Comparative testing against competitive products;
Product elimination or product line simplification;

2.2.4 PROMOTIONAL PLANNING

Research is concerned with the selection and effectiveness of persuasive communications. Three main areas are identified below.

Sales force planning
Determining sales areas;
Testing alternative selling techniques and messages;
Setting sales targets;
Evaluating sales performance;
Evaluating sales compensation system;
Making selling operations more productive.

Advertising planning
Message design and content;
Pre-testing ads;
Post-testing ads e.g. awareness, comprehension, recall, attitude shifts, brand switching effects;
Advertising weight-of-expenditure tests;
Media selection, media scheduling, media research;
Advertising effectiveness.

Other promotional planning
Selection;
Pre- and post-testing of 'below the line' expenditure;
Public relations and publicity effects on awareness/attitude;
Exhibition effectiveness research;
Direct mail effectiveness research.

2.2.5   DISTRIBUTION PLANNING

Research is concerned with the formulation and effectiveness of distribution policy.

Channel selection;
Distribution cost analysis;
Wholesaler/retailer margin;
Incentive policy;
Dealer sales levels;
Distribution achievement;
Penetration levels;
Stock checks;
Inventory policy.

2.2.6   PRICE PLANNING

Research may be used as one of the inputs to price selection.

Analysis of what problems the organization has and the uses to which research can be put will establish whether there is a need for research. The next step is to know what types of research information can be acquired.

2.3   WHAT TYPES OF RESEARCH DATA ARE THERE?

The collection of research data may be a *continuous* or occasional (*ad hoc*) activity of the organization. Usually there is a requirement for both approaches since they serve different purposes. Some information is already available and simply needs organizing if it exists within the organization (*internal*), or tracking down if it is available from elsewhere (*external*). These activities form the basis of *desk or secondary research*. Other data needs collecting and organizing before being usable and this is known as *field or primary research*. In many markets (mainly for consumers) standardized services carry out primary research on a regular basis and the user simply buys the information produced or the service offered. The term '*off-the-peg*' is used to describe this type of research. Most organizations will also have a need for data more specifically geared to particular problems and this is when '*made-to-measure*' research is required.

These six types of research are introduced briefly in this section and discussed more fully in later chapters.

2.3.1 CONTINUOUS RESEARCH

Any type of research may be organized so as to produce a continuous stream of data. The advantage of doing this is that it indicates trends and measures performance over time. This is particularly valuable in enabling an organization to spot changes in the market before they present themselves as serious problems. Continuous research forms an important element in any management information system and will probably include desk research and 'off-the-peg' services. It is essential for the organization which aspires to being 'pro-active' (making things happen) rather than 'reactive' (responding to things that have already happened).

2.3.2 'AD HOC' RESEARCH

'One-off' research studies meet those information needs that cannot be identified in advance. A new opportunity may suddenly arise or some specific problem need to be explored. Any type of research data might be used in an *ad hoc* study but it is most likely to include 'made-to-measure' research surveys.

2.3.3 DESK RESEARCH

Desk research is so called because it refers to that type of research data that can be acquired and worked upon mainly by sitting at a desk. That is to say, it is research data already extant, having been produced for some other purpose and by some other person or body. It is commonly referred to as secondary research because the user is the secondary user of the data and this term reflects the fact that it may not precisely meet his need nor be sufficiently recent to be wholly useful. Desk research makes a good starting point for any research programme because it is generally quick and cheap to acquire and can be readily assimilated. Whilst a scan of appropriate desk research sources may not produce an answer to the problem, it is extremely useful as a familiarization process and in generating ideas which will help to formulate and refine any subsequent collation of primary data.

Internal desk research

This represents the most sensible starting point for any organization, and should come before going to great lengths of resource expenditure in acquiring data from outside. Much useful information is generated within all organizations simply in the course of their normal operations. A simple analysis of accounting data should indicate: what is being sold, in what sizes, at what prices, and to whom in terms of geographical area, type of customer and so on. The key to making use of internal desk research sources is to organize the collection of data in such a way that it is not only useful but also usable. The acquisition, organization and use of internal desk research sources are more fully explored in Chapter 3.

External desk research

The Government is a major producer of all kinds of external research data. Useful external research data is also available from trade organizations, trade publications, banks, and many official bodies. The acquisition and use of external desk research data is discussed in Chapter 4.

Both internal and external desk research have limitations for decision makers. Internal desk research by definition is data confined to the organization's own activities. External desk research is characteristically of too general a nature to be applicable to any specific problem. Field research can overcome both these limitations.

2.3.4 FIELD RESEARCH

Field research is so called because it is concerned with the generation and collection of original data from the field of operation or intended operation for the organization. The organization determines exactly what information is necessary and from whom it needs the information and then sets about acquiring it. The data is thus specific to the purpose for which it has been acquired, and is often called primary research for this reason. There are two kinds of primary research, 'off-the-peg' services and 'made-to-measure' research.

'Off-the-peg' research services

A considerable amount of original research data is continually being generated by research organizations. Either the data itself or the system for collecting it may be bought 'off-the-peg'. The two types of service referred to are *'syndicated research'* and *'omnibus research'*.

Syndicated research   This is research, which is of value to a number of organizations, but which would be too expensive for any of them to collect individually. The data is therefore collected by a research agency and sold to all the organizations who have a use for it. This system means that effectively the organizations are sharing the costs of generating the kind of original data they require.

'Omnibus' research   When regular surveys of defined populations are being undertaken the agency doing the field-work may make the service available as an 'Omnibus' for other organizations to climb aboard. They may each add a few questions to the questionnaire. Those questions and the answers to them will be entirely confidential to the paying client but the respondents will find themselves answering a large number of questions about a possibly diverse range of subjects. Omnibus research represents an extremely cost-effective half-way house between carrying out a complete survey and buying the data already available

from external desk research or syndicated services. It gives the advantage of being able to specify the questions without having to bear all the costs of field-work.

Acquisition of both types of 'off-the-peg' research service is discussed in Chapter 4.

'Made-to-measure' research surveys
This is the type of research which most often comes to mind when managers think of using research. The organization wishing to acquire information decides what it wants to know, and usually briefs a research agency to acquire that information for it. The research agency will design an appropriate questionnaire, organize a team of professional interviewers to collect answers to the questions, process the data when the questionnaires are returned to the office and produce a report for the original client. The whole survey and its findings are guaranteed confidential to the organization which pays for them. This is the most expensive type of research data but should also be the most useful, since like other custom-built items it is designed and produced to meet exactly the requirements of the buyer. The design of 'made-to-measure' research surveys is discussed in Chapter 5. Technical aspects of data collection, sampling, questionnaire design, field-work, and data analysis and interpretation are discussed in Chapters 6-10 respectively.

2.4   HOW CAN THE ORGANIZATION OBTAIN THE RESEARCH IT NEEDS?

2.4.1   GETTING STARTED

In getting started as a research user a logical progression would be to begin with internal and external desk research. Any appropriate syndicated services should be considered for purchase, or a few basic market data questions included on an omnibus survey. These research activities are likely to be followed by 'made-to-measure' field research. This order of research progression reflects the order in which data are most readily acquired. It demands an increasing level of commitment in terms of cost and personnel involved in acquiring the data, and an increasing level of research knowledge in both acquiring and using data. The quality of information acquired also increases as one moves from one type of research to the next, and this may be in step with the ability of the user to handle it.

RESOURCES

An essential point to note for the organization wishing to use research data is that it is equally important to set up an adequate system for using the data when it has been acquired, as it is to set up the information-acquisition system in the first place. As with all other services an organization needs, acquiring useful and usable information costs both time and money. If research is to be used effectively by the organization, then someone within it must be designated as having a primary responsibility for this and be given time to discharge that responsibility properly. The acquisition of market research data costs money and the information product is like most other products, in that the organization seriously wanting to get started on using market research intelligently must be prepared to devote adequate personnel and financial resources to it. Some suggestions follow as to what this might mean in practice.

Internal desk research
This requires a statistical assistant to design and operate an internal information system, a data handling system (usually a computer) and an executive to use output.

External desk research
This requires a research assistant within the organization to identify sources, acquire, organize and report on the data. Alternatively, a specialist desk research organization may be used. In this case the main resource requirement on the

client organization is that of money to pay for it. The growth of specialist desk research agencies is relatively new. They are mainly used by industrial organizations for whom desk research usually represents a more important aspect of their overall research programme.

'Off-the-peg' field research
This requires an executive with a need for such a service, the ability to identify appropriate sources and money to pay for the services available.

'Made-to-measure' field research
This requires an executive within the organization with responsibility for defining the need for research and briefing and commissioning a research agency to conduct it. Money is needed to pay for the technical expertise of a research agency.

Some research can be carried out by executives within a user organization. Exploratory interviews in industrial or trade research and postal surveys are the most commonly used do-it-yourself research methods because they are possible and practical. However, the fact that they are apparently easy to do means that, as in do-it-yourself in many other areas, a great deal of bad workmanship can result! If an organization does plan to do its own marketing research then the executives concerned will need to know rather more about it than could possibly be covered in a short introductory book such as this. Suggestions for improving personal research expertise are offered in Chapter 15.

Research techniques almost always commissioned from research agencies are those involving large-scale interviewing or telephone research surveys because these require more routine time and womanpower than most organizations are likely to wish to handle, or are able to do, cost effectively. Group discussions and consumer depth interviews are normally also commissioned from research agencies since they require specialist expertise for successful application and interpretation.

2.5 SUMMARY

Any organization is likely to have a need to use marketing research in making resource allocation decisions. The first step is to define precisely why the research is needed, and some examples and suggestions about research applications are given. The next step is to realize what types of research data are available and six types of research are introduced: continuous research, *ad hoc* research, internal and external desk research, 'off-the-peg' and 'made-to-measure' field research. Finally, the organization needs a method for getting started and appropriate resources for the acquisition of research data, and these are discussed.

3 Marketing Research Begins at Home

3.1 INTRODUCTION

Many organizations make judgements, prepare plans and reach decisions with little or no contribution from formal marketing research. This chapter indicates ways in which organization of data readily available from sources within the firm can produce information of great practical relevance. The purpose of an internal information system is to produce a continuous stream of data which can:

(a) measure current performance;
(b) identify the characteristics of current performance;
(c) establish a base line for change;
(d) form a basis for comparison – over time, over industry, etc.
(e) suggest a basis for resource allocation – geographic, profitability, product, etc.
(f) indicate trends;
(g) monitor and track performance;
(h) signal change;
(i) provide an early warning detection system;
(j) form a basis for operating control systems;
(k) highlight performance problem areas;
(l) provide information resources;
(m) indicate areas for further research.

The aim of an internal information system is to keep the organization informed about its own performance; to be able to anticipate change in its own competitive and technological environment; and as a guideline to focus and monitor company effort.

3.2   WHAT CAN BE DONE AT HOME?

For most organizations new to marketing research the budget available is limited. It therefore makes sense to begin by making use of data which is already available. This has the advantage of being quick and relatively cheap to obtain in addition to being private to the organization and highly relevant and specific to its products, markets and performance.

Three examples illustrate the major categories for 'research which begins at home'.

3.2.1   *DATA PRODUCED IN THE NORMAL COURSE OF RUNNING THE ORGANIZATION*

A builders' merchant based in a small market town in the South and serving a wide area of the South of England was considering opening a second branch as a result of the success of the established operation. The problem was to decide where to site the new branch so as to increase sales rather than switch them from one branch to the other. Possibilities were five conurbations within fifty miles of the home branch. The decision was made by undertaking a detailed analysis of invoices which indicated where current customers were based. Factors were taken into account in order to estimate the potential demand in the areas under review together with an analysis of the likely impact on the current operation of transferring trade to another location.

This example involved the analysis of sales records. Other data which may be useful in making decisions about the more effective or efficient running of an organization could include production records, distribution statistics or cost data.

3.2.2   *DATA ACQUIRED THROUGH PERSONAL CONTACTS*

The sales representative of a carpet manufacturer was told

by one of the retailers whom he was visiting that in his opinion there might be a market for carpet designs in the Laura Ashley/Habitat style. He reasoned that many other household soft furnishings were in this style, but it was not well represented within existing carpet ranges. The representative mentioned it to one or two other retailers whom he was visiting, and finding further support for the idea passed it on to the design manager. The design manager, who also filled the role of marketing controller for the company, commissioned a consumer market research survey which confirmed that such a market existed. The end result was a successful range of new patterns.

As this example illustrates, information picked up during the normal course of a day by sales representatives, by attendance of executives at conferences and meetings, and by customer suggestion and complaints, made either direct to the firm or via the medium of its retailer and distributor network, can be of value if the organization responds appropriately.

3.2.3 ACCUMULATED RESEARCH INFORMATION

A vinyl manufacturer was planning to launch a new material for covering furnishings. The material had the appearance and feel qualities of cloth combined with the durability and washability of vinyl. The manufacturer felt that there must be a strong market for this material which combined the advantages of both cloth and vinyl. Some years previously the company had launched a floor covering material that had been unsuccessful. Research into the reasons for failure indicated certain areas of pre-market preparation and launch activity which had contributed to the downfail of the product. One of the executives involved in the launch of the new furnishing product remembered to look up the old research report on the floor-covering failure. The information contained in it was extremely useful to the company in ensuring that the same mistakes were not repeated and that where lessons could be learned they were applied in the approach to launching the new furnishing material.

This example illustrates how a library of past research projects and marketing information stored by the organization can enable it to learn from past experiences and so improve performance.

3.3 WHAT GOES INTO AN INTERNAL INFORMATION SYSTEM?

Together, the three types of data illustrated can provide an internal desk research information system. This is a system which produces useful and usable information through organized methods for collecting, storing, retrieving and reporting on data available from within the firm. The first category of data illustrated is called 'operating data' because it is produced as a result of the operation of the organization. The second data category is called 'market intelligence' because it refers to intelligence information acquired by individuals who work for the organization as a result of the personal contacts they make. Market intelligence differs from marketing research by being less systematic or representative in the selection of sources from which information is acquired. The last category is accumulated research and marketing information and this forms the basis for setting up an internal 'information library'.

These three aspects of an internal desk research information system are discussed in the following sections.

3.3.1 OPERATING DATA

It is perhaps surprising that many companies start by commissioning outside marketing research before organizing an internal desk research system. An entirely human reason is that it is often easier to commission an outside research agency than to persuade heads of functional departments, like accounting and production, to produce records in a form that is of value in marketing decision-making.

An earthenware manufacturer made a range of tableware such as plates, cups and saucers and so on, together with a range of earthenware mugs. Having been very successful it was keen to open a second factory. The decision it had to make was how much of the new capacity should be devoted to the tableware and how much to mugs. The first piece of information required was to know what proportion each of these lines currently contributed to turnover and profit. Unfortunately the company's accounting system only produced customer invoices indicating a final cash figure. Customers of different sizes were given different discounts, but these were not shown on invoices. Prices had changed several times during previous years but goods supplied were not itemized. No records of production output or breakages were kept. Any goods remaining at the end of the week were taken away by jobbers with only a cash value being recorded. As a result, the company had no internal data on which to base its decision.

The current widespread availability of computers and micro computers means that basic record-keeping, which would have provided this company with at least a starting point for its decision-making problem, is relatively easy to undertake. The first step is for the researcher to co-operate with relevant departments to ensure that appropriate records are instituted and maintained. The critical factor in this lies in the design of record-keeping in such a way that the statistics produced will be useful both to the originating department and to the management decision maker.

Decisions about the form in which the data is to be produced, its frequency of production and how it is to be analysed need to be taken before the system is initiated. No data collection system should be initiated that will not or cannot be used. This is the quickest way to ensure that any research will never be taken seriously by the organization. One factor to be taken into account may be the time period for record-keeping: for example, it is quite common to use four-week periods (i.e. thirteen 'months' per year). These are more comparable than calendar months, having the same number of working days in them on a year-on-year basis which is often not the case when calendar months are used. Differences in the number of working days can account for apparent sales fluctuations in year-on-year monthly comparisons. Examples of data useful to the researcher include sales statistics, expenditure and operations statistics.

Sales statistics
These may be produced in a number of ways, each of which can provide useful data for management. Analysis may be by:

(a) Product/product group – this will indicate the importance of each product and item in the product range and their effect on overall company performance. Trend data will indicate which products are growing and which declining.

(b) Markets – this is particularly important in industrial organizations where analysis of sales data by industrial application of the customer, perhaps using Standard Industrial Classification (SIC), will indicate the relative importance of, and trends in, the company's major markets.

(c) Outlets – analysis of sales by different types of outlet will indicate their relative importance, trends and the mix, for demand analysis. In the confectioner/tobacconist/newsagent (CTN) market the growth of the new generation of minimarket CTN's, and the increasing importance of do-it-yourself (DIY) stores as opposed to the traditional paint retailer or the more recent supermarket entrant to paint retailing, indicates a possible need for re-organization of the marketing effort to take account of different outlets for the company's products. Statistics on the regional distribution of outlets may have implications for other marketing activity such as sales and advertising, or for re-organizing the regional outlet pattern.

(d) Geographic area – there are a number of ways in which sales may be analysed with respect to geographic area. The area may be a country for multinational firms, or a sales area or representative territory when selling is an important element of the marketing effort. I.B.A. TV areas are used for analysis of consumer markets in which television advertising is used. Another advantage of using the I.B.A. TV areas is that much published data, including that on media audiences and readership, is available based on TV areas. Using area analysis, performance can be measured and compared and decreases and increases spotted and dealt with. Implications for regional allocation of marketing effort can be drawn from this analysis.

(e) Time period – analysis of sales by time will enable seasonal demand to be plotted and therefore anticipated. Year-on-year or period-on-period performance comparisons can be made.

(f) Size of orders – calculation of average orders by size may have a direct bearing on profit per order handled. This could form the basis for calculation of standard delivery charges or standard levels of costs to be applied to small orders. Incentives for order size to be increased may result from this type of analysis.

These examples give some indication of the value in simply analysing sales records in a variety of ways, each of which might have different decision-making implications. But sales statistics are only half the story when the company's real concern is about profit and so a second set of data records are needed to complete the picture.

Expenditure statistics
Analysis of expenditure statistics can be used to calculate relationships between areas of expenditure and income. This will increase efficiency by leading to optimization of various areas of expenditure against incomes. Expenditures on promotion, sales force, packaging, despatch, or invoicing, may be analysed against sales turnover to indicate the relationship between sales and each particular area. This

might be used in budget allocation for future years. The same expenditure statistics may be analysed against specific product sales. This forms a basis for the allocation of effort devoted to, or overheads charged against, these products. A more fruitful analysis might be to look at items of expenditure against profit generated. A sales promotion may have produced an increase in sales turnover yet have had no effect at all on profit. The upheaval that sales promotion activity often produces in the production system may be shown to be not worthwhile with this kind of analysis.

Another area of expenditure which can be analysed in a number of ways is advertising expenditure. This may be set against product sales revenue, profit, market type or media. The outcome of any of these analyses will prove useful for planning decisions. Analysis of advertising expenditure by product line may well indicate that most advertising expenditure goes on the biggest product lines. This is particularly likely to be the case when advertising budgets are determined on the basis of sales turnover. Analysis may indicate that greater response could be achieved by diverting advertising expenditure to smaller products with greater potential for growth. This could result in a greater increase in overall profitability.

The value of all these kinds of expenditure analysis lies in the fact that they can increase the organization's perception of what relationships do and do not exist between various types of expenditure and resultant effects in the market-place.

Operations statistics
Statistical records may be kept on almost any area of an organization's operations and analysis of them can indicate more profitable, more efficient, or more effective ways of operating. For example:

(a) *Stock control statistics*: Stock records will indicate stocks being run down or built up, or bottle necks in the stock system. Calculations can be made of the amount of investment tied up in stock at any particular moment in time. In these days when additional profit is hard to achieve by increasing sales volume, analysis of stock inefficiencies may make a greater contribution to an overall increase in profitability than any marketing activity.

(b) *Transport statistics*: Maintenance of statistics on mileage, routes covered, vehicle maintenance, and so on, will often lead to more economical handling of a company's distribution and transport system.

All the statistics referred to above should be maintained continuously over time in order for the manager to be able to spot trends or change in the market-place and deal with it. The danger inherent in producing any continuous set of data is the problem of 'information overload'. This occurs when the system is generating more information than the manager can cope with reading, never mind responding to! Some mechanism needs to be introduced to ensure that the manager's attention is only attracted to continuous sets of statistics when some action may be necessary. This normally involves setting out guidelines which will enable management to identify and deal with only exceptional developments. An instruction may be given that the manager himself will only see the information if the data for any time period are outside an operating norm of, say, 10% either way. Statistics based on operations data are also used to calculate 'operating ratios'. These are an input to assessing the efficiencies of different operations, and to allocating budgets for those areas.

The data generated from operating data can prove extremely useful in indicating the performance of the company. They are not appropriate for identifying changes in the external environment which do not necessarily show themselves in company sales. It is for this reason that the market intelligence system is particularly useful.

3.3.2   MARKET INTELLIGENCE

Sources of information such as personal contacts, feedback

from the trade and from the sales force, informal store checks and monitoring of competitors' products and publicity efforts can be extremely useful. A problem with market intelligence data lies in the procedures used for its collection. Most sales people would argue, often rightly, that additional paper work reduces profitable selling time. At the same time sales people are keen to be the first to report some new market-place development to the organization, particularly when they know the organization will respond to that information.

This indicates two key points in the design of market intelligence systems. First, the reporting system should be as straightforward as possible and organized in such a way as to minimize the work involved in reporting. Secondly, the response mechanism to market intelligence must be good and known to the individuals making reports. The single most important incentive for members of the organization to participate in a market intelligence system is the feeling that it is of real value to the organization and does feed into its decision-making procedures.

Exactly what type of market intelligence may be of value will depend on the organization but the most commonly collected areas are those already referred to. In the more rapidly developing industries it may be that the market intelligence system would be extended to include feedback from conferences and meetings at which new technology is discussed. Other avenues for feedback of useful snippets of intelligence gathered through personal contact may suggest themselves.

3.3.3 INFORMATION LIBRARY

When an organization is starting to develop a research facility then it makes sense to ensure that research undertaken is classified and stored in such a way that it is usable and utilized on future occasions. Reading past research studies can be extremely helpful in indicating ways in which the same problem may be approached again. If it is appropriate to update the piece of research then the earlier work will serve as a bench-mark indicating change. If an earlier piece of research used a method which did not work very well then the same mistakes can be avoided. There is usually something to learn about where the product is now in the market-place from an analysis of how it got there.

Sometimes, new executives in the organization will come up with ideas which have been tried before. Although there may be good reasons for believing that something which did or did not work on some occasion in the past may or may not work now, it is nevertheless of value for the new executive to know when something has been tried before and what the circumstances and outcomes were. With the fairly rapid turnover of both marketing and market research executives it is useful to have a retrieval system operating so that when a manager intends to carry out some research in a particular area there is ready access to any previous work done. It is still common practice in organizations that copies of research reports are kept only by the managers who have commissioned them and are not readily accessible by, or made available to, other members of the same organization. The establishment of an information library will rectify this.

Another important function for the information library will be to acquire, store and retrieve external desk research information, and this is discussed in Chapter 4.

3.4 SUMMARY

Organizations are typically rich in information, which would prove extremely useful if it were available in an appropriate form or collected, evaluated and retrievable in some systematic way. This forms the basis of an internal information system to produce continuous data which can be used for measuring, evaluating, monitoring and controlling performance. Three aspects of an information system are discussed: operating data, which flows from normal operating procedures; market intelligence, which derives from normal personal contacts; and the establishment of an information library, which stores past research data and acquires new information from external desk research sources.

4 'Off-the-Peg' Research

4.1 INTRODUCTION

Much of the data that a company new to marketing research might want to know is probably already in existence. Such things as: overall market size and structure, basic information about consumer spending patterns, major social and economic trends, financial data about customer firms, competitor firms, supplier firms, markets which are growing and profitable, markets in decline or unprofitable, and so on. The purpose of this chapter is to give some indication of the vast amount of 'off-the-peg' data available, and an idea about where to locate the appropriate 'pegs'. Once an organization has identified relevant data sources, it will often continue to obtain updating information, and as discussed in the last chapter this forms an important part of the organization's information system.

There are four main types of 'off-the-peg' research:

1 Research using the very large body of already published data, usually termed 'Secondary desk research'.

2 Research using data available from regular market surveys, often referred to as 'Syndicated research'.

3 Research in which the method of data collection is syndicated, but the data is not, called 'Omnibus research'.

4 Research making use of specialist expertise available from research agencies, discussed under the heading 'Specialist research services'.

This chapter considers each type of research in turn. Inevitably, some of the specific information sources and contact data given in this chapter will become outdated.

Nevertheless, the general points made, and major sources indicated, will prove of value as a guide to 'off-the-peg' research for some years beyond the date of publication.

4.2 SECONDARY DESK RESEARCH

4.2.1 INTRODUCTION

Secondary desk research uses data that has already been published by someone else, at some other time period, usually for some other reason than the present researcher has in mind. The researcher is therefore a secondary user of already existing data which can be obtained and worked on at a desk. This accounts for its name. The most characteristic thing about secondary data is the vast amount available. Because it is so overwhelming in its range and sometimes complexity, secondary data is often overlooked as a source of research information. However, much specific data is already in existence on markets, and companies operating within those markets. It is therefore worthwhile any organization making a determined attempt to identify relevant secondary data sources for its own use.

Secondary data is relatively quick and cheap to obtain. Once obtained, a regular series of updating information can be acquired from the same source. At best, secondary data may provide the complete answer to a problem. At worst, it will save the organization time and money when it comes to carrying out a piece of original field research. Secondary data can define the scope or direction of a field research survey and indicate the type and range of information which might be available. It will suggest possible methods for carrying out field research. If past research survey are found to be too out of date for the information to be of current relevance, they may at least provide a basis for comparison with a new survey replicating the method. This will give the added insight of market change data to an original piece of research. There are a number of possible sources for published secondary data.

4.2.2 SOURCES

Government published data

The Government publishes a great deal of information regularly on almost every aspect of British economic, social, commercial, and financial life. It is always worth checking what Government information is available for any research problem under review, since this will probably be the cheapest way of obtaining the information. Only the costs of publication are covered by the price of the various reports produced.

Trade published data

When information is required about a particular trade or industry there are four sources likely to have appropriate information available in published form.

(a) *Trade Associations*. These exist in most industries, for example, The Electrical Contractors' Association or The British Federation of Builders' Merchants. These associations normally carry an information library staffed with appropriate information specialists.

(b) *Trade Press*. Any trade of sufficient size will have newspapers and journals relevant to that industry. These will maintain a library of past items of news and information which can be consulted to provide a background picture for any particular aspect under consideration.

(c) *Professional Institutes*. Most professions have an Institute, for example, the Institute of Marketing, Institute of Cost and Management Accountants, British Institute of Management, and so on. These organizations are equipped with libraries and information services available to members. They also provide a service to non-members of those professions, usually for a small charge.

(d) *Chambers of Commerce*. If the problem under consideration refers to a particular regional location, contact with the local Chamber of Commerce for the area may prove particularly useful. The quality of information available from Chambers of Commerce varies, but the larger Chambers provide quite comprehensive and relevant information on many aspects of business in their areas.

Financial institutions' published data
Regular reports on various industries, their performance, their financial record, trends and potential are produced by the major banks and leading stock brokers. These should always be checked to see whether a relevant report has recently been published.

Press published data
The 'quality' press and the financial and economic press regularly produce industrial and commercial reports on various aspects of business, companies and products. Information services of the relevant press can be contacted to discover whether a report is available.

Foreign and international organizations' published data
All the data referred to as being available for the United Kingdom are available for most well-developed economies via a variety of foreign and international data-producing organizations. The Statistics and Market Intelligence Library in London maintains a library of world statistics and this provides an excellent starting point for any investigation into overseas markets.

Specialist organizations
A number of specialized organizations exist to provide the type of desk research information obtainable through published sources. These organizations act as 'Information Brokers' and produce relevant abstracts and digests of statistics and news items to subscribers.

4.2.3   FINDING THE PEGS

Generally speaking the most difficult part of a desk research survey using secondary sources for the beginner is actually beginning. This section will therefore concentrate on indicating some of the more general starting points for a desk research survey. Once the research survey is under way each source uncovered, or contact made, will generally lead on to the next. Following up these leads will provide the depth of information the researcher may need in his particular area of interest.

The section that follows suggests various leads. It begins by indicating some of the books available which list information sources and classify them. It goes on to suggest sources for some of the more commonly required types of information: about companies, about industries, and about markets. It then comments on and identifies some Government statistics. The section concludes with a list of some of the information services available to give help on data collection using secondary sources.

Where to Start Looking

This section includes lists of information sources, and directories. Where available, telephone numbers are included rather than addresses.

Wills, G. & Tupper E. *Sources of U.K. Marketing Information*, 2nd edn, (Ernest Benn Ltd: London, 1975).

Described as the 'sole comprehensive source reference for marketing data.' Alphabetic index of sources by product groups, services and industries. Sections on: prime sources, marketing environment, market data, media data, organizations providing marketing research services, marketing journals and abstracts.

Hull, C. *Principal Sources of Marketing Information*, (*The Times* Information and Marketing Intelligence Unit: London, 1976) (Tel: 01 837 1234).

Lists main sources of published information useful to marketing personnel. Includes government departments, trade associations, research bodies. Notes general sources, and those specific to industries.

Harvey, J. M. *Statistics Europe: Sources for Social, Economic and Market Research*, 4th edn, (CBD Research Ltd:

Beckenham, 1981) (Tel: 01 650 7745).

Covers all countries of Western and Eastern Europe. Designed to enable researcher to identify appropriate published sources of statistics, find where they can be consulted or obtained, and to locate 'live' sources from which to augment them.

Published Data on European Industrial Markets (Industrial Aids Ltd. London, 1983) (Tel: 01 730 5288).

Particularly useful for industrial markets. Lists industrial market research reports available for purchase, by subject, with source and cost. Also lists data sources for UK and International industrial market statistics. Information repeated for twenty West European countries and eight East European countries.

The Marketing Year Book (Annual) (Institute of Marketing: Cookham) (Tel: 06285 24922)

Mainly lists specialist organizations providing a variety of marketing services e.g. advertising, promotion, packaging, exhibitions, consumer, trade, technical and professional publications, directories, broadcasting. Includes some marketing statistics and sources of information.

The Market Research Society Year Book (Annual) (Market Research Society: London) (Tel: 01 235 4709)

Mainly useful for comprehensive lists of organizations providing market research services in Great Britain.

International Directory of Market Research Organizations, 6th edn, (Market Research Society: British Overseas Trade Board, 1982) (Tel: 01 235 4709).

Information on almost 1300 market research organizations operating in over sixty countries.

International Directory of Published Market Research (British Overseas Trade Board/Arlington Management Publications Ltd:) (Tel: 01-930-3638)

Classified list of over 6000 market research studies covering over 100 countries.

The Grocer Marketing Directory, 24th edn, (William Reed Ltd: 1978) (Tel: 01 407 6981)
Lists Multiple shops, Co-operative Societies, Wholesale and Trade Organizations in the grocery business.

Information about Companies
This section includes sources of data about companies: their existence, location, type of business, ownership, performance, financial and commercial statistics.

Kompass Products and Services (Vol. 1)
Lists suppliers of most products.
Company Information (Vol. 2)
Lists Company names and locations with information about each company and its products.

'Who Owns Whom' (Annual) (Dun & Bradstreet Ltd: London) (Tel: 01 628 3691)
Shows ownership of subsidiary and associate companies, including those owned by official bodies like government and nationalized companies.

Europes 5,000 Largest Companies (Dun & Bradstreet Ltd: London) (Tel: 01 628 3691)
Lists industrial and trading companies with headquarters location, industry type and financial performance data.

The Hambro Company Guide (half yearly) (Investment Evaluator (UK) Ltd: London) (Tel: 01 628 3744)
Provides full information on all 2000 companies listed in back pages of the *Financial Times*. Grading system from 'blue-chip' to 'take-care' investment potential. Useful to assess performance of suppliers, customers and potential new clients.

Extel Handbook of Market Leaders (half yearly) (Extel Statistical Services Ltd: London) (Tel: 01 253 3400)
Financial and commercial data on all companies in

Financial Times Actuaries All-Share Index.

Jane's Major Companies of Europe (Jane's Yearbook: London)
Lists activity, management and financial performance.

McCarthy Information Ltd, Warminster (Tel: 0985 215151)
Subscription service providing daily or weekly information sheets containing items from leading newspapers and financial journals, with news and comment on companies and industries.

Information about Industries
Industrial Performance Analysis, 7th edn, (Inter Company Comparisons Ltd: 1982) (Tel: 01 638 2946)
A financial analysis of major UK industry and commerce sectors. Useful for managers wishing to place their own company's performance in perspective, or wishing to check on sector performance for possible diversification, etc.

The A–Z of U.K. Marketing Data (Euromonitor Publications Ltd: London) (Tel: 01 242 0042)
A digest of marketing facts about market size, structure and trends for 500 consumer products.

MGN Marketing Manual of the United Kingdom (Annual) (Mirror Group Newspapers, London) (Tel: 01 353 0246)
A compilation of consumer marketing data from published sources. Social and economic, market-place, media and advertising data.

European Marketing Data and Statistics (Annual) (Euromonitor Publications Ltd: London) (Tel: 01 242 0042)
General population, social, economic, marketing and media information for thirty European countries.

Information about Markets
Subscription Services
These are designed to provide the latest information regularly. An annual charge is made for the service.

Individual reports and back copies are usually available.

Market Intelligence (Monthly) (Mintel Publications Ltd:)
(Tel: 01 839 1542)
Each issue contains a detailed market report on about five
markets. e.g. September 1982: carbonates, DIY, chemicals, hotels, radios, sweet spreads. Always worth checking to see if relevant reports are available.

Other Mintel Services
Retail Intelligence (Monthly): Like *Marketing Intelligence*
but about retailing rather than products.
Daily Digest: daily information on subject profile
specified.
Monthly Digests on twelve different market areas.
Special subject reports also available e.g. the gardening
market, the kitchen report.

Home, Office, Leisure Market Assessment (Bi-monthly) (BLA
Management Services Group Ltd:) (Tel: 01 278 9517)
Reports on markets indicated by title. Reprints of past
reports available.

Keynote Publications Ltd, London (Tel: 01 588 2698)
Market reports compiled from a variety of published
sources.

Retail Business (Monthly) (Economist Intelligence Unit,
London) (Tel: 01 493 6711)
Monthly reports on a number of markets. Check for
topics required.

Euromonitor Publications Ltd, London (Tel: 01 242 0042)
Various market reports available.
Market Research Great Britain (Monthly)
Each monthly magazine contains five articles on U.K.
consumer markets and products, selected to give com-
prehensive review of markets each year. Back issues to
1960 for trend data.
Market Research Europe (Bi-monthly)
Each issue contains up to ten articles on Western Europe's

major markets. Back issues to 1968 for trend data.

Business Surveys Ltd, Dorking (Tel: 0306 87857)
Research Index. A comprehensive reference to articles and news items of financial interest appearing in over 100 periodicals and the national press.
Section 1 (pink pages) – industrial and commercial news by products and industry.
Section 2 (blue pages) – articles about particular companies.
Reports Index (Monthly)
A monthly listing of new research reports, where to obtain them and cost. Indexed.

Nielsen Market Information Manual 1982 (A. C. Nielsen Company, Ltd: Oxford, 1982) (Tel: 0865 64851)
Two years' data covering over 250 markets for products sold in grocers, off-licences, pharmacies, confectioners, and cash and carry outlets. Plus economic, population and advertising data.

Nielsen Researcher (Quarterly) Free. (A. C. Nielsen Company Ltd: Oxford) (Tel: 0865 64851)
Short market analyses based on information from Nielsen Retail Index Service.

The Food and Drink Forecast (Quarterly) (The Food and Drink Industries Forecasting Group, Bath House (3rd floor), 56 Holborn Viaduct, London EC1A 2EX)
Comprehensive guide to sales, expenditure, price, brand share, advertising and regional usage trends in fifty major UK food and drink markets.

Also see 'Data for Sale' section of Market Research Society monthly Newsletter (Tel: 01 235 4709) advertising 'off-the-peg' research studies in a range of markets: consumer, industrial, trade and service.

Government Statistics
Government Statistics: A Brief Guide to Sources (Annual) (Available free from Central Statistical Office, Great

George Street, London SW1P 3AQ).

Each department of the Government Statistical Service prepares and publishes its own statistics. This small guide lists the most important statistics by subject, shows which departments are responsible for which statistics, together with contact addresses and telephone numbers. This information is not reproduced here since it is available free, and any reader interested should write for a copy.

Guide to Official Statistics (Annual) (1982 – £25.00) (Central Statistical Office, Great George Street, London SW1P 3AQ) (Tel: 01 928 1321)

Covers all official and significant non-official sources of statistics, both regular and occasional, published during the last ten years, making it a document of prime importance to users of these statistics. Aims to give the user a broad indication of whether the statistics he wants have been compiled and if so, where they have been published. Does not contain statistics, but indicates where to find them. A mine of information. Available in all main public libraries.

As will be seen from the *Guide to Official Statistics*, a vast wealth of information is available from the Government Statistical Service, and each Department contains experts who are keen to encourage use of its statistics. 'Departmental Contact Points' are listed in both Guides above. There are literally hundreds of sources of Government statistics and no attempt is made here to list them – that is what the *Guide to Official Statistics* seeks to do in 538 A4 pages of small print! A few of the more general titles are listed as examples:

British Business (Weekly) (HMSO, PO Box 276, London SW8 5DT) (01 928 6977)

Contains news and items from the Departments of Industry and Trade about many aspects of business, including overseas items.

Social Trends (Annual)
Statistical series about people relating to social policies and conditions which provide a picture of some significant ways in which our society is changing. Background information on society.

Family Expenditure Survey (Annual)
Data on characteristics, incomes and expenditure of private households in the UK. Trend data useful for indicating change in patterns of expenditure.

The General Household Survey Continuous sample survey. Provides a regular picture of changing social conditions in most aspects of everyday life.

New Earnings Survey (Annual)
Indicates earnings and hours worked by industry, occupation, region, age, and sex.

Employment Gazette (Monthly) Main publication of the Department of Employment.
Regular monthly statistics and articles on all aspects of labour and employment.

Business Monitor, Department of Industry Business Statistics Office. (Tel: 0633 56111 ext 2973)
Information about manufacturing industries, their markets and the industries they buy from, and about the retail and wholesale trades. For list of all *Business Monitors*, contact the telephone number above.

Digest of Tourist Statistics (British Tourist Authority: London)
Most Government Departments produce statistics relevant to their field of operation. This is one example and presents basic facts relating to tourism to and within the United Kingdom.

For specific topics of interest, consult 'Subject List' of 'Guide to Official Statistics'. Taking 'Tourism' as an example, the Guide lists over 100 services which may contain relevant statistics.

Information Services

Statistics and Market Intelligence Library (Export House, 50 Ludgate Hill, London EC4M 7HU) (Tel: 01 248 5757)

National reference library for public use of UK statistics, and referral centre to sources of information in the Government Statistical Service.

Large collection of material on overseas markets.

Economic, social, industry and market data held for all countries of the world. Telephone and trade directories (except UK), market surveys, development plans and mail order catalogues.

British Overseas Trade Board's Export Marketing Research Scheme (Export Marketing Research, BOTB, Export House, 50 Ludgate Hill, London EC4M 7HU). (Tel: 01 248 7263)

Free professional advice and, in approved cases, financial support, to help UK firms and trade associations undertake marketing research overseas for exports.

Statistics and Market Research (Monthly) (Birmingham Public Libraries) (Tel: 021 235 4531)

Guide to current articles on most markets. Photocopies available. Contact 'Quick Reference and Commercial Information Department'.

Other *Specialist Business Libraries* may be worth contacting, particularly if easily accessible e.g. City of London, Manchester Business School, Universities of Coventry and Warwick. Advice on which libraries to contact for special subjects may be obtained from *ASLIB* (Association of Special Libraries and Information Bureau) 3, Belgrave Square, London, SW1X 8PL.

Commission of The European Community, 8 Shorey's Gate, London SW1 (Tel: 01 222 8122)

Provides on-line information service on EEC statistics.

Mintel Information Service: London (01 839 1542)

Provides information service to client specifications.

CMIS (Comprehensive Marketing Information Systems) (A. C.

Neilsen Co. Ltd: Oxford) (Tel: 0865 64851)
Provides information service to client specifications.

4.2.4 USING SECONDARY DATA

Whenever secondary data sources are being used a number of points need to be checked.

(a) Who is producing the data? This is a relevant question because, particularly with information from trade associations, the possibility of bias is present. An association which exists on members' subscriptions, with the objective of furthering members' interests, is unlikely to publish data that is against those members' interests. This is not to say that they will publish false data, but simply that they may not publish data which gives both sides of every question relevant to members' interests.

(b) Why was the information collected in the first place? Answering this question will give greater insight into the nature, and therefore value, of the data which has been collected.

(c) How was the information collected? From the chapters in this book on methods of data collection (Chapters 6–10) it will be apparent that the value of information for use in making a decision is partly determined by the method used in collecting the data. In deciding how useful a particular item of secondary information is, it is therefore necessary to consult the technical appendix of the report to see how the data was collected.

(d) When was the information collected? A particular problem with Government statistics is that they may not be published until eighteen months or even longer after the time period in which the data was collected. Depending on the nature of the data and the market to which it refers, this may be a serious limitation in using the statistics.

Sources of secondary data will vary widely in terms of: reliability of the data, how specific it is to a particular problem, how recent the information is, the amount of bias or vested interest in the data source and, particularly when using press report services, the amount of useful information hidden in the verbiage. Nevertheless, the desk researcher can almost always produce an extremely useful background report on any industry, in a relatively short space of time, and at a relatively low cost. It is recommended that a desk research survey of secondary sources be carried out before any major field research survey is undertaken.

4.3   SYNDICATED RESEARCH SERVICES

The origins of the syndicated research services came when a group of manufacturers all interested in data on a particular market formed a syndicate to buy a research survey jointly providing that data on a continuous basis. Alternatively, a research agency might suggest the idea to a number of companies with common data needs. No single manufacturer could afford the costs of the research survey, but by clubbing together, research costs are shared and information is available to all members of the syndicate. Over time, the original services have proved useful to a wider number of manufacturers than those forming the original syndicate and, because the surveys have been continuous, they have become the property of the research agencies who provide them. In this sense the term 'syndicated' is a hangover from the origins of these services, rather than a description of their current ownership.

In practice nowadays, most syndicated research services are owned by the research companies who run them. An association of users of a service may meet to ensure that user interests are expressed in the method of collection and presentation of the data. Most syndicated research surveys are continuous panels and the advantages of these as a method of data collection are discussed in Chapter 6. (Where this is not the method used, then this is indicated for the service listed below.)

The main problem for the intending user of syndicated

research services is to identify what services are available and which companies provide them. The Market Research Society, 15 Belgrave Square, London SW1X 8PF (Tel: 01 235 4709) produces an annual year book containing a list of organizations providing marketing research services in Great Britain. Off-prints of the list are available on request. The list in 1983 contained 199 organizations, and the intending buyer of 'off-the-peg' research services should consult this book. Not all marketing research organizations supply syndicated services, and so the following index and list of suppliers of syndicated research services was compiled from an analysis of the *MRS Year Book* to give an idea of the range available. The index lists topics covered. Full details of the services offered, the method by which the data is collected, and costs of the services can be obtained from the organizations named, whose telephone numbers are given.

4.3.1 INDEX TO SYNDICATED RESEARCH SERVICES

Note: numbers refer to the full listing which follows.

4.3.2   SYNDICATED RESEARCH SERVICE

1 *ACE (Advertising Campaign Effectiveness)*. IPC Magazines, London.

   To assess impact of advertising campaigns particularly in women's magazines and on TV.

2 *AGB Index Ltd*. Berkhamsted (Tel: 04427 3311) Established 1977.

   Measures personal financial activity of panel of 10 000 individuals aged 16 and over.

3 *Agridata Ltd*. London (Tel: 01 258 0470)

   Usage of animal health products, fertilizers and crop chemicals among a panel of 4000 British farmers.

   Attwood Statistics Ltd. Berkhamsted (Tel: 04427 3311) Established 1948

4 *Household panel* provides continuous information for a wide range of products in regular weekly, quarterly and half yearly reports.

5 *AMSAC*: A panel of individuals (rather than households) providing data on product purchasing, usage, influence and attitudes.

6 *Auditplan*, Croydon (Tel: 01 686 3051)

   Specialist retail audit panels which can provide data analysed by client, sales area, specialist retail outlets and at specific times, like product launch.

   Audits of Great Britain Ltd. Ruislip/Harrow Lane (Tel: 01 868 4422) for Home Audit; 01 997 8484 for all other services.

7 *Television Consumer Audit (TCA)* of packaged foods in 7000 homes. Covers groceries, frozen food and meat.

8 *Home Audit of Consumer Durables* in 25 000 homes quarterly.

9 *Toiletries and Cosmetics Purchasing Index (TCPl)* 10 000 adults.

10 *Personal Purchasing Index (PPI)* 10 000 adults and 2000 children in 3000 households reporting on purchases such as clothes, drinks, snacks, films, cards, etc.

11   *Television Audience Research* operated for BARB (Broadcasters' Audience Research Board).

12   *Retail Services*, measuring retailer performance, shares of trade, etc, performance in product fields covered by panels.

13   *Prices Audit: Grocery* – prices and distribution check of named retail chains in 600 grocery stores.

14   *Prices Audit: Electrical Appliance* – prices and distribution check of named retail chains in 1100 electrical outlets.

British Market Research Bureau Ltd. London (Tel: 01 567 3060)

15   *Target Group Index (TGI)* an annual report of 24 000 self-completion questionnaires from a random sample of respondents (not a panel), covering the usage of hundreds of product groups and thousands of brands. Gives basic market usage data combined with demographics and media usage for brand users. Covers most consumer markets.

16   *Holiday Booking Index.* A regular survey of travel agents and tour operators.

17   *BARS* – record sales of top fifty records each week based on panel data.

18   *FORTE* – record purchases by individuals.

Carrick James Market Research, London (Tel: 01 636 8822)

19   *Wavelength.* Tracking study of trends among 6–15 year olds 4000 interviews annually (not a panel).

City Research Associates Ltd, London (Tel: 01 251 4549).

20   *General Insurance Broking.*

21   *Institutional Stockbroking.*

22   *Public Sector Pension Funds.*

23   *Life Assurance Advisers.*

CMR Ltd, London (Tel: 01 734 6245)

24   *National Hair Salon Survey.* On products used in ladies' hair salons.

Cocks Williamson Associates Ltd. London (Tel: 01 359 0200)

25   *Barometer 1* (in partnership with IED in Paris) An

international bi-annual monitor of attitudes and behaviour patterns among 8–14 year olds.

European Data and Research Ltd, London (Tel: 01 353 4513)

26   *U.K. Jewellery Trade Retail Audit*

Forecast (Market Research) Ltd, London (Tel: 01 480 5275).

27   *Motorists' Diary Panel.*

28   *Storecheck* – national distribution check in grocers, chemists and cash and carry.

Gordon Simmons Trade Research, London (Tel: 01 240 0256)

29   *Confectionery survey.* Recording purchases among 1000 outlets.

30   *Retailer Index.* Covering major multiples.

Industrial Market Research Ltd, London (Tel: 01 834 7814).

31   *Syndicated reports.* Available in a range of industrial markets

John McCormick Marketing Associates Ltd. London (Tel: 01 723 3484).

32   *Grocery buyers survey* – annual syndicated survey assessing manufacturers' performance.

Media Audits Ltd. London (Tel: 01 353 9585).

33   *Television Cost/Rating Index* – Regular monitoring of value obtained in TV advertisement buying.

34   *Press Buying Index* – Regular monitoring of value obtained in press advertisement buying.

MIL Research Group Ltd, London (Tel: 01 637 1444)

35   *Pharmaceutical Development Service* – A continuous survey.

36   *Veterinary Indices in Britain, Holland, and France* – A continuous survey.

37   *Building Division* – A continuous survey among architects.

MMI Medical Market Investigations Ltd, Bishops Stortford (Tel: 0279 57170).

38   *Audit of Diagnostic Kits and Reagents used in Laboratories*

(half yearly).
39 *Bulletin of Medical Marketing Information* (monthly).
40 *Directories of Health Centres, Private Hospitals, Health Services and Intensive Care Units* – Produced annually *A. C. Neilsen Co. Ltd*: Oxford – (Tel: 0865 64851)
41 *Neilsen Retail Index Services* – Shop audits covering groceries, chemists, confectioners/tobacconists/ newsagents, off licences, and cash and carry whole- salers. Covers consumer sales, retail purchases and stocks, distribution, retail prices etc.
NOP Market Research Ltd, London (Tel: 01 836 1511)
42 Continuous financial study.
Produce Studies Ltd. Newbury (Tel: 0635 46112)
43 *FARMSTAT* – Farming panel.
Professional Studies Group Ltd. London (Tel: 01 584 8535)
44 *Prescribing Trends*. Monthly data on G.P. prescribing.
45 *Baby Monitor* – weekly interviews, quarterly reports.
Public Attitude Surveys Research Ltd: High Wycombe (Tel: 0944 32771)
46 *PAS Beer Market* – continuous monitoring of drink- ers' attitudes and consumption habits.
RBL Medical Research Ltd: London (Tel: 01 488 1366)
47 *Patient panel UK.*
48 *AMOS – (Assessment of Market Opportunity and Size)* An international service.
Research Surveys of Great Britain Ltd. (RSGB) London (Tel: 01 997 5555).
49 *ACT* – Advertising Campaign Tracking Service.
50 *JICRAR* – National media survey on radio audiences.
51 *JICMARS* – Readership of medical publications among G.P.'s.
Retail Audits Ltd: Wembley (Tel: 01 902 8887)
52 *Retail Audit Panels and Distribution checks.* Covering the following outlet types: grocers, CTN's, hard- ware, DIY specialists, builders merchants, paint and wallpaper specialists, garages, automotive outlets, toy shops, department stores, stationers, gardening outlets, sports shops, variety chain stores, public

houses and other licensed premises.

Social Surveys (Gallup Poll) Ltd: London (Tel: 01 794 0461).

53   *Meals away from home.* – Continuous national survey.
54   *Consumer Confidence Index.*

Stats M.R. Ltd: London (Tel: 01 388 0221).

55   *Retail Audit and Distribution check.* Panels covering the following outlets: grocers, chemists, hardware, liquor and special CTN's trades.

System Three (Scotland) Ltd: Edinburgh (Tel: 031 556 9462).

56   *Scotcheck.* Integrated and repeated package of consumer and trade measures.
57   *Scottish Market Reports* – On individual markets.

Taylor Nelson and Associates Ltd: Epsom (Tel: 01 394 0191).

58   *Family food panel.*
59   *Monitor (social trends).*
60   *Business Opinions Study.*

Taylor Nelson (Medical and Social Surveys) Ltd: Epsom (Tel: 01 394 0191)

61   *Monitor* – Attitudes to medication and health care amongst G.P.'s and general public.
62   *Scriptcount* – Fortnightly audit of 800 chemists giving market information on all leading medications.
63   *Scriptlink* – An audit of G.P. attitudes to selected drugs.

Television Advertising Bureau (Surveys) Ltd (TABS): London (Tel: 01 629 0424).

64   *TABS National Brand Health Monitor.* 500 adults per week providing continuous campaign performance measurement and press versus T.V. effectiveness on multi-brand, multi-area basis.
65   *TABS on-air testing* – Large target market samples providing in-home reactions to live TV.
66   *TABS TVR laydown plans* – To help advertisers stretch TV budgets.

Technical and Medical Studies Ltd (TMS): London (Tel: 01

724 0811).

67   *Quarterly audits.* In laboratories and hospitals covering pathology and disposables.

Trade Studies Ltd: Wembley (Tel: 01 902 8887)

68   *Trade Voice* – Syndicated continuous data on retail and business outlets.

Travel and Tourism Research: London (Tel: 01 251 4549).

69   *North American and Channel Island package holidays.* Syndicated studies.

4.4   OMNIBUS RESEARCH SURVEYS

Omnibus Research represents a middle ground between 'off-the-peg' research services, where the data has already been collected and the researcher simply buys what is available, and primary research, where the researcher has to collect the information for himself. Omnibus Research describes regular research surveys which are being undertaken with a stated frequency and a decided method, using a set number of respondents and sampling points. Quite literally, the field-work 'Omnibus' is running, and the client is invited to board the bus by adding a few questions of his own to the questionnaire. The Omnibus user has the advantages of original question design, privacy of information and representativeness of sample, without having to bear all the field-work costs alone. He pays only for the number of questions included, and this is a very cheap form of original survey research. Omnibus research is particularly suitable for fairly robust data, e.g. the usage and purchase of products. It is less reliable for attitudinal and opinion data. This is because an omnibus survey might last for forty minutes or even more. During that time the respondent might be asked about six or more entirely different topics, which could range from voting intentions through bank account ownership, holiday-taking and purchase of hair-care products. The miscellaneous mix of bed-fellows, who might come together in a single questionnaire, means that if more than superficial data is required the respondent is unlikely to be in a frame of mind to give sufficient concentration to any single topic for reliable attitudinal data to be produced. For straightforward questions, where top of the head answers are perfectly acceptable, for example, 'When did you last buy . . . ?' 'Do you own . . . ?' or 'Have you ever . . . ?', omnibus surveys can provide good original data at a fraction of the cost of a 'made-to-measure' survey.

A list of organizations providing omnibus research services is published as an advertising feature in the Market Research Society Newsletter each month. A copy of this can be obtained from the Market Research Society (Tel: 01 235 4709) and will identify companies currently offering services. The list which follows was compiled from the *Market Research Society Year Book* and supplemented with data from the Market Research Society Newsletter. The Index which precedes the list illustrates the range of omnibus research services available.

4.4.1   INDEX TO OMNIBUS RESEARCH SERVICES

4.4.2   OMNIBUS RESEARCH SERVICES AND SUPPLIERS

Audience Selection: London (Tel: 01 481 1512)

1   *Weekend Omnibus*: 1500 respondents every fortnight. Entry deadline Friday noon, results Monday noon.

British Market Research Bureau Ltd: London (Tel: 01 567 3060).

2   *ACCESS*: 1000 adults weekly, stratified by ACORN.

Carrick James Market Research: London (Tel: 01 734 7171).

3   *National Parents' Survey*: 500 mothers of 3–6 year olds and 800 mothers of 7–14 year olds, bi-monthly.

4   *National Childrens' Survey*: 1100 7–17 year olds, monthly.

City Research Associates Ltd: London (Tel: 01 251 4549).

5   *City Omnibus*: 100 investment analysts and managers, per month.

EMS European Surveys Ltd: London (Tel: 01 388 7487)

6   *1100 adults*, monthly.

ESA Market Research Ltd: London (Tel: 01 481 1512).

7   *CTN Store check*: 1220 CTN outlets visited every two months.

European Data and Research Ltd: London (Tel: 01 353 4513).

8   *'Eurobus'* – European Omnibus.

Forecast Market Research Ltd: London (Tel: 01 481 1512).

9   *Grocers/Chemists/Drug stores*: 3200 outlets visited every two months.

Lansdowne Market Research Ltd: Ireland (Tel: Dublin 68277),

10   *Ireland*: Monthly survey of 1400 adults in the Republic of Ireland.

Marplan Ltd: London (Tel: 01 928 1200).

11   *Marplan Omnibus*: 2000 adults.

12   *Q 15*: 1500 adults aged 15+.

MAS Survey Research Ltd: London (Tel: 01 240 2861).

13   *OmniMAS*: 2400 adults weekly.

MILPRO Ltd: London (Tel: 01 637 1444).

14   *MILPRO Baby Monitor*: Interviews mothers weekly, reports quarterly.

MRF Medical Research Factors Ltd: Wallington (Tel: 01 773 0037).

15   *MRO (Medical Research Omnibus)*: 200–400 G.P's monthly.

NOP Market Research Ltd: London (Tel: 01 836 1511).

16   *Random Omnibus*: 2000 adults weekly, based on random sampling.

17   *Quota Omnibus*: based on quota sampling.

18   *8000 Omnibus.*

Research Surveys of Great Britain Ltd (RSGB): London (Tel: 01 997 5555).

19   *Weekly omnibus*: adult sample. 2000 weekly.

20   *Motoring omnibus*: 1000 motorists monthly.

21   *Baby Products Survey*: 700 mothers with a baby under 2 years old, bi-monthly omnibus.

22   *Baby Panel*: 1150 mothers with a baby under 2 years old. 2-week diaries of purchases.

23   *Octobus*: 8000 adults monthly.

24   *Catering Omnibus:* 600 catering establishments, bi-annually.

Sample Surveys Ltd: London (Tel: 01 229 1403).

25   *Omnicar*: motoring omnibus.

Social Surveys (Gallup Poll) Ltd: London (Tel: 01 794 0461).

26   *Gallup personal omnibus*: 2000 adults weekly.

27   *Gallup telephone omnibus*: 1000 interviews nationally. Results in four working days.

28   *European omnibus*: EEC + seven other European countries, weekly, fortnightly, monthly or quarterly.

System Three (Scotland) Ltd: Edinburgh (Tel: 031 556 9462).

29   *Scottish Opinion Survey* (S.O.S.): 1000 adults, monthly.

Travel and Tourism Research: London (Tel: 01 251 4549).

30   *Travel Agents' Omnibus Survey*: 200 +ABTA Travel Agents.

Ulster Marketing Surveys Ltd: Belfast (Tel: Belfast 231060).

31   *Ulster Omnibus*: 1100 adults quarterly.

Overseas Omnibuses: see MRS Newsletter (Tel: 01 235 4709).

32 *Examples from November* 1982 issue show omnibuses being carried out in: Indonesia, France, Cameroun, Switzerland, Japan, worldwide 'Flexibus' in thirty-five countries.

4.5 SPECIALIST RESEARCH SERVICES

4.5.1 TYPES OF RESEARCH OFFERED VIA THE MARKET RESEARCH SOCIETY

In addition to the syndicated data and omnibus research services which can be bought 'off-the-peg', marketing research organizations also provide a wide range of specialist research facilities. In this case a client is buying 'off-the-peg' expertise in a particular area of research. The kind of specialist techniques which have been developed and are available for purchase are shown in detail in the Market Research Society free booklet *Organisations Providing Market Research Services in Great Britain*. An indication of the range of 'off-the-peg' expertise available is given by simply listing the key to types of research offered from the booklet. Specialist research services exist for: advertising, agriculture, children's, data processing, employee attitude, executive consultancy, executive interviews, fieldwork and coding, financial, industrial, international, media, motoring, continuous consumer panels, pharmaceutical, packaging, price, product testing, qualitative, retail audits, tourism, trade, test markets.

More detailed reading of the entries for the 210 firms listed indicates that there is an organization offering specialist expertise in almost every market of any size: consumer, trade, industrial or service, for both public and private organizations. Special research techniques are also available for a wide variety of applications like company acquisitions, telephone research, postal research, business research, name testing, market modelling, sales forecasting, colour and design research, transport studies, retail location, and so on. The *Market Research Society Newsletter* also contains an advertising feature on 'Data for Sale'. A recent issue featured the following 'off-the-peg' data:

Distribution checks in all types of retail outlet.

Surveys three times a year among truck dealers in the UK and France.

Children and teenagers: data on a range of relevant markets.

Reports and data bases for over 100 consumer products in 16 European markets plus the USA.

Holiday brochure availability.

Retail price checks/new product availability in range of retail outlets.

As this section indicates, a wide range of specialist research services exists, and information about them is contained in the Market Research Society publications: *Organisations Providing Market Research Services in Great Britain* (annual) and the *Market Research Society Newsletter* (monthly). Both can be obtained free on request to: The Market Research Society, 15 Belgrave Square, London SW1X 8PF. (Tel: 01 235 4709). The MRS also publishes a series of guides and notes on research in many European and other overseas countries.

4.5.2   CONSUMER CLASSIFICATION SYSTEMS

Social grading or social class

Social grading is a system of classifying the UK population according to the occupation of the head of household and allocating people to one of six social grades. These are also referred to as 'social classes', and are shown in Table 4.1. The system was used before the 1939–45 war, and is still the major classification system used today. The reason for its widespread use is that members of each social group or class do show broadly similar patterns of behaviour, consumption, life-style, attitudes and media use in many situations.

This can help to explain differences in use of, or response to, all kinds of products, services and therefore gives a basis for comparison. It is also relatively easy to apply in research surveys, and so is used in most surveys and marketing activity. However, the very fact that it is a pre-war classification system highlights its current social grading deficiencies. Although the process of social change is slow (and hence the system still has broad relevance in many situations), since the war there has been considerable social change resulting in more social diversity. For many situations the system of social grading is no longer relevant and so cannot help in explaining or understanding consumer behaviour.

% population 15+*	Social grade	Social status	Head of household's occupation
3	A	Upper middle class	Higher managerial, administrative or professional
13	B	Middle class	Intermediate managerial, administrative or professional
23	C1	Lower middle class	Supervisory or clerical, and junior managerial, administrative or professional
32	C2	Skilled working class	Skilled manual workers
19	D	Working class	Semi and unskilled manual workers
10	E	Those at lowest levels of subsistence	State pensioners or windows (no other earner), casual or lowest-grade workers

*Source: JICNARS National Readership Survey, 1981.

Sagacity

This is a system of classification pioneered by Research Services Ltd (01 903 8511). Its basic thesis is that in addition to differences, between groups of people accounted for by social grading, other important differences in aspirations and behaviour patterns are accounted for by general income

Figure 4.1 *Sagacity groupings*

The basic thesis of the SAGACITY grouping is that people have different aspirations and behaviour patterns as they go through their life-cycle. Four main stages of life-cycles are defined which are sub-divided by income and occupation groups.

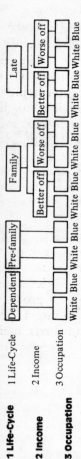

1 Life-Cycle

2 Income

3 Occupation

Descriptive notations for each of the twelve groups are described below together with their size as a percentage of total adult population

Dependent. White (DW) 6%
Mainly under 24s living at home or full-time student, where head of household is an ABC1 occupation group.

Dependent Blue (DB) 10%
Mainly under 24s living at home or full-time student, where head of household is a C2DE occupation group.

Pre-family. White (PFW) 4%
Under 35s who have established their own household but have no children and where the head of household is in an ABC1 occupation group.

Pre-family, Blue (PFB) 4%
Under 35s who have established their own household but have no children and where the head of household is in a C2DE occupation group.

Family, Better off, White (FW+) 6%
Housewives and heads of household, under 65, with one or more children in the household in the 'better off' income group and where the head of household is in an ABC1 occupation group (63% are AB).

Family, Better off, Blue (FB+) 8%
Housewives and heads of household, under 65, with one or more children in the household, in the 'better off' income group and where the head of household is in a C2DE occupation group. (80% are C2).

Family, Worse off, (FW−) 8%
Housewives and heads of household, under 65 with one or more children

in the household, in the 'worse off' income group and where the head of household is in an ABC1 occupation group (70% are C1).

Family, Worse off, Blue (FB−) 14%
Housewives and heads of household, under 65, with one or more children in the household in the 'worse off' income group and where the head of household is in a C2DE occupation group (53% are DE).

Late, Better off, White (LW+) 5%
Includes all adults whose children have left home or who are over 35 and childless, are in the 'better off' income group and where the head of household is in an ABC1 occupation group (61% are AB).

Late, Better off, Blue (LB+) 6%
Includes all adults whose children have left home or who are over 35 and childless, are in the 'better off' income group and where the head of household is in a C2DE occupation group (72% are C2).

Late, Worse off, White (LW−) 9%
Includes all adults whose children have left home or who are over 35 and childless, are in the 'worse off' income group and where the head of household is in an ABC1 occupation group (67% are C1).

Late, Worse off, Blue (LB−) 20%
Includes all adults whose children have left home or who are over 35 and childless, are in the 'worse off' income group and where the head of household is in a C2DE occupation group (72% are DE).

Source: Research Services Ltd, 1981.

level and by the stage of life individuals are at in the 'family life cycle'. Figure 4.1 describes them briefly, and indicates their size as a percentage of the total adult population.

ACORN

Described by *The Sunday Times* (31 October 1982) as 'a new computerized research system that is taking the marketing world by storm', ACORN is an 'off-the-peg' service offered by C.A.C.I. Market Analysis Group (Tel: 01 404 0834). Its title is an acronym for 'A Classification of Residential Neighbourhoods', and it divides the country into thirty-six types of neighbourhood based on enumeration districts (average population about 460). The full ACORN profile based on 1981 census data is shown in Table 4.2. The system reflects the fact that people living in particular types of neighbourhood tend to exhibit broadly smiliar patterns of behaviour. ACORN is linked with syndicated services like TG1 (BMRB), Monitor (Taylor Nelson), National Readership Survey, Home Audit (AGB), TCA (AGB), and with the post-code system. This means it can be used to identify areas of relevance for most product and service groups, and direct communication to those areas is possible through the post-codes.

ACORN has been used by local authorities to isolate areas of deprivation, and by marketing firms seeking to identify areas of greatest demand for their products and services. Major retailers, banks and building societies use the service for branch location, and the mix of products appropriate to each branch. It is also used to target local advertising, posters, leaflet distribution and direct mail. Researchers can also use the system to select representative samples for questionnaire surveys.

Although still a relatively new service, the widespread applicability and usage of ACORN in researching consumers has led to the suggestion that it may eventually supersede the system of social grading based on occupation of the head of household.

Table 4.2 **The ACORN Classification**

1981 ACORN Profile Great Britain **ACORN Groups**		1981 Population	%
A	Agricultural Areas	1 811 485	3.4
B	Modern Family Housing, Higher Incomes	8 667 137	16.2
C	Older Housing of Intermediate Status	9 420 477	17.6
D	Poor Quality Older Terraced Housing	2 320 846	4.3
E	Better-off Council Estates	6 976 570	13.0
F	Less Well-off Council Estates	5 032 657	9.4
G	Poorest Council Estates	4 048 658	7.6
H	Multi-Racial Areas	2 086 026	3.9
I	High Status Non-Family Areas	2 248 207	4.2
J	Affluent Suburban Housing	8 514 878	15.9
K	Better-off Retirement Areas	2 041 338	3.8
U	Unclassified	388 632	0.7
ACORN Types			
A	1	Agricultural Villages	1 376 427	2.6
A	2	Areas of Farms and Smallholdings	435 058	0.8
B	3	Cheap Modern Private Housing	2 209 759	4.1
B	4	Recent Private Housing, Young Families	1 648 534	3.1
B	5	Modern Private Housing, Older Children	3 121 453	5.8
B	6	New Detached Houses, Young Families	1 404 893	2.6
B	7	Military Bases	282 498	0.5
C	8	Mixed Owner-Occupied and Council Estates	1 880 142	3.5
C	9	Small Town Centres and Flats Above Shops	2 157 360	4.0
C	10	Villages with Non-Farm Employment	2 463 246	4.6
C	11	Older Private Housing, Skilled Workers	2 919 729	5.5
D	12	Unimproved Terraces with Old People	1 351 877	2.5
D	13	Pre-1914 Terraces, Low Income Families	762 266	1.4
D	14	Tenement Flats Lacking Amenities	206 703	0.4
E	15	Council Estates, Well-off Older Workers	1 916 242	3.6
E	16	Recent Council Estates	1 392 961	2.6
E	17	Council Estates, Well-off Young Workers	2 615 376	4.9

E	18	Small Council Houses, Often Scottish	1 051 991	2.0
F	19	Low Rise Estates in Industrial Towns	2 538 119	4.7
F	20	Inter-War Council Estates, Older People	1 667 994	3.1
F	21	Council Housing for the Elderly	826 544	1.5
G	22	New Council Estates in Inner Cities	1 079 351	2.0
G	23	Overspill Estates, High Unemployment	1 729 757	3.2
G	24	Council Estates with Overcrowding	868 141	1.6
G	25	Council Estates with Worst Poverty	371 409	0.7
H	26	Multi-Occupied Terraces, Poor Asians	204 493	0.4
H	27	Owner-Occupied Terraces with Asians	577 871	1.1
H	28	Multi-Let Housing with Afro-Caribbeans	387 169	0.7
H	29	Better-off Multi-Ethnic Areas	916 493	1.7
I	30	High Status Areas, Few Children	1 129 079	2.1
I	31	Multi-Let Big Old Houses and Flats	822 017	1.5
I	32	Furnished Flats, Mostly Single People	297 111	0.6
J	33	Inter-War Semis, White Collar Workers	3 054 032	5.7
J	34	Spacious Inter-War Semis, Big Gardens	2 676 598	5.0
J	35	Villages with Wealthy Older Commuters	1 533 756	2.9
J	36	Detached Houses, Exclusive Suburbs	1 250 492	2.3
K	37	Private Houses, Well-off Elderly	1 199 703	2.2
K	38	Private Flats with Single Pensioners	841 635	1.6
U	39	Unclassified	388 632	0.7
Area	Total		53 556 911	100.0

4.6 SUMMARY

Before embarking on original research, an organization is well advised to discover whether the data it requires is already available. There are four sources for 'off-the-peg' research data. Secondary desk research includes the use of published data from a range of identified sources covering data about companies, industries and markets. Syndicated research services produce current market data which is available for purchase, and an index to, and list of, services and suppliers is given. Omnibus research services provide an 'off-the-peg' vehicle for asking questions of specified groups. An index to, and list of, services and suppliers is given. Expertise exists in many research areas, and the types of specialist research services available via the Market Research Society are mentioned. The section concludes with a brief introduction to three commonly used consumer classification systems: social grading, sagacity and ACORN.

5 'Made-to-Measure' Research

5.1 INTRODUCTION

Chapters 3 and 4 were concerned with the use of data from within the organization, or data and specific services already available 'off-the-peg' from outside bodies. Inevitably, there are many situations for which existing information is too specific, too general, too out-of-date, not available, or in some other way inappropriate for providing a solution to the problem with which a manager is faced. This is when it is necessary to consider generating original first-hand data, which is collected with the special data requirement the manager has, as its sole objective. This type of research is referred to as 'primary' research, because it is first-hand. It is also known as 'field research', because it generally involves going out into the market place, or field, to gather data. The term 'made-to-measure' research underlines the fact that the research programme is tailored to meet the precise information needs for which it is required.

5.2 BUYING A 'MADE-TO-MEASURE' RESEARCH SURVEY IS JUST LIKE BUYING A 'MADE-TO-MEASURE' SUIT

The Suit	The Research Survey
People decide to get a new suit when the old one wears out, or there is a special occasion, or a new fashion is introduced. They may decide to get a quote from a tailor. This tailor will ask:	Organizations decide to use research when things go wrong, or they decide to enter a new market, or launch a new product. They may decide to get a quote

1 What does Sir want the suit for?

2 Let us take Sir's measurements.

3 Did Sir have any particular style in mind?

4 Did Sir have any particular colour in mind?

5 Did Sir have any particular material in mind?

6 Did Sir have any particular cutter in mind?

7 Should it be machine-stitched or hand-stitched?

8 Will he give the job to the tailor, or decide to get it done at home? Tailor-made or hand-made? Depends on cost, how big a job it is, and how good a job he could get done at home.

9 Will the suit be worn?

10 Will he like it, and get another one, or decide something was wrong with it that should be changed next time – the colour or material, perhaps. If it's bad enough, maybe he'll change the tailor!

In buying a suit, the client decides what he wants the suit for, and the measurements will fit him closely, although the tailor will measure up. He is likely to take the tailor's advice on technical aspects of the suit, although it helps to know something about these things if you're going to get a good job, say on material qualities. Whether it's worn when it arrives depends on whether it's really what was wanted, and both the client and the tailor will learn from the experience. Whether a tailor is really necessary depends on whether professional expertise is worth paying for.

from a research agency. The agency will ask:

What is the problem?

What data is needed to solve it?

How will the data be collected?

Who will provide the data?

How will the questions be asked?

Who will ask the questions?

What will happen to the answers?

Will he give the job to a research agency, or get it done within the organization? Agency job or in-house job? Depends on cost, how big the job is, and how much relevant expertise there is in-house.

What action will result?

What will be learned from the process? Was it a good piece of research or not? Should the sampling procedure be improved, or the questionnaire? Should the research agency be used again?

In buying research, the client defines the problem and the data will be needed to fit the problem, although the research agency may suggest data requirements. The client will probably take the agency's advice on technical aspects of the survey, although it helps to know something about these things if you're going to get a good job, say on data collection methods or questionnaire design. Whether the survey results are used in decision-making depends on whether they are really what was needed, and both the client and the agency will learn from the experience. Whether an agency is really necessary depends on whether professional expertise is worth paying for.

5.3   THE 'MADE-TO-MEASURE' RESEARCH PROCESS

It is helpful to begin with an overall view of the research process. Six stages in the research process are identified, and twelve related questions which must be given consideration. These form the framework within which the content of this and the following five chapters are set.

Table 5.1   The 'made-to-measure' research process: six stages, twelve questions

Stage	Question	Chapter
1 Defining the research required	1 What is the problem?	5
	2 What data are needed to solve it?	5
2 Planning the research	3 How will the data be collected?	6
	4 Who will provide the data?	7
	5 How will the questions be asked?	8
	6 Who will ask the questions?	9
	7 What will happen to the answers?	10
	8 Will the plan work?	
3 Carrying out the field-work	9 Is it going according to schedule?	(9)
4 Analysing, interpreting and reporting	10 What are the results?	(10)
5 Using the research	11 What action will result?	
6 Feedback	12 What can be learned from the process?	

A clear definition of the problem, and the data needed to produce a solution to it, is the starting point of the research process. It is also the most important part of the process from the point of view of the manager who must play a dominant role in it if the research is to produce the right kind of data for his needs. This chapter is concerned with defining the research requirement, and deals with questions 1 and 2: What is the problem? and, 'What data are needed to solve it?

The next stage is the planning stage. At this point decisions must be made about technical aspects of the research survey. In practice, the manager who requires research information is unlikely to have more than a controlling involvement in the research process from stages 2–4. The research itself and the major technical decisions about research method, sampling, questionnaire design, field-work, data analysis and report writing, are usually undertaken by research professionals either within the research department of an organization, or in research agencies.

The manager who needs to commission and use research will be more effective in making use of a tool if he knows more about it. Each of the significant decision areas in the planning and operation of research surveys is explained in the following chapters. Research method in Chapter 6, sampling procedures in Chapter 7, questionnaire design in Chapter 8, field-work in Chapter 9, and analysis, inter-pretation and reporting of results in Chapter 10.

The aim of these chapters is to enable the non-research manager to become a more informed research user and buyer, and to equip him with appropriate criteria for judging research quality. This will allow him to deal more competently and confidently with research agency per-sonnel, and the matter of selecting a good research agency to carry out the research is covered in Chapter 11.

Stage 5, using the research, is the subject of Chapter 14 where a range of research applications in making marketing decisions are dealt with. Stage 6, feedback, is always important, but perhaps particularly so for the new research user. After carrying out a 'made-to-measure' research survey, it should be critically analysed by the manager himself in order to learn from it. Approaches, methods or techniques which worked well can be noted for use again in similar circumstances, and vice versa for those aspects of the research process which did not work so well. It is always helpful to share this analysis with the research agency, if one were involved, in order to build a constructively developing and improving research expertise relevant to the organization's specific needs, within the agency. Alternatively, of course, it may be that sharing the post-research analysis with an agency may explain to them why they are unlikely to be involved again! The purpose of critical feedback from the research process is for the manager to develop his personal skills and experience as a research user ready for when the process begins again from Stage 1.

5.4 STAGE 1: DEFINING THE RESEARCH REQUIRED

Before any research programme can be undertaken, its scope and objectives must be defined. Too often, research surveys are undertaken with insufficient clarification of their objectives, with the result that the findings are found to be too vague, too narrow, or entirely inappropriate. The responsibility for defining the research objectives lies mainly with the manager who initiates the research, and wishes to apply its results in decision-making. A non-specialist manager may know very little about research, but is likely to be the only person with a clear idea of why the research is needed and how the findings will be used. If this is not communicated adequately to the researcher, the research programme which follows may be entirely misdirected.

Answering the following questions can help in arriving at a more precise definition of the research required.

5.4.1 STAGE 1: QUESTION 1 'WHAT IS THE PROBLEM?'

This should be stated as specifically as possible. For example, a cinema chain faced with the problem of declining audiences decided that its problem was, 'to identify ways in which more people could be attracted to attend the cinema'. An alternative statement of the problem which was rejected was 'to discover why cinema audiences are declining'. Although the two are obviously very closely related, the outcome of the research as defined was specifically directed to be action-orientated in its findings, in a way that the more general statement was not.

5.4.2 STAGE 1: QUESTION 2 'WHAT DATA ARE NEEDED TO FIND A SOLUTION?'

Deciding the data requirement
The first step is to review the information that already exists. In the cinema example, there was already some data about cinema attendance. The present state of knowledge should form the starting point for the search for new information, since it can often guide further research into those areas most likely to be fruitful in producing worthwhile data. Cinema audiences were known to be typically young, and so it was clear that the views of this group must be adequately represented in the survey.

The second step involves generating a list of necessary information. In doing this, it is important to distinguish between what is *essential* to know, and what it would be *nice* to know, and to delete the latter. This can be accomplished by going back over the first list of necessary information and deleting from it those bits of information which are inessential. The resultant list of essential information now forms the basis for deriving research survey objectives, and makes it possible to redefine the original problem in marketing research terms.

The cinema chain management realized that although they already knew what kind of people attend the cinema, and how often, the further information they needed concerned people's attitudes and motivations for cinema-going. This information would enable them to identify what factors attract people to the cinema.

A 'crunch' question in deciding whether a research

survey is really required is to ask 'What would happen without the information?' If the answer to the question indicates that the absence of research information will not materially affect the decision-making process, then the research programme should not be undertaken. It may well be that other routes to problem solution may be more effective, less costly, less time-consuming, and maybe all three! Wasting money on research is as undesirable as wasting it on any other area of business, and just as easy.

If a research survey is to be undertaken, then a definition of who or what is to be surveyed must be drawn up. All decisions about survey content and coverage must be made explicit. For example, in a survey about farms, the group to be surveyed was 'all farms'. Specifically excluded was 'small holdings'. This made it quite clear to the researcher how the terms were defined. In this example, the definition of 'farms' would be further improved by greater precision: including the minimum acreage, or minimum turnover to be considered, and indicating whether all arable, dairy and mixed farms were included, and how other specific classifications were to be treated.

The outcome of this procedure should be a clear and concise written statement of the objectives of the proposed research survey, and its scope. To complete the definition of the research required, any constraints must be clearly spelled out at this early stage, since they are likely materially to affect the nature of the research which can be undertaken. The two most important constraints are time and money. If the decision for which the research input is required has to be made by a particular deadline, then this must be made clear at the outset, for it will affect the choice of research method. Some methods are more time-consuming than others. Similarly, if the budget available for research is limited, then the amount which can be spent must be stated in broad terms. As with any other commodity, in research one gets largely what one pays for. An organization not prepared to spend much cannot expect to get very much good research information. Hundreds of pounds saved in research costs must be weighed against possibly hundreds of thousands of pounds lost in the results of wrong decisions.

The high marketing costs of failure, and the damage done to a company's reputation in the market-place as a result of wrong decisions, are illustrated by the following rather painful example. A manufacturer of industrial contract materials produced a new flooring material. The success of the product was very important to the organization because markets for most of their product ranges were in decline. Management had high hopes for the new product which produced a more durable floor with a better finish than existing materials, although it was more expensive. Laying the flooring required a completely different technique to that of traditional floorings, but it was not a complicated process. The manufacturer felt that an industrial market research survey to predict demand for the new material would be too expensive, but some 'market research' was required in view of the importance of the new product launch to the company as a whole. As a result, six good customers for the company's products were given samples of the new material and asked to try it out. Some time later, one of the company executives called on the customers and asked how they rated the material. The customers confirmed the company's own view that it was a good material. On the strength of this 'research', the product was launched nationally. It was a flop. The 'research exercise' was repeated with different customers. They also reported liking the material, and it was relaunched. Another flop. Finally, in desperation, the company undertook a formal survey of the market for flooring materials to discover whether there was a market niche for this material, and if so, how to relaunch the product into it for the third time.

Their research indicated that the conservatism of the building trade was a major stumbling block. The benefits of the new material all came in use. When a floor was being laid the product was seen as expensive and the differences required in laying technique met with resistance from the floor-layers. The company discovered that to make a success of this product their marketing should be aimed at architects so that they would specify the new material for its good appearance and durability. Builders, to whom the product had been launched, could see little reason for bothering with it. At the same time, the instructions could be vastly improved so as to make it clear that the material was *different* to lay, but not difficult and not any more time-consuming than traditional materials. The message was clear: it was a good product, but needed marketing in ways which the company had not previously been aware of.

If a company cannot afford, or does not wish to pay for, the type of research necessary for a particular decision, then it may be better to have no research at all than an inappropriately small research programme. Beautifully presented research reports have a way of being believed by those who wish to do so, however uncertain the data base. At least with no research information at all a company knows that its decisions have no affirmative background, and they are therefore more likely to be made with greater caution.

The research required can now be defined in terms of its objectives, scope and practical constraints. This definition forms the framework within which the research itself will take place. It is therefore essential for the manager to satisfy himself that the data requirement is correctly specified. In this situation, 'more heads are better than one' and it is a useful discipline to discuss a proposed project with others. This has a number of advantages. First, the project benefits from additional input: new and useful suggestions. Secondly, it benefits from external criticism: points not as clearly defined as they should be will be queried. Thirdly, the very process of articulating and defending the approach to others is most valuable in clarifying and distilling the essence of the research required.

This emphasis on the need for careful consideration at the definitive stage of a research project is because it is the easiest stage to skimp in practice, and one of the most damaging to the final outcome if not done properly. Research which starts off unsure where it is going is unlikely to arrive in the right place! Defining the research required is a task which the decision-maker himself must be really precise about. The main means by which control can be exercised over the execution of the project is via the framework of a clear, and correctly expressed statement of the research required.

Deciding the type of data

From the starting point of a well-defined statement of the research required, the next step is to consider what kind of research data would be most useful in improving the decision to be made. Research is often categorized as being either 'qualitative' or 'quantitative', and the distinction is an important one.

Qualitative research Qualitative research is so called because its emphasis lies in producing data which is rich in insight, understanding, explanation and depth of information, but which cannot be justified statistically. Qualitative research is typically carried out with only a few respondents – often less than fifty individuals may be surveyed. Whilst the findings from this number of people may be very important to the researcher in giving clues to the thinking of other members of the target group under investigation, the data base is far too small to make statements like, '10% thought this . . .' and, '15% did that . . .'. It is in this sense then, that the data is qualitative rather than quantitative: the emphasis is on meaning rather than number.

The main methods used in qualitative research are depth interviews, and group discussions and these are described in Chapter 6. Their relatively small-scale means that qualitative studies can generally be completed more quickly and less-expensively than quantitative surveys. They can be used early in the research process to generate hypotheses which a subsequent quantitative survey will investigate further.

Quantitative research   Quantitative research is the kind of research which the layman brings to mind with a stereotype picture of a researcher, with questionnaire and clipboard, interviewing people in the street. It involves the research techniques of representative samples, questionnaires, interviewers, data processing, and so on. These are all necessary to make it possible to express the results quantitatively, with statements like, '25% of the population own . . .' and, '37% of machine tool buyers think . . .'. The word 'population' is used here in the research sense, meaning 'the whole group under consideration'. It can, therefore, refer to the human population of the country, but the 'populations' considered by management decision-makers are usually more restricted than that. They may include only the buyers of the company's products, all housewives aged 16–45, or all main-frame computer owners. The 'population' being surveyed may be non-buyers, or potential buyers of a product or service not yet launched, and so on. The definition of the population being considered must be quite specifically described for the purposes of each particular research survey.

If a population is to be surveyed it would be unacceptably expensive, time-consuming and difficult to organize a census, in which questions are asked of every individual in the target population. It is also unnecessary, since sampling theory makes it possible to select a limited number of respondents who are representative of the whole group, i.e. a sample. Carrying out a sample survey is cheaper, quicker and more efficient than a census, but equally effective if an appropriate procedure is used for selecting the sample. Details of sampling techniques are discussed in Chapter 7. It is important to note that as well as being representative, the sample must be sufficiently large for statistical generalizations from it to be valid. In consumer research surveys this usually means several hundred respondents, and for large surveys several thousand. Industrial and other specialized surveys often have smaller, but still adequate, samples. Questionnaires are the device used to ensure that all respondents are asked precisely the same question, so that their responses can be added together meaningfully. Questionnaire design is considered in Chapter 8, and techniques of interviewing and data processing in Chapters 9 and 10 respectively.

The outcome of the research procedure outlined is that the researcher is able to use the results from this type of sample survey to predict, with a known level of statistical accuracy, what the result would be if the whole group being considered had been asked the questions, whether that be all housewives, all drivers, all retired persons, and so on. The practical limitations of the questionnaire itself – it cannot be too long or respondents will refuse co-operation – mean that data collected this way cannot usually produce the richness of insight which comes from the qualitative approach, but the results have the great advantage of producing quantitative estimates of known reliability. When the decision to be taken is itself a quantitative one, for example, deciding production levels for the next period, or the levels of social amenities to be provided, then quantitative research is the most appropriate route to providing information input to the decision-making process. In general, the scale of quantitative research means that it is more expensive and rather more time-consuming than qualitative research. A survey of 500 consumer respondents might take 2–3 months from commissioning to final report.

In a major study, both qualitative and quantitative approaches may be used. For example, if information is needed about a subject with which a manager is largely unfamiliar, he might begin with a qualitative survey. This will generate ideas and insights, and give sufficient familiarity with the area under study to make it possible to formulate a more systematic approach to data collection. It may even be possible to develop research hypotheses from qualitative research which can be tested using an experimental approach. The great advantage of initiating a research programme with qualitative methods is that little prior knowledge of the area is required. On the basis of the knowledge gained in this way, a quantitative follow-up study can be designed to measure the importance of variables identified in the initial study. Qualitative research used in this way is referred to as 'exploratory research'.

Alternatively, in an area with which a manager is already familiar, the research programme may begin with a large-scale quantitative study. In the course of this study some findings may emerge for which there is no apparent explanation. In this case, qualitative research may be used to generate explanations of findings from quantitative studies.

Deciding the research method

It is apparent from the preceding section that the type of data produced depends not only upon the approach decided on, but also on the method of data collection used. Different methods will produce data of differing depth, breadth, quantity and content as well as differing in levels of accuracy, speed and cost. In this section the types of method in common use are introduced, and in Chapter 6 the methods themselves are described.

There are many ways of categorizing the various methods of collecting data. The descriptions 'primary or secondary', and 'qualitative or quantitative' have already been referred to. The scheme used here classifies methods as employing *interviews, observation,* or *experiments* as the means of data collection. For the research user, it is important to have some feel for what each method can accomplish, in order to select those appropriate for the needs of a particular problem.

Interview research   The basic assumption of all interviewing techniques is that to get information about people, you simply ask them for it. This could be information about what type of people they are, how they behave (usually in terms of purchase behaviour) or what their likes, dislikes, attitudes and opinions about the subject under study may be. Very often, this basic assumption is a realistic one, which explains why interviewing is the most commonly used technique of social research – i.e. any research concerned with people. The advantage of interviewing techniques is that it is often possible to discover not only *what* people are, do or think, but also *why* this may be so. This makes it a very rich data source in terms of the quantity and quality of data generated.

There are, however, occasions when the basic assumption is unjustified, and people either will not or cannot give, or will falsify, the information required. Some categories of information cannot be gathered by the interview method and other approaches are needed.

There may be occasions when people cannot say what they do, often because the information, which is so important to a decision-maker, is of such trivial interest to the individual that it simply is not recalled. A manufacturer may wish to know exactly how many packets of biscuits, and of what type, each household buys in a month, and whether this changes over the year. Only the individual whose biscuit-buying behaviour is unusually regular and stable would be able to answer such a question accurately. For those households where biscuits are bought as required, and where several different types may be bought in the course of a year, the best answer to the question could only be an approximation. Manufacturers facing increasingly tight profit margins may find the difference between decisions based on purchase approximations and reality is the difference between profit and loss.

Observation research   It is for situations such as this that observation techniques are particularly valuable. The 'retail audit' method of research is based on observation of the stocks in a retail outlet. The amounts delivered, as shown by invoices, are added to the amount in stock last time an observation was made, minus the amount in stock for this observation. The difference is the amount of the product which has been purchased in the intervening period. Such information avoids the possibility of error introduced by bad memory.

Observation techniques are also used a great deal in social planning: in traffic counts, for example, or observation of hospital out-patient departments to investigate ways of minimizing waiting time, and therefore saving the space taken by large waiting areas. Increasingly, observation is being undertaken by electrical apparatus rather than people, as in store layout investigations using cameras, or television-watching measurement using SET meters. As well as overcoming the limitations of memory, the other important advantage of observation as a method of data collection is that the behaviour of the individual is not influenced by the research process. For behaviour which the individual feels reflects badly on him, like smoking or drinking, observation may give a more accurate picture than personal interviewing.

The main limitation of observation methods is that whilst they may provide good information on 'what' people do, they offer no explanation as to why that might be so. If observation data is interpreted subjectively with incorrect explanations of the behaviour observed, then the advantages gained by use of the method are lost. For this reason, observation methods are often combined with other sources of data. The management of a chain of bingo halls initially assumed that regular attenders were primarily gamblers and more could be attracted with higher prizes. When this approach failed, subsequent group discussion indicated that many people play bingo for its social benefits. More money spent on decor and 'ambience' would attract higher attendance from this group, who were put off by the rather seedy appearance of some bingo halls.

Research experiments   Research experiments involve a more rigorous approach to research design than is necessary in straightforward interview or observation research surveys. The point of research experiments is that they make it possible for the experimenter to investigate cause-and-effect relationships between variables. What factors influence sales, and by how much, for example? Since almost all real life situations, particularly sales, are the outcome of the interaction of many variables, it is necessary for the research programme to be designed in such a way that the variables under test can be controlled by the experimenter and the effects of other identified variables measured independently. To identify the effect of advertising on sales, for example, price, distribution levels and external factors like the weather, must also be measured to isolate their effects. When a number of interacting variables are under consideration, specific experimental approaches need to be employed to make it possible to isolate statistically the effects being measured. Some of the experimental approaches in common use are discussed in Chapter 13.

Although these are the most technically complex studies to mount, they are the most rewarding because they make cause-and-effect relationships statistically explicit. For the manager wishing to exercise control through decision-making, such knowledge is invaluable. Knowing how responsive a market is to advertising, price cuts, and so on, makes for greater marketing precision. The difficulty in practice lies in the fact that the more important management problems are typically multivariate. Even if the manager were able to identify all the relevant variables, many of them would be difficult to measure precisely, for example, the 'innovativeness' of buyers in an industrial market. Interaction between variables, like price and sales support, will also complicate the picture. The more complex and imprecise the measurement of variables becomes, the less easy it is to justify the time and expense which experimental research demands.

5.5   SUMMARY

'Made-to-measure' research surveys are designed to meet the precise data needs for solving a particular problem. The first stage is to define the research required, and this begins with precise specification of the problem. It is followed by specification of the data required to answer the problem. Decisions must be made about whether qualitative or quantitative data, or both, will be needed. The method to be used in generating the data must also be determined and three approaches are introduced: interview research, observation research and research experiments.

6 How are the Data Collected?

6.1 INTRODUCTION

This chapter reviews the main methods of data collection for primary research. Interview methods are the most widely used, and there are a number of ways in which interviews can be conducted. These methods involve personal, face-to-face contact between the interviewer and the respondent, and can therefore be both expensive and time-consuming. The non-personal contact research methods attempt to overcome these problems, but in doing so, of course, other problems arise. The major non-personal contact methods are: postal research, diary panels, telephone research and observation research.

6.2 INTERVIEW METHODS

Interviews are the most flexible of data collection methods. They are of general application for differing information requirements and differing situations and as a result are very widely used. They can be divided into two categories: those which require direct personal contact between the inter-viewer and respondents, and those where the contact is via non-personal and indirect means, like postal questionnaires or the telephone.

6.2.1 INTERVIEWING INDIVIDUALS

The advantage of the personal contact methods is that they normally produce a high response rate, and this means that error, which might be introduced by many people refusing to co-operate in the survey, is minimized. The main disadvantage of the personal contact interview is that it is expensive. Survey costs are influenced by the complexity of information sought, the nature of the sample and the ease with which effective replies can be gathered. To give some idea of the level of cost likely to be involved, in 1984 the cost per completed interview for a 20-minute structured questionnaire administered to consumers was £10–12. This includes all executive and administrative overheads. A survey of 500 consumer respondents commissioned from a research agency in which they are required to present a research design proposal, design the questionnaire, carry out the fieldwork, analyse the data and prepare a report, would result in a bill of the order of £5000–6000. For industrial research, which requires more technically quali-fied and skilled interviewers and where respondents are more difficult to obtain, the cost could be very much higher per completed interview, although generally smaller sample sizes used in industrial research may compensate for this. Personal interviews may be carried out in a number of ways as follows.

Fully structured interviews
In fully structured interviews, the situation is 'structured' or controlled through the medium of the questionnaire. The interviewer must read out the questions and notes to respondents exactly as they appear on the questionnaire form, and may not add anything else, even by way of explanation to the respondent. This ensures that the responses, from many individuals, are given to precisely the same question, even though many interviewers may be involved in the data-gathering process. Also, in a fully structured interview, the respondent may only give one of the responses already listed on the questionnaire. This means that neither the interviewer nor the respondent may introduce material not previously originated by the re-searcher in designing the questionnaire.

Such questionnaires are used most commonly in 'head-counting' exercises, when the researcher wants to answer the question, 'How many people do this, or think that?' Fully structured questions are easy to ask and easy to answer. This makes it possible to use less technically qualified interviewers, since there is very little they can do to bias the answers. Interviews can also be completed more quickly. Both these factors will reduce field-work costs, which is why fully-structured questions are used whenever possible. Another practical advantage is that data-processing and analysis of answers to this type of question are relatively straightforward. Responses can be 'pre-coded' on the questionnaire, and all the interviewer has to do is to put a ring round the code number of the answer given. The completed questionnaire can go straight into the data-processing department where those numbers will be punched directly from the questionnaire for machine analysis. The elimination of any intervening coding process between field-work and punchroom is important in reducing both the time and costs of research.

The main limitation of fully-structured questionnaires is that they can only collect the data made possible by the content of the questionnaire. The respondent may only choose one of the answers given, not provide his own. If the questionnaire designer has erred, the final data collected will be erroneous. For example, a question may be presented in the form, 'Which of these six items is most important to you when considering purchase of a video-recorder?' and go on to list on a show-card six possible factors which seem to the questionnaire designer to be the most important. The answers will make it possible to rank those six factors in order of their importance to respondents. However, if there is some other factor equally as important as the six selected, because respondents are given no opportunity for making this point, it will not be discovered. Many research designers attempt to get over this problem by adding an 'Other response' category, but this too has limitations, as will be discussed in Chapter 8. In summary, then, there are practical advantages to using fully structured interviews, but the onus for the quality of data produced is most fully on the questionnaire designer who is responsible for providing all the possible answers as well as the questions.

Semi-structured interviews
In semi-structured interviews, fully-structured questions described above are combined with 'open-ended' questions. These questions are easy to design and to ask, but require more of the respondent in answering, and of the interviewer in recording those answers. Structure is still present from the interviewer's point of view, in that the question wording shown on the questionnaire may not be departed from. The respondent is free to answer in whatever way he pleases, since no direction or structure is implied by the question. For example, 'What factors would you personally take into account when considering purchase of a video recorder?' This is followed by a space in which the interviewer is instructed to write down exactly what the respondent says. The interviewer may be required to encourage the respondent to think about the question by using probing questions like 'What other factors are there?' after one or two have been given. The use of interview 'probes' demands a higher level of technical expertise from the interviewer than in fully-structured questioning. The use of open-ended questions and probes in questionnaire surveys goes some way to making it possible to collect both qualitative and quantitative data in the same survey. The main difficulty lies in analysing and interpreting the responses to open-ended questions. This is discussed more fully in Chapter 8.

Unstructured interviews
In this type of interview, neither the interviewer nor the respondent are bound by the structure of a questionnaire. The interviewer has only a checklist of questions which must be asked, or topics which must be covered. She is normally free to word the questions as she pleases, and to

vary the order in which the questions are asked rather than disrupt the 'flow' of the respondent's answer. The respondent answers often at considerable length, and is encouraged to explore all his thoughts on a particular topic. Unstructured interviews are often used in industrial marketing research, for example, in surveys of managerial, professional or technical groups such as purchasing managers, architects, data processing managers or civil engineers. Unstructured interviews are used to provide qualitative data. They also make it possible to identify the relevant points that must be included in subsequent structured or semi-structured interviews if quantification of the data is needed.

Depth interviews
This approach to the interview situation has been borrowed from the methods of psychoanalysis. It is called 'depth research' because the pattern of questioning encourages the respondent to go deeper and deeper into his levels of thought. Respondents move beyond the first thoughts generated by structured and semi-structured interviews, on to second and further thoughts, where the real motives and explanations for behaviour often lie. This is why depth research is used as one of the tools of motivation research.

It is obvious from the description given that the quality of depth research is largely in the hands of the interviewer, and depth research interviewers need to be experts at using the technique. They normally have specialist, and often psychological, training in the methods of depth interviewing. Since the method is so time-consuming and requires such a high calibre of specialist skill, it is usual for fewer than fifteen depth interviews to be carried out in any particular survey, particularly if it is a survey of consumers. Costs per completed interview of this type of research are very much higher than for fully or semi-structured interviews at around £200–220 per interview in 1984. Analysis of depth interviews, which are often recorded on tape with the agreement of the respondent, is also a specialist task, usually carried out by the same person who carried out the interviews. This individual has both the behavioural science expertise to interpret the findings, and the advantage of having been present at the interview, which means that nuances of the interview situation can be included in its interpretation. The costs quoted would include all preparation and design of the field-work and subsequent analysis and reporting.

6.2.2 ATTITUDE MEASUREMENT

Attitude and behaviour

In order to make good decisions, it is often helpful to understand why the group, who will be affected by those decisions, behaves the way it does. The attempt to understand behaviour brings us to a consideration of attitudes. An 'attitude' is 'a predisposition to act in a particular way'. Knowing attitudes can therefore be useful in predicting what people are likely to do, as well as explaining what they have done. Indeed, it was the belief that individuals with favourable attitudes towards products or services were more likely to buy them that led to the importance of attitude measurement as a method of data collection. Unfortunately for decision-makers, attitudes do not operate quite as simply or directly as that, in influencing behaviour. Strong personal or social influences may cause an individual not to act in accordance with his general attitude. When the behaviour is relatively unimportant to the individual he may act first, and form an attitude later, based on the outcome of the action. However, for actions which are costly or important to the individual there is evidence that attitudes often precede behaviour. Hence the management decision-maker's interest in attitude measurement.

For example, a factory manager may *believe* a fire safety manufacturer's claims that its products will reduce the risk of fire in the factory. He may *feel* a greater sense of security and less anxiety if safety equipment were installed. This would make him favourably *disposed towards* the idea of *installing* the equipment. He may not do so, of course. The cost or disruption of installing the equipment may be too high, or his levels of anxiety about fire risk may be too low, and prevent him taking any action at all. Bringing the factory manager to the point of being *favourably disposed* towards the idea of installing fire safety equipment is a first step for the equipment manufacturer. He will want to measure what the factory manager's *beliefs* about the efficiency of the equipment are and how he *feels* about the idea of installing it.

This example illustrates the three components to attitude:

Attitude =
- Cognitive component: What the individual *knows or believes* about an object or act
- Affective component: What the individual *feels emotionally* about an object or act
- Conative component: How the individual is *disposed to behave* towards an object or act.

An important assumption of attitude measurement techniques is that 'attitudes' are multi-dimensional. That is to say, about most objects, we note more than one aspect, and our decisions to buy are often a compromise between the different aspects which make up our attitudes. The researcher is interested in uncovering all the relevant aspects of attitude towards a particular brand or service, and identifying which will be most important in a particular choice situation. For this reason, attitude measurement often involves the use of scales which measure many dimensions of attitude to the same object, be it a product, brand, service or act. Two of the scaling techniques commonly used in attitude measurement are Likert scales, and Semantic differential scales.

Likert scales

A list of attitude statements about the topic under investigation is generated from depth and semi-structured interviews. This list is then tested on a sample of, say, 100 respondents. Each respondent is asked to score every

INTRODUCTION Now I would like you to think about building
materials and the effect they create in your local environment.

Q.1 SHOW CARD B

Using a phrase from this card how do you feel about the appearance of <u>New</u> buildings in your local environment?	CODE
	(22)
EXTREMELY STRONGLY	1
VERY STRONGLY	2
QUITE STRONGLY	3
NOT VERY STRONGLY	4
NOT AT ALL STRONGLY	5
DK/NOT INTERESTED	6

SHOW CARD B

EXTREMELY STRONGLY

VERY STRONGLY

QUITE STRONGLY

NOT VERY STRONGLY

NOT AT ALL STRONGLY

Figure 6.1 Likert Scales. *These are used to qualify the respondents' reaction to a question on a scale ranging from one extreme to the other, for example, from* very good *through* good, fair, poor *to* very poor.

statement on a five-point scale:

agree strongly;
agree slightly;
neither agree nor disagree;
disagree slightly;
disagree strongly.

Results from the sample are analysed and some statements are eliminated from the scale, so that the statements remaining are those which discriminate best in measuring attitudes to the topic under test. The scale is then administered to a representative sample of respondents, usually as part of a wider questionnaire survey. Responses are scored from 1 to 5. The final result is an average score which represents overall attitude on the subject and measures the degree of respondents' feeling about it. However, since the score total can be arrived at in a number of ways, it is usually useful to look at the pattern of responses as well as the total. (In the example shown in Figure 6.1, it would be interesting to see how different age or social class groups in the sample answered the question, as well as looking at the overall response.)

Statistical analysis (*see* Chapter 10 Section 2.8) of this multi-dimensional data can also identify groups of responses which have something in common. If these grouped responses are held by a sufficient number of the sample, they can indicate separate market segments. Since the attitude clusters of these segments are different, it follows that they are likely to respond to different marketing approaches. This information is extremely useful to the marketing planner.

Semantic differential scales
As their title suggests, these scales 'measure the difference between words'. Prior research with members of the target group is undertaken to generate the 'constructs' or dimensions which people use when thinking about products and services. The semantic differential scale presents these bi-

	Strongly agree	Agree	Agree with neither	Agree	Strongly agree		No opinion
Has a pleasant smell	□ 5	□ 4	□ 3	□ 2	□ 1	Has a rather unpleasant smell	□ (58)
Contains pure ingredients	□ 5	□ 4	□ 3	□ 2	□ 1	Does not contain pure ingredients	□ (59)
Leaves the skin feeling smooth	□ 5	□ 4	□ 3	□ 2	□ 1	Does not leave the skin feeling smooth	□ (60)
Is a good cleanser	□ 5	□ 4	□ 3	□ 2	□ 1	Is not a good cleanser	□ (61)
Leaves the skin soft and supple	□ 5	□ 4	□ 3	□ 2	□ 1	Does not leave the skin soft and supple	□ (62)
Is easily absorbed	□ 5	□ 4	□ 3	□ 2	□ 1	Is not easily absorbed	□ (63)
Is good value for money	□ 5	□ 4	□ 3	□ 2	□ 1	Is poor value for money	□ (64)
Is a natural product	□ 5	□ 4	□ 3	□ 2	□ 1	An artificial product	□ (65)
Is a good overall moisturizer	□ 5	□ 4	□ 3	□ 2	□ 1	Is not a good overall moisturizer	□ (66)
Is a good quality product	□ 5	□ 4	□ 3	□ 2	□ 1	Is a poor quality product	□ (67)
Suitable for all skin types	□ 5	□ 4	□ 3	□ 2	□ 1	Is only suitable for certain skin types	□ (68)

Figure 6.2 Example of a self-completion attitude battery for a skin care product, and showing brand profiles constructed from it.

	Strongly agree	Agree	Agree with neither	Agree	Strongly agree		No opinion
Is a product for younger women	5	4	3	2	1	Is a product for older women	(69)
Is a product for women with active social lives	5	4	3	2	1	Is a product for women who are homely	(74)
Is a product for women who are really confident	5	4	3	2	1	Is a product for women who are rather anxious	(71)
Is for women who have a modern outlook	5	4	3	2	1	Is for women who are a bit behind the times	(72)
Is a product for conscientious mums	5	4	3	2	1	Is a product for mums who are less conscientious	(73)
Is a product for women who love feminine things	5	4	3	2	1	Is a product for women who are less interested in feminine things	(74)
Is a product for women who take especial care of their skin	5	4	3	2	1	Is a product for women who do not take especial care of their skin	(75)
Is a product for the sort of person I would like as a friend	5	4	3	2	1	Is a product for the sort of person I wouldn't like as a friend	(76)
Is a product for career women	5	4	3	2	1	Is a product for the ordinary housewife	(77)

———— Brand profile for Brand A

— — — Brand profile for Brand B

Figure 6.2 (cont.)

polar constructs on a scale, with up to 20 scales on a page, forming an 'attitude battery'. At the top of the page appears the name of a brand, and respondents are asked to rate that brand on each of the scales. Figure 6.2 shows an example.

If a representative sample of respondents is asked to complete the same attitude battery, then the results can be computed, and a 'Brand Profile' drawn. Brand profiles can also be drawn for other brands used in the exercise, and this can help to explain the strengths and weaknesses of brands in the market-place, particularly when considered in conjunction with their sales figures. It is also useful to add to the attitude-battery scaling exercise a set of ratings for 'your ideal brand'. The profile for this can be compared to the profile achieved for the company's brand in order to pin-point ways in which the company's product differs most from the consumer's ideal. (Figure 6.2 shows on the attitude battery the profiles that might result for two brands of skin care product.)

The data from semantic differential scaling can also be plotted on two dimensions simultaneously, showing how competing products, brands or services relate to each other in the consumer's mind. This technique can be carried out on a computer (*see* Chapter 10, Section 2.8) to make multi-dimensional maps of the consumer's positioning of products, and is called '*perceptual mapping*'. It can indicate close competitors which the manufacturer may not have identified. In a perceptual mapping exercise on food, the closest competitor to lamb chops was found to be fish fingers, from a survey of housewives. It also indicates products which the manufacturer may have believed to be competitive, but which the consumer does not perceive as such. For example, a holiday survey indicated that short-break holidays in the UK are not seen by consumers as an alternative to two-week package holidays abroad. If bought at all, short UK holidays would be in addition to, rather than instead of, package holidays abroad. This kind of information is very illuminating both about market behaviour and for marketing strategy. (Figure 6.3 shows a hypothetical perceptual map for canned beers.)

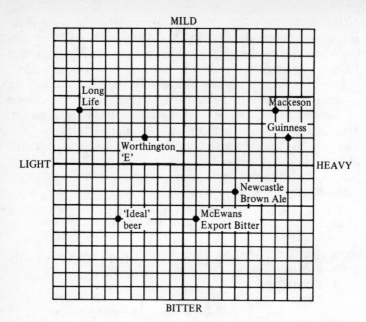

Figure 6.3 A perceptual map

6.2.3   PROJECTIVE TECHNIQUES

The interviewing techniques discussed so far rely on the basic assumption that, if you want to know what people do or think and why this is so, then go out and ask them. In some cases, however, this basic assumption is unjustified. People may not tell you what they do or why they do it, either because they do not wish to do so – they may feel the information is too personal, or reflects on them badly – or because they are unable to do so – the information you require may be difficult to articulate, or if it is to do with motives for action it may be impossible to verbalize consciously when so many motives lie within the realm of the subconscious. In order to overcome the problems of difficulty in articulating complex or subconscious motivations, researchers have 'borrowed' some approaches and techniques originated by clinical psychologists in their studies of mentally disturbed individuals, who have similar problems in explaining their behaviour to others. These techniques are often called 'projective techniques'. They set up a situation in which the individual is required to bring his own point of view to interpret or complete an ambiguous stimulus provided by the researcher. In these situations respondents draw on their own attitudes, opinions and motivations and 'project' them in their reaction to the stimulus. Thus, although they may not be talking about themselves consciously, respondents reveal to researchers what their own views are. Some of the techniques used are briefly described to illustrate the way in which the approach works.

(a) Third person   This is sometimes referred to as 'friendly martian'. This is particularly useful for products and services in which the individual has very little interest, and if asked what his own approach is might answer, 'I just don't think about it'. The question requires him to explain what someone else, or a 'friendly martian' might do. For example, 'Suppose someone living round here wanted to buy a car, how would he go about it? What next? How would he decide which manufacturer? Which retailer?, etc.' The 'friendly martian' version of the question would go, 'Suppose a friendly martian were to land and ask you how he should set about buying a car round here, what would you suggest?'

(b) Word association   This is based on the assumption that if a question is answered quickly and spontaneously, subconscious thoughts are revealed, because the conscious mind does not have enough time to think up something else. This approach is sometimes used to test proposed brand names and ensure that they have favourable and appropriate associations for the new product or service. 'What is the first thing that comes into your mind when you hear the word "Lymeswold?"' was used to test the brand

name for a new cheese. Test names are normally included in a list of other words.

(c) Sentence completion As in the previous technique, the individual is asked to respond without thinking so that underlying attitudes and motives are more likely to be revealed. 'Men who drink lager are . . . ?' 'People who have American Express credit cards . . . ? 'People who go to art galleries . . . ?'

(d) Thematic apperception These are usually referred to as 'TAT tests', or 'picture interpretation'. The individual is shown a picture and asked to say what is going on in the picture, what happened just beforehand, what will happen next, or is asked to tell a story based on the picture. The original clinical Thematic Apperception Test used twenty standard cards, but when used in market research it is more usual for fewer pictures to be used, and for them to relate to the specific topic under investigation. In a picture interpretation test used by a public library, a picture was shown of an individual going into a library. Both users and non-users of libraries were asked to describe the events which had led up to that individual going to the library, what would happen whilst he was in the library, and what would happen next. Comparison of the responses was revealing about differences in attitude among library users and non-users, and suggested ways in which non-users might be attracted to use the library services.

(e) Story completion In this technique the respondent is told a story giving an outline of a set of events. He is asked to say what he might have done in a similar situation, or to complete the story by relating what will happen next. He might also be asked to give reasons for the behaviour of the people described in the story.

(f) Cartoon completion This test shows the respondent a cartoon drawing in which one individual is talking to

another. The speech of one of the individuals is shown in a 'balloon', and the 'balloon' for the reply of the other individual is left blank. The respondent is asked to fill in that reply. An example might show two housewives talking as one of them unpacks her shopping basket, as she takes out a particular product, her friend asks, 'Why did you buy that brand?', and the respondent in providing a reply will give clues to purchase motivation.

(g) Psychodrama This is also called 'fantasy situations'. Respondents are asked to imagine that they are products or services themselves, and to describe their feelings about being used. Examples commonly quoted are motor cars, lawn-mowers or boxes of chocolates. This is intended to uncover people's attitudes towards the products. Whether using the lawn-mower is an inconvenient chore, or an enjoyable fresh-air experience, for example. An alternative approach is to ask the individual to imagine that a particular brand is a person, and then to describe what that person would be like. When repeated for other brands in the market, this provides considerable insight into the mental images which consumers have of the various brands. 'If "Charlie" perfume were a woman, what would she be like?' 'How would she differ from "Chanel" if she were a woman?'

A major reservation with these projective techniques lies in the fact that answers given by respondents can rarely be taken at face value: some interpretation is usually necessary. This opens up the possibility of misinterpretation. Trained psychologists are usually employed both to carry out and to interpret the projective techniques used in motivational research, but it should be recognized that these methods are most valuable in the extent to which they provide insights and clues, rather than answers.

6.2.4 INTERVIEWING GROUPS

Situations in which people are interviewed in groups always produce qualitative data, i.e. findings which cannot be treated statistically. This is because they are typically carried out on a small scale, and because the method does not allow for the collection of individual responses which could be summed. Three approaches are described here and, of these, group discussions are by far the most commonly used.

Group discussions

A group discussion usually consists of about eight respondents and an interviewer, usually called a 'group moderator'. The role of the moderator is to introduce the topics for discussion, and then only to intervene in the conversation in order to guide the discussion on to other topics or to curtail discussion which gets too far away from the subject. The aim is to get the group members to discuss the topic among themselves, unlike the individual interview situation when the dialogue consists of questions from the interviewer and answers from the respondent. Here, the members of the group stimulate, encourage and spark ideas off each other. It is this process of group interaction which makes group discussion so rich in content. In addition to the spontaneity and frankness generated in group comments, it is also interesting to observe the process by which a group concensus is arrived at when there is an initial wide diversity of opinion within the group. To maximize contribution from each of the group members, it is important to ensure that members of the group are sufficiently similar in 'status' to feel free to make their points without inhibition. This usually implies that working class and middle class respondents should not be mixed in the same group, and that doctors and hospital consultants should be interviewed in separate groups, and so on. Whenever any members of a group are unduly influenced by the views of other members of the group, the process of free discussion is inhibited, and the point of the exercise lost. Another role for the moderator is therefore to ensure that individuals with a powerful personality do not dominate the group to the exclusion of points of view that do not match their own.

Group discussions are commonly held at the outset of the research process since they give such a good 'feel' for the topic being discussed, and can throw up possibilities for more structured investigation later in the research process. Often, only four to eight groups may be held, and each group lasts one to two hours, normally. Such small-scale research means that care must be taken not to generalize too much from so few respondents, even though they will have been selected for their representativeness of the wider group being studied. Care is also necessary in the interpretation, organization and reporting of data generated in group discussions, which are usually tape-recorded. This is normally carried out by the group moderator personally.

The quality of data from group discussions is very largely in the hands of the group moderator, who conducts, interprets and reports on the whole exercise. Group moderation is a skilled task, for which psychological training is useful and experience is essential. An advantage of the small-scale nature of group discussion is that it is a fairly speedy form of research. The whole process from briefing the moderator to final report may take only a matter of three to six weeks. It is also a relatively inexpensive form of research, particularly considering the richness of its output. The 1984 cost was around £700 per group, including recruiting and paying group members, organizing an appropriate venue (usually a house in the neighbourhood from which respondents are recruited, or a hotel for professional people), providing refreshments to put group members at ease, tape content analysis and reporting. A typical four group survey of housewives would therefore cost around £3000. Industrial, professional or other specialist groups are likely to be more expensive. The additional costs come from using an hotel venue, more substantial refreshments, higher payments to group attenders and generally longer duration of groups which may extend to three or even four hours.

Synectics

These are a special form of group discussion, in which the aim is to generate creativity, rather than to collect existing thoughts and attitudes. Synectics are therefore most commonly used to generate new product ideas, or new ideas about provision of services. They were originally used in high technology markets and carried out using highly qualified technical respondents. More recently, they have also been applied in consumer markets using quite 'ordinary' consumers to generate new product possibilities, with some degree of success. Although it is rare for non-technical respondents to achieve completely innovative idea 'breakthroughs', they can produce valuable insights into the way in which new product development might go, and suggest a general outline of what a new product might be like. Synectic groups, even with consumers, are rather more intensive, and usually longer, than group discussions, lasting three to four hours. The group structure is different, in that group members are selected deliberately to reflect difference rather than similarity. In the purest form of this method group members are screened for 'high creativity'. They may also meet on more than one occasion, and so increase the generative capacity of the group.

Large group testing

This method is sometimes used for groups who may be difficult to convene because they are widely dispersed. A large group are brought together, and some questions asked of the whole group, to which they are usually required to write down the answers. This can provide useful demographic and background data about the group members, together with their individual responses to a few questions. The large group is then broken down into a number of smaller groups for group discussions in which the same and other questions can be explored in more depth. It can also be seen whether on exposure to other points of view, individuals are prepared to change their originally stated positions. Large group testing is not a very commonly used form of research. It has most application in industrial and professional research, where it might be possible to apply the method at a conference.

6.3   POSTAL RESEARCH

In postal research the respondent is sent a questionnaire for self-completion through the post. The category also includes other means of distribution like leaving questionnaires in hotel rooms, or giving them out as people enter museums or department stores. Perhaps 'self-completion' is a better descriptive term since the essence of the method is that the individual completes the questionnaire on his own, and then returns it either through the post, or by leaving it at an indicated place. The fact that many of those sent or given self-completion questionnaires fail to return them is the major limitation of postal research. Response rates as low as 10% of completed questionnaires are not uncommon, although the range is very wide. When topics are of particular interest to the sample the response may be much greater. An industrial distributor in a recent survey of customers achieved 85% response, although this is unusually high. A well-run postal survey of interest to respondents, not too demanding of them, with some specific incentive for completion and with follow-up reminders can expect to achieve a response rate of over 50%.

Self-completion questionnaires work best when they are fully pre-coded so that all the respondent has to do is to tick boxes. The layout should be clear and spacious. If the appearance of the questionnaire suggests that a lot of time will be needed to fill it in, it is less likely to be returned. For these reasons, the type of data which can be collected using postal research is limited both in quantity and quality. When a postal survey is used, evidence suggests that a covering letter explaining the purpose of the survey, and suggesting advantages for the respondent in co-operating, has a very important influence on the response rate.

Normally, a second questionnaire is sent about three weeks after the first to non-responders, and then a third. These follow-ups are useful in pushing up the overall response rate. Some argue that separate analysis of the late responders from early responders will reveal differences in response, and that non-responders are likely to be further in the direction of late responders. This allows some subjective estimation to be made of the likely bias present in data from a non-representative sample. Essentially, those who return the questionnaire are self-selected, rather than selected by the researcher, and so may not be representative of the whole group. The lower the response rate, the more of a limitation this becomes. In practice, there is often a bias in such respondents, since individuals who feel more strongly about the topic under investigation are more likely to complete and return questionnaires about it.

Despite this limitation, postal research is quite widely used, and there are a number of reasons why this is so. It can reach all types of people, in all geographic areas, for the same cost, and does not involve personal interviewers. This makes it much less expensive than other methods. It is also comparatively speedy, since the majority of questionnaires will be returned in the first few weeks if they are going to be returned at all. Sometimes, postal research can be used to reach respondents who would not see an interviewer or accept a telephone call, particularly senior business and professional people. For certain basic factual types of data, postal research may be quite useful, and in these circumstances its advantages over other methods are most evident. The method is often used in industrial research. This is particularly so when an industrial supplier wants to identify ways in which his services to customers could be improved. Customers are generally quite ready to respond to this type of research which is in the interests of both parties. Whether postal research can be used depends on whether an appropriate and up-to-date mailing list exists. Once again, this explains why the method is used in business research since either customer lists can be used, or classified business directories, which make it possible to mail to selected types of company, or regions. Whether for industrial or consumer application, postal surveys are most readily completed by enthusiasts and so certain subjects are more likely to be successful in using this method than others: those addressed to specialist groups or concerned with hobbies, for example.

6.4 DIARY PANELS

In the methods discussed so far it has been assumed that the research is being carried out on an *ad hoc* basis, i.e. a 'one-off' piece of research carried out when the decision-maker has a particular need for a piece of information. However, there are situations in which it is useful to have a continuous series of measurements of the same piece of data, so that any change can be monitored. This is particularly true, for instance, when the decision-maker wishes to discover what effects his decisions have, for example, about price changes, advertising campaigns, and so on.

One of the most important sources of continuous data are the diary panels. These are usually run by independent market research agencies, who sell the results to interested companies. Increasingly, the media are also setting up diary panels whose results are available not only to the media owner, but also to advertisers who use the medium. This service has been run for television for some time, and in recent years diary panels have been set up by a number of local newspapers, and by local commercial radio stations. The way in which a diary panel operates is that a representative sample of respondents are selected and visited by an interviewer. If they agree to co-operate they are recruited on to the panel and left a diary. In this they record the behaviour of themselves and sometimes other members of the family as well, relevant to the subject of the panel. Examples of panel data available are those on buying of household consumer goods, personal consumer goods like toiletries, baby products, and motoring products. (Figure

Figure 6.4

Field — Tick below if none bought	Full Brand Name and Manufacturer									
Powdered Cold Drinks inc. Fruit Juices & Squashes (exclude milkshake powders) **17**							Flavour			
Fruit Squashes, Cordials & Fruit Drinks (to be diluted) exc. Tins & 'Fizzy' **17**						Flavour		Low Calorie Yes ¦ No		
Fruit Juice INC: Sparkling Fruit Juices. (Record frozen fruit juice in "Frozen Fruit Juice" field) **42**		Type of Container: Jar ¦ Tin ¦ Carton ¦ Bottle			Is 'Longlife' stated on pack? Yes ¦ No		Flavour as stated on pack e.g. Apple, Ruby Red Grapefruit.			
Flour **94**	Manufacturer	Brand		Self-raising	Bread	Plain	Not Stated	White	Brown/Wheatmeal	Stoneground Wholewheat
Sugar **27**		Preserving	Granulated	Extra Sup. fine	Caster	Cube	Icing	Demerara	Other Light ¦ Brown Other	Crystal
Bread Mixes & Bread Roll Mixes **62**								Bread ¦ Bread Roll	White	Brown
Cake / Sandwich / Sponge / Dry Pastry / Cheesecake } Mixes **62**	Brand	Type e.g. Sponge Mix			Flavour			Sachet ¦ Carton ¦ Bag		
Fruit Pie Fillings in Cans and Bottles (Exclude Tinned Fruit) (Record Jams in "Jams, Preserves" field) **12**		Flavour						Is Pie Filling stated on pack? Yes ¦ No		
Flavoured Savoury Pasta/Noodles (For serving as a vegetable) **D3**		Type & Flavour e.g. Herb & Chicken								
Plain and Savoury Rice **C3**		Long Grain/ Patna	Short Grain/ Pudding	Other Plain state type	White ¦ Brown		Savoury -- please state full details			
EXCESS — Field Name	Write Full Product Description as for Main Entry									

Weight printed on pack	Number of Packs Bought	Total Money Spent			Name and Type of Shop e.g. Grocer, Chemist Greengrocer, Delivery Van etc.	Shop Code	Offers & Promotions 18 e.g. competitions, send aways, coupons, price reductions, banded packs, soiled goods. If there is no offer or promotion write 'NO OFFER'.
		£	(p)	½p			

10

✱✱SAVOURY SNACKS✱✱

Please write in number bought in each shop type

A = Woolworths
B = Sweet Shop/Newsagent
C = Large Grocer/Supermarket
D = Small Grocer
E = Anywhere else (Include Tuck Shop

		A	B	C	D	E			A	B	C	D	E
BATTLE BAGS	Battle Tanks						HORROR BAGS	Bat					
	Cheese 'n' Onion												
	Fighter Planes							Bones					
	Salt n Vinegar												
CHIPSTICKS	Ready Salted							Claws					
	Salt 'n' Vinegar							Fangs					
CHEESEY CRUNCHIES							HULA HOOPS	Original					
COUNTRY CRUNCH	Crispy Bacon							Barbeque					
	Slightly Salted						KP MINICHIPS						
CRACKLES							MONSTER MUNCH	Roast Beef					
FARMER BROWN	Salt & Vinegar							Pickled Onion					
	Bacon							Saucy					
FOOTBALL CRAZY								Tomato					
FRAZZLES	Bacon						ONION FRIES						
	Bacon 'n' Tomato Sauce						OUTER SPACERS	Beef Burger Rockets					
Walkers FRENCH FRIES	Ready Salted							Chutney Starships					
	Salt 'n' Vinegar							Hot Dog Modules					
	Worcester Sauce							Pickled Onion Space Stations					
GRIDDLES	Beef						PIGLETS	Bacon & Bean					
	Fried Onion							Smokey Bacon					
	Prawn Cocktail							Pickled Onion					
							QUAVERS	Cheese					
								Spicey					
								Ham					

There are more snacks on the opposite page.

Figure 6.5

✳✳SAVOURY SNACKS✳✳

Please write number bought in each shop type

A = Woolworths   D = Small Grocer
B = Sweet Shop/   E = Anywhere else (Include Tuck Shop)
C = Large Grocer/
    Supermarket

	A	B	C	D	E			A	B	C	D	E
RANCHEROS Bacon						**SNAPS**	Crispy Bacon					
Hamburger							Salt 'n' Vinegar					
							Savoury Cheese					
RINGOS Beef							Spicy Tomato					
Cheese & Onion						**SUPER HEROS**	Spiderman Salt 'n'Vinegar					
Salt & Vinegar							Captain America Barbecuded Beef					
SAVOURS						**TWISTS**	Ready Salted					
SKIPS Prawn Cocktail							Salt & Vinegar					
Spicy Sauce						**WICKERS**	Chicken					
Sweet 'n' Sour							Prawn Cocktail					
Tomato						**WOTSITS**	Beefy					
							Cheesey					
SKY DIVERS Beef							Gammon					
Cheese & Onion							Saucy Tomato					
Salt & Vinegar						**100's 1000's**	Bacon					
							Beef					

Please use the section below for any savoury snacks which are similar to the ones listed above but are another brand or manufacturer.

BRAND NAME/ MANUFACTURER'S NAME	**FLAVOUR**	Please write number bought in each shop type				
		A	B	C	D	E

6.4 shows a page from the Television Consumer Audit diary, operated by AGB.) Sometimes specific companies may set up short-term panels to monitor the effects of some particularly important decisions, as in test marketing or launching a new product. The diary is usually returned to the research company on a weekly basis, and reports are available of monthly or quarterly data.

Diary panels are an excellent method of providing regular data on a range of behaviours that would otherwise be difficult to collect. This is particularly true for buying of items that are easily forgotten, like chocolate, confectionary, and other small purchases. (Figure 6.5 shows a page from a diary used in the Personal Purchases panel run by AGB.) They are also extremely valuable in that they are 'single-source' data, i.e. the behaviour of the same individual is monitored over time, and this makes it possible to do some very interesting analyses of 'brand switching' behaviour. That is, the way in which the same consumers choose different brands or a small range of brands over time. Media-use data is also sometimes recorded, which adds further to the value of the data.

When diary panel data are used in conjunction with retail audits (*see* Section 6.6.2) they are particularly useful in identifying market segments. Retail audits measure what is being bought; diary panels describe who is buying. Diary panels are also useful in showing differences in response among different consumers, say to price, pack or advertising changes, and this represents a useful diagnostic tool. Most of the syndicated panel research surveys available are listed in Section 4.3.

There are two main problems in diary panel data. The first is a concern over whether membership of the panel distorts the behaviour of the members: the 'guinea-pig' effect. Does someone recruited to the television-viewing panel exhibit atypically high viewing of documentary and news programmes rather than soap operas and sports programmes? Tests which have been done on this aspect of panel behaviour suggest that it may happen with new panel members, but that the effect quickly wears off. Research companies therefore exclude the first four weeks' diaries of new panel members from analysis. The second problem with diary panels lies in maintaining interest in the membership of the panel, since, if the drop-out rate becomes too high, the advantages of continuous data from the same individuals are lost. Research companies operate incentive schemes both to encourage prompt return of diaries and to keep interest in and involvement with the panel going. This might take the form of regular 'lucky draws' and a points system which can be used to buy items from a catalogue.

Companies which decide to operate a panel 'in-house' of customers or trade intermediaries will need to give careful consideration to the cost and mechanics of operating the panel and handling the data generated, since both can escalate beyond expectations.

6.5   TELEPHONE RESEARCH

The great advantage of telephone research is its speed and relative economy compared to personal interviewing, particularly when only a limited amount of information is required. It has the added advantage for industrial research that individuals difficult to reach by personal interview – the more senior executives – may respond to telephone surveys which are less demanding of their time. Until recently, telephone interviewing was a method used primarily in industrial research.

And important constraint on its use in consumer research in the UK has been the fact that until recently less than half the households in the country owned telephones. This fact, combined with the number of unlisted numbers created problems in selecting a representative sample. Telephone owners tend to be better off and more middle class than the population as a whole. However, for products and services aimed at this group, and in London where penetration of telephone ownership is greater than in other parts of the country, telephone research among consumers is possible and growing. In 1979 a number of telephone panels were set up by Marplan Ltd. The organizers claim that by including panel members who are reached at work, and by using personal interviews to recruit a representative sample of the population, not of telephone owners, their panel represents 75% of all under 65s. The fact that telephone owners tend to be more affluent means that this group was representative of 80% of net income. For most marketing purposes this makes the panel quite adequate in terms of its representativeness. However, for social research the 'affluence bias' of telephone panels is likely to make their use inappropriate. The swiftness of the method was illustrated by a survey of attitudes to the Royal Family carried out for *NOW!* magazine during its brief life. The idea was discussed and a questionnaire with twenty-four questions drawn up on Day 1. 961 respondents were surveyed on Day 2. Results were keyed directly on to computer disc, and were printed out the same night. A report based on the tabulations was completed on Day 3. A complete survey had been carried out within forty-eight hours of the idea being born.

From its small beginnings in 1979, telephone research among consumers has grown rapidly. Ownership of telephones has continued to increase giving greater representativeness of samples. By 1982 a number of research companies had set up telephone research facilities, and CATI (computer-assisted telephone interviewing) was described as 'acronym of the year' in the *Market Research Society Newsletter*. A survey carried out in August of that year suggested that people generally like the idea of telephone interviewing. CATI systems offer the chance to combine the cost and flexibility advantages of telephone contact with the increased control, and hence improved data quality, of the computerized interview. The systems operate by showing the questionnaire on a visual display unit from which the interviewer reads the questions. Answers are keyed in directly to the computer by the interviewer, and the next question is displayed on the screen. Since the computer can handle complex question-naire routing systems (if answer to Q. 15 is 'Yes' then go to Q. 16, if 'No' go to Q. 27) by only displaying the correct next question, possibility for interviewer error is reduced. It seems clear that developments in telephone interviewing will continue to be made as the system establishes itself. For agencies offering telephone interviewing services, the *Market Research Society Newsletter* should be consulted (Tel: 01 235 4709).

6.6 OBSERVATION RESEARCH

The quality of data collected using interview methods is dependent on individuals being willing and able to report their behaviour or attitudes verbally. In certain circum-stances people may be unable to do this not because they are unwilling to do so, but simply because they do not mentally record the data required, and are therefore unable to report it. An example of this would be if you wished to know what items a housewife had taken from a supermarket shelf and considered purchasing, but had not actually purchased; or if you wished to know the path an individual had taken around an art gallery, what exhibits he stopped to look at, and for how long. In both instances it would be highly unlikely that the individuals concerned could give an accurate account of their behaviour. Such information can be quite readily obtained by observation. Observation techniques are also widely used by social researchers, in road planning and underpass-siting for pedestrians, for example. They can be used by industrial firms to check interest in exhibition stands. The method is therefore of wide application, and where the data required is about what people do rather than why they do it, this can provide accurate data, free of the possible biases of interviewer effect and faulty memory. These advantages make observation especially useful in collecting data about routine consumer behaviour on a continuous basis.

6.6.1 OBSERVATION PANELS

There are a number of panels in operation in which observation is the primary method of data collection. These cover household consumer goods, shopping behaviour and television viewing. For the first of these a panel of informants is recruited who agree to allow an auditor to come into the home each week and check what products are in the house in the product fields being investigated. Informants are given a plastic bin in which to place discarded wrappers and packets of products used during the week. From this data both purchase and usage rates can be calculated. These are sometimes referred to as 'pantry checks' and 'dustbin checks'. The research company collates the data and presents monthly reports to clients purchasing the service. Shopping behaviour is observed by recruiting a panel of housewives who agree to do all their shopping in a travelling shop. This is a caravan laid out inside to look like a supermarket. The housewife simply shops in the usual way. From time to time new brands are introduced on to the shelves to test how the housewife reacts to them in a purchase choice situation, and more importantly, whether she buys the product next time or goes back to her original brand.

One of the advantages of observation techniques is that in an age of sophisticated electronic technology it is not always necessary for an individual to collect the data, since this can be done using the appropriate hardware. Television viewing is a case in point. A meter-recording device (the SET meter is one widely used) is attached to the television. It records when the set is on, and which channel it is tuned to. This gives a measure of 'sets tuned'. To convert this to 'viewers', co-operating households agree to complete a diary which records who is present in the room in 15-minute time segments. Observation by hardware is also useful for all kinds of 'flow counts'. For example, to investigate traffic and pedestrian flows past poster sites, or round supermarkets, exhibitions, and so on. Usually the recording periods are randomized to give flow patterns on different days of the week and at different times of day.

6.6.2 RETAIL AUDITS

An important application of the 'audit' method of observation research is in the field of trade research. An example of this is that organized by A. C. Nielsen Co. Ltd. A representative sample of around 2000 grocery shops are recruited to the panel. At each visit auditors record the amount of stock in the shop, and check invoices for deliveries made since the last visit. Sales in the intervening period can then be calculated. A similar method is employed by Nielsen covering chemists, CTN, DIY, home appliances, liquor and cash and carry trades. This is an important service for manufacturers of products covered, since it is one of the ways in which they can measure consumer sales reaction to advertising, price changes, and other marketing tactics. Ex-factory sales do not provide this kind of feedback because of the length of the marketing channel, which may include stock buffers at both wholesale and retail outlets. This can mean that after leaving the factory it could be six weeks before a product reaches the retail outlet shelf. The introduction of direct electronic links from checkout points is likely to improve the quality and speed of retail audit data. Other research agencies also produce retail audit data and are listed in Section 4.3, since they are usually made available on a syndicated basis, as is Nielsen data.

6.7 SUMMARY

Interviews involving personal contact between interviewer and respondents, are the most versatile and widely-used method of primary data collection. They may be carried out in a variety of ways, and descriptions are given of types of individual interview, attitude measurement and projective techniques. Group interviewing methods, of which group discussions are the most important, are also mentioned. The non-personal research methods covered are postal research, diary panels, telephone research and the observation methods of panels and retail audits.

7 Who Provides the Information

7.1 INTRODUCTION

This chapter is concerned with sampling: the process of actually selecting those individuals whose views will be collected in the survey in order to be representative of the whole group whose views are being sought. Good sampling practice is the key to the ability of large-scale quantitative surveys to represent the views of the population being studied to a known and calculable degree of accuracy. Sampling theory has at its heart probability theory and it is on probability theory that the validity of large-scale surveys rests. If you like, it is probability theory which allows large-scale market research surveys to 'work'. A complete understanding of sampling theory therefore demands an understanding of basic statistical and probability theory. However it is possible for an individual without a statistical background to appreciate what sampling theory is able to do and how samples are selected without necessarily getting involved in the intricacies of the statistical basis for this. Those wishing to read a statistical treatment of sampling are recommended to the appropriate chapters in Worcester and Downham, and Ehrenberg, listed in Chapter 15. This chapter will answer four questions:

1. What is a sample?
2. Why use a sample?
3. How is the sample selected?
4. How big does the sample need to be?

In Section 7.4 describing how samples are selected the three main methods of sampling will be discussed: random sampling, quota sampling, and judgement sampling.

7.2   WHAT IS A SAMPLE?

A sample is a limited number taken from a large group for testing and analysis, on the assumption that the sample can be taken as representative of the whole group. Most people are familiar with the concept of sampling and its application in many everyday areas of life. For example, we take a sip or a bite of food in order to determine whether or not we are going to enjoy it. We are also familiar with the idea that scientists wishing to check the quality of a production batch will take a small sample from a large batch of product, and subject the sample to analysis in order to determine the constituents and their proportions in the whole batch. It is exactly this procedure which the marketing researcher is seeking to apply when sampling is used in survey research. From the example given it is easy to see that the major constituents of the production batch will only be represented in the correct proportions if the sample selected by the scientist for test was from a well-mixed batch, i.e. is representative of the whole content of the batch. It is the techniques of sample selection that seek to ensure that the members of a survey sample are truly representative of all the members of the population from which they are derived. This therefore underlines the importance of correct sampling procedures in research. Without them the sample selected will not be representative and the answers gathered from them will not be a good guide to what the population of interest would say if all were asked.

7.3   WHY USE A SAMPLE?

In survey research, samples are used to make an estimate of what the whole population of interest is like or thinks or does. In theory it would be possible to measure or to question all members of the population of interest, but in practice this would prove difficult. It is the practical advantages which account for the fact that samples are the normal method of collecting data rather than censuses in which everyone must be included. Obviously, the smaller the number of people from whom data is to be collected the cheaper and quicker it will be. Analysis of the data will be more manageable and control of the whole procedure more effectively achieved. Added to these highly practical advantages is the fact that good sampling procedures allow a high degree of precision in estimating the results which would have been achieved from a census, and so the argument for sampling becomes overwhelming and explains its almost universal usage.

7.4 HOW IS THE SAMPLE SELECTED?

Samples are selected from populations and the term 'sample' has already been explained. In marketing research, use of the term 'population' refers to the whole group whose views are to be represented. For example, some surveys are actually interested in the views of the general population of the country. More commonly, marketing researchers are interested in the views of populations with characteristics of special relevance, for example, the population of motorists, the population of housewives, the population of retail outlets for a particular type of goods, the population of suppliers of a particular type of industrial machinery, the population of professional groups such as architects, or users of social services, and so on.

Data collected from the sample are referred to as 'statistics' and these sample statistics are used to estimate the 'population parameter'. That is to say, results obtained from a sample are used to calculate the results which would have been obtained from the underlying population had a census been used. The degree to which it is possible to use sample statistics in order to estimate population parameters with an acceptable degree of accuracy depends on the sampling procedures used and on the size of the sample.

The three main methods used in selecting samples are called *random sampling, quota sampling,* and *judgement sampling.* The method whose statistical validity forms the foundation for the whole practice of survey research is random sampling and for this reason it is the best known and most commonly described method of sampling. However, in practice, quota sampling has been found to give perfectly acceptable results for commercial purposes and at a cheaper cost than random sampling. Quota sampling is therefore the most commonly applied sample selection method in market research, despite its lack of statistical purity. Judgement sampling is also commonly applied in practice simply because, as its title suggests, it is often the most sensible way of approaching the sample selection problem although it has theoretical limitations. Because of the lack of statistical purity in their manner of sample selection, quota and judgement sampling methods are sometimes referred to as 'non-probability' sampling procedures, and, referring to the element of personal discretion used, they are also called 'purposive' sampling procedures.

7.4.1   RANDOM SAMPLING

Random sampling, based on statistical probability theory, has two characteristics which make it extremely useful in practice to the decision-maker. These are that it is possible to calculate the 'level of confidence' and 'limits of accuracy' of the results.

The 'level of confidence' refers to the fact that from a randomly drawn sample it is possible to work out the statistical probability that the sample is a good one. Very much like that famous toothpaste 'ring of confidence', it is heartening for a decision-maker to hear from the researchers, 'these results are correct to the 95% level of confidence'. What they are in effect saying is, 'there is only a one in twenty chance that this sample is a bad one'. The 95% level is the most commonly used level of confidence in research and most decision-makers in organizational settings are quite happy with data in which they can be assured of having a 95% level of confidence, simply because so much other uncertainty surrounds the decision-making environment.

The second practical outcome of sound sampling practice referred to is the 'limits of accuracy'. Common sense dictates that when a thousand respondents are used to calculate the views of the three million members of the population whom they represent, then the calculation is likely to be only an approximate one. This is to say, sample statistics can be used to calculate population parameters only within certain 'limits of accuracy' rather than with spot-on precision. It also makes common sense that the more respondents included in the sample, then the more accurate the calculation of the population parameters is likely to be i.e. the larger the size of the sample the narrower the range of 'limits of accuracy'. The relationship, however, is not in direct proportion. From a sample of 1000, results may be within limits of accuracy of + or −10%. To reduce that by half i.e. to results of + or −5%, it would be necessary to include four times as many individuals in the sample i.e. 4000 respondents. This point about the relationship between sample size and accuracy is considered further in Section 7.5.

The third, and important, practical advantage of sampling theory is that the level of confidence and limits of accuracy required in the results can be decided in advance of the survey. Use of the appropriate statistical calculations make it possible to determine what size of sample will be required in order to produce findings to those specifications. Whilst it is not essential to be able to perform personally the statistical calculations referred to, it is important to note that the quality and validity of the findings from large-scale quantitative research surveys is determined by the appropriateness with which these calculations are carried out and statistical concepts applied.

This book aims only to introduce marketing research and does not expect the reader to be equipped with a statistical background. Nor is it felt feasible or desirable to attempt to teach that statistical background in an introductory book. In the author's experience it is those horrifying pages of statistical calculations which cause managers who started off with an interest in learning more about marketing research to decide that perhaps the subject is not for them! However, the author is also aware of the desire of managers in very many types of organization to undertake their own research. Advice to the would-be 'do-it-yourself' researcher is that he needs to know far more about sampling theory and practice than the introduction given in this chapter will provide. The same advice holds for students of market research. The purpose of the following explanation of sample selection procedures is to provide a basis for understanding why particular selection techniques are used in sample surveys and to judge their appropriateness. It will also give an appreciation of the advantages and limitations of each method.

To summarize, the great advantage of random sampling techniques is that they allow statistical calculation of the appropriate sample size for pre-determined levels of confidence (usually set at the 95% level) and limits of accuracy (set to meet requirements of the decision to be made). It must be stressed that these calculations are only possible when random sampling techniques are used because random sampling is the only one of the three methods discussed in this chapter which is based on probability theory from which the appropriate calculations derive. So random sampling may be called 'probability sampling'.

The Sampling Frame

A randomly drawn sample is one in which every member of the population has a calculable chance of being included in the sample. If every member of the population is to have a chance of being included in the sample then it follows that every member of the population must be known in order to have that chance. So the first step in drawing a random sample is to make a list of all the members of the population and this is referred to as the 'sampling frame'. The term 'frame' is used rather than 'list' because for certain types of samples the frame may be a map rather than an actual list. It is at this point that many attempts to apply random sampling techniques will flounder, simply because a sampling frame cannot be constructed. Commonly used frames are: the electoral register, for sampling households or adults over eighteen; trade directories, for sampling manufacturing, retailing and other organizations; and customer lists, for sampling the customers of a particular firm. Difficulties arise, however, when the population to be sampled cannot be listed, for example, owners of video recorders, buyers of office supplies, or people who have taken more than one holiday in the past twelve months. Even when a sampling frame can be constructed it may turn out to be unusable in practice because of: out of date addresses, incompleteness, duplication of entries, lack of geographical clustering, or poor list organization. The greater any of these problems then the less reliable is the frame as a basis for sampling. If the frame itself is not representative of the population of interest then any sample drawn from it will not be.

Simple random sampling

The point of any random sampling procedure is that there should be no personal influence in the selection of individuals to be interviewed. The simplest way to achieve this in theory is to cut up the population list into separate individuals, put all the strips of paper into a large container or tombola drum, give them a good mix around and then draw out the number required. Whilst straightforward in theory, this procedure is less so in practice particularly on a windy day! Nowadays the most common method of drawing a simple random sample is to assign a number to every item on the list and to select the required number at random by using random number tables. (These are available in books rather like logarithm books. The numbers in them are produced by electronic means and checked for randomness.)

Systematic (quasi-) random sampling

The most commonly used method of systematic random sampling is to select every '*n*'th number from the frame by dividing the number of items on the list by the number required in the eventual sample. In our earlier example if the sampling frame contained 3 000 000 names and if we required 1000 respondents then dividing 3 000 000 by 1000 would indicate that every 3000th name on the list must be selected. This is achieved by selecting the first name at random out of the first 3000 names and thereafter selecting every 3000th. So using a simple random method the first number selected might be the 111 thereafter the second number would be 3111 the third number 6111, and so on, and by the time the end of the list was reached 1000 names would have been drawn from it.

Random sample interviewing

Since the whole point of random sampling is that respondents are selected without any personal bias creeping into the process, then it is equally important that the individuals selected are actually included in the samples by being interviewed. In practice this means that interviewers must call back on the address they are given until they make contact with the individual named and it is normal procedure to insist that three call-backs are made by the interviewer before giving up on an individual. It is the need for call-backs in the field which is one of the reasons why random sampling is the most expensive form of sampling to use, but if the named individuals are not contacted then the whole point of the use of a random sampling selection procedure is lost.

Practical limitations of simple random sampling

Whilst simple random sampling methods may be the most elegant in theory they often turn out to be the most expensive to apply in practice and there are a number of reasons for this. First, there is the time and expense involved in drawing up the sampling frame in the first place, particularly if it is a large one which has to be compiled from a number of different sources. Secondly, for a national sample it would be quite reasonable to expect that the respondents selected would be randomly distributed on a national basis. This will make the cost of field-work very high since separate trips will need to be made to each location and, as has already been mentioned, up to three call-backs may have to be made in each location. In order to overcome these limitations two refinements in methods of random sampling have been developed. They are quite widely used in commercial research practice and have been found to yield results of acceptable accuracy, bearing in mind that most research is done in order to represent the views of typical members of the population under consideration rather than unusual members of it.

Random route sampling

In this form of sampling the district within which an interviewer will work is determined by random methods. However, within that district the interviewers must follow a prescribed 'route'. That is to say they are given a set of instructions like, 'Take the first turning on the right, the third on the left', and so on. The instructions contain details about where to start trying to obtain interviews and how many houses to leave before trying again after a successful interview has been achieved. The practical advantage of this system is that interviewers do not make a call-back if they get no reply and this therefore reduces the time and cost involved in the survey. The possibility of bias arising from the fact of some individuals being more likely to be found at home than others is overcome by setting controls on the numbers of, say, working women who must be included in each interviewer's required number of interviews.

Random location sampling

In simple and systematic random sampling procedures the final sampling unit selected is the individual to be interviewed. In random location sampling the sample is selected in such a way that the final unit of selection is a geographical unit rather than an individual. The interviewer must complete a given number of interviews within the geographical area, which is usually an enumerator district of about 150–200 homes. Which actual respondents should be selected within that location is determined by giving the interviewer a target number of individuals meeting specified age, sex, class and other relevant characteristic requirements. These targets are called 'quotas' and are further explained in Section 7.4 under 'quota sampling'. Random location sampling is a hybrid between random sampling and quota sampling which attempts to combine the best aspect of both these sampling methods. That is to say, the objectivity of random sampling combined with the cost efficiency of quota sampling.

Stratification

The point of sampling is to represent the characteristics of the population of interest in the correct proportions, but because a sample is being used only an estimate of the characteristics of interest can be derived from it rather than a precise value. However, it is often the case that certain characteristics of the population of interest are already known. In the case of the general population these characteristics are known from census data. In industrial and trade research certain characteristics of the population may be known from existing secondary sources, or from previous original research data. When the proportions of certain important and relevant characteristics in the population being surveyed are known with certainty, then it makes sense to use this information as a way of improving the quality of the sample. The technique used to do this is 'stratification'. For stratified samples, the sampling frame is re-arranged so that particular attributes of the population are grouped together in their known proportions. The sample is then selected by a random method from each group or 'stratum' in the same proportion in which the stratum exists in the population. One of the most common stratification systems used is to stratify by geographical regions, taking account of population density. The proportion of survey respondents within each region is then calculated in proportion to the percentage of the population living in that region. By ensuring that each known segment of the population of interest is correctly reflected in the make-up of the sample, one possible source of inaccuracy in the sample is avoided.

The method of stratification is commonly applied in sampling wherever possible since it improves the accuracy of the sample. Age, sex, region and social class are four commonly used stratification variables in much commercial market research. In industrial research, manufacturers may be stratified by SIC grouping or by number of employees, or size of turnover. In trade research, retail outlets may be stratified by size of turnover, percentage of retail trade, square footage of floor space, and so on. Whenever the proportions of relevant characteristics about the population are known with certainty then it makes sense to apply them. This method of determining the allocation of a sample of respondents is also referred to as 'proportionate sampling'. This is because it has the effect of ensuring that important characteristics of the population are proportionately represented in the sample.

Multi-stage sampling

The method of stratification referred to above is often used as a basis for multi-stage sampling. This is a refinement of the random sampling technique which attempts to reduce the cost of random sampling at both the selection and field-work stages, without losing the element of randomness. In the case of sampling UK households, for example, at the first stage of the process a simple random sample may be taken of all parliamentary constituencies in Great Britain. For each constituency selected at the first stage a list of wards is compiled and a simple random sample selected of wards within each constituency. At the third stage each ward is divided into groups of streets known as polling districts and a simple random sample taken of these streets. It is this technique which forms the basis for random location sampling since the group of streets selected at the third stage form the areas used for interviewers to carry out their quota of interviews. The process could go one stage further and the selection of individual respondents be made from lists of names and addresses for the polling districts identified at the previous stage.

An advantage of multi-stage sampling is that compilation of the sampling frame is very much reduced. Even when the individual sampling unit is of names and addresses this does not arise from the need for a complete listing of all addresses in the UK in the first place. At the first stage the frame is restricted simply to a list of constituencies, electoral registers of names and addresses only being required for a limited number of areas at the final stage. A second advantage of the technique is that the final interviews end up being geographically clustered. This considerably reduces the administrative and travelling costs of carrying out the field-work in these areas.

Weighting
It may be that the research user is not equally interested in the views of members of all sub-groups of the population, or that he is particularly interested in analysing the views of just one small sub-group. In a general survey about television advertising during 1981 some information was required from owners of video recorders about its effects on their exposure to television adverts. At the time, only 4% of homes had a video recorder, so in the sample of 1000 respondents, only 40 of them could be expected to be within this sub-group and this would not be enough for detailed analysis of their views alone. In order to have a minimum of 100 respondents in this minority group for detailed analysis, it would be necessary to start off with an original sample two and a half times as big, that is to say of 2500. This would have obviously undesirable effects on the timing and costs of the survey. An alternative way of

overcoming the problem was simply to increase the number of respondents in the minority group to 100 without changing the rest of the sample. That is to say the total sample size was actually 1060 respondents, of whom 100 were video recorder owners.

For the purpose of analysing results of the whole sample then obviously the sub-group of video recorder owners would have two and a half times more representation than any other group. To correct this imbalance when analysing the content of the survey as a whole, results from this group were weighted downwards by a factor of two and a half. However, with 100 respondents there was a sufficient number for a limited amount of analysis within the responses of that group. They could therefore be used for separate consideration as a group.

The procedure described is known as 'weighting'. It may be used, as in the example, to explore the particular views of minority groups without over-inflating the total size of the sample. It can also be used to reduce the number of respondents selected from particularly large sub-groups of the population, so as to reduce the overall cost of the survey. Results from this group are then weighted up by the factor with which they have been under-represented in the original sample.

A trade survey of grocers' attitudes was carried out in 1981 using Nielsen data. This indicated that co-operative and multiple shops each accounted for 9% of all grocers, the remaining 82% being independent grocers. The sample included 100 respondents from each type of outlet. In analysing the results for grocers generally, weighting factors were applied to reduce the input from co-operative and multiple shop respondents and to increase that of independent grocers. Each sub-group could also be analysed separately to identify differences between them. Had the sample wished to take account of differences in turnover rather than number of shops, the weighting factors would be based on Nielsen data showing that for share of turnover co-operatives represent 15%, multiples

59% and independents 26%.

7.4.2   QUOTA SAMPLING

In order to be sure that respondents to a random sample are genuinely representative of the population from which they are drawn, it is common practice to calculate the proportions of respondents by age, sex, class, region and so on and check that these are in line with the known figures of census data. Since this has become routine procedure for checking the accuracy of random samples it is a very short mental step from there to suggest that if applying the proportions of known characteristics of the population to the results of random samples is valid as a check for their accuracy, then why not simply select the sample so as to represent those characteristics in the known proportions in the first place? It is this reasoning which forms the basis for quota sampling. The reasoning is that if the known characteristcs of the population are represented in the correct proportions then all other data collected will be represented in the correct proportions. Stating its underlying assumption in this way also illustrates the main area for criticism of quota samples. It could happen that even though known and measurable characteristics are distributed in the correct proportions, unknown characteristics relevant to the subject of the survey may not be.

A quota sample based on interviewing people at home is likely to under-represent those who go out a lot. A quota sample based on interviewing people in the street may under-represent those who do not go out a lot. If behaviour relevant to going out or not going out is important to the context of a quota sample survey, perhaps it is about leisure activity in general, or frequency of visits to pubs, or amount of TV viewing, then important aspects of the data may be misrepresented, resulting in the collection of biased data which will mislead the decision-maker. When the significance of the limitations of the sampling procedure is as obvious as in the example suggested, then common sense can go a considerable way to overcoming this disadvantage. The theoretical danger of quota sampling is that some hidden bias may exist which will not be discovered.

Quota sampling is considerably influenced by the researcher, in ways that random sampling is not. In the first place, the researcher determines which characteristics should be used as a basis for setting quotas. Next, the actual selection of respondents is left to the interviewer rather than determined by the sample selection procedure as in random sampling. In quota sampling the interviewer is presented with a set of target interviews to complete, and the interviews are described in terms of the characteristics of the respondents required. For examples, the interviewer may be told that she has to complete 30 interviews in 3–4 days' work; the 30 interviews to be completed as shown in Figure 7.1.

Once she has these quotas it is up to the interviewer to locate the appropriate number and type of people within her working area in the required time. Most interviewers knowing their area well will know exactly where to go in order to collect the type and age of person specified. Everyone knows for their own home town where the middle class area is and the working class area. One can think of the place one would go to if one were particularly interested in collecting the views of younger people or of older people. Applying exactly that kind of local knowledge the interviewers quickly and efficiently complete the quota set for them. The problem is that by selecting respondents from such stereotyped areas they are not entirely representative of the whole population, which is more mixed than the method described might reflect. What of the middle class individual living in a generally working class area, or vice versa? What of the young person not to be found with the majority of young people, and so on?

Recognizing that a possible weakness in the validity of quota sampling lies in the degree to which the interviewer is able to influence the selection of final respondents, hybrid systems of sample selection have been developed. In

Figure 7.1 Quota sheet.
Your assignment is to interview 30 respondents to the sex, age and class quotas detailed below.

Sex

	Required	Achieved	Total
Male	15		
Female	15		
			30

Age

	Required	Achieved	Total
16–34	13		
35–54	12		
55+	5		
			30

Class

	Required	Achieved	Total
ABC1	12		
C2	11		
DE	7		
			30

random location sampling the interviewer is given a quota of interviews to complete, but may only do this within an area of named streets. Other quota controls may be established, perhaps to limit the proportion of respondents with easy-to-interview occupations like men working on outside jobs or public transport. Quota controls are also used to get the correct proportion of working housewives, and of other characteristics relevant to the purpose of the survey.

The great advantage of quota sampling is its quickness and cheapness, both in generating the sample in the first place and in completing and controlling the field-work. In order to select the sample, no sampling frame needs to be devised. This is not only a saving in cost and time, but in certain circumstances makes sampling possible when a sampling frame cannot be established and yet some important characteristics, of the population to be sampled, are known. In industrial and trade research, quota sampling is particularly useful since sampling frames are often difficult to construct yet the major characteristics of an industry or trade may be known. Another advantage of quota sampling is that it overcomes one of the problems of random sampling, in that although sampling frames may be quickly outdated the population characteristics used as the basis of allocating quota samples are far more stable.

In carrying out the field-work the most important advantage of quota sampling is that interviewers do not have to find named individuals. It is this which accounts for the greatest cost and time-saving of the method. The interviewer simply screens likely individuals with a small number of classification questions and, if they meet the requirements of her quota, she goes on to complete the full interview. If they do not meet the quota requirement she terminates the interview and continues knocking on doors or stopping other individuals in the street until she finds someone who does. This reduces the costs of quota sampling by about one-third to one-half that of random sampling.

As far as the quality of data is concerned, studies which have tested the results of quota samples against those of random samples have suggested that for the majority of commercial purposes these are perfectly acceptable. In these applications the cost benefits of the method outweigh the theoretical disadvantages, provided adequate control is exercised. This will include adequate training of interviewers for their important role in this type of sample selection procedure. The cost saving made in the application of quota rather than random sampling can be used to improve the quality of the data generated in other ways, say by increasing the sample size. Quota sampling is mainly used as an acceptable but cheaper alternative to random sampling for the purposes of most *ad hoc* market research surveys. The fact that this is the major method now in use appears to underwrite its widespread acceptability. Presumably its army of regular users have found that the system works well in practice. For social surveys, however, when it is often the views of minorities rather than majorities which it is required to represent, it is possible that quota sampling may not be sufficiently sensitive.

7.4.3   JUDGEMENT SAMPLING

Judgement sampling is a move further away from the unbiased attempt to produce a representative sample of the population to be surveyed. Theoretically speaking it is only the random sampling methods which do this. Quota sampling is an attempt to replicate what random sampling achieves at a lower cost, and it has some success in doing this. An element of judgement comes into the method in deciding which quota controls should be used in selection of the sample. Nevertheless, the basic aim of the method is to attain the representativeness of random samples.

Judgement sampling, like quota sampling, is a form of purposive sampling but differs from quota sampling and from random sampling in that the attempt to achieve statistical representativeness of the population as a whole is largely abandoned. The aim, of course, is still to produce data representative of the population to be sampled but judgement is used in the sample selection procedure in order to make the data more useful to the decision-maker.

Judgement sampling is commonly applied in industrial and trade research when a few large manufacturers or retailers may dominate a market. In this case the sample might include all the major manufacturers or retailers in a trade and then a sample of the other organizations. This will ensure that those major organizations, whose activities are of such significance in the market-place that any survey not including all of them could not hope to give a valid picture of what is happening in that market, are not left out. A manufacturer of china included all the major department store buyers in a sample together with a random sample of specialist china outlets. The purpose here, as is usually the case in trade and industrial research, was to give additional weight to the views of more important members of the trade in terms of their size or share of turnover. A similar approach may be taken by an industrial supplier surveying his own customers. Once again he may wish to seek the views of all his important customers and sample the rest.

Judgement sampling may be the only practical approach for sampling populations if no sampling frame can be constructed for random sampling and insufficient data is available about the population for quota sampling. This is often the case in the preliminary stages of a survey and judgement sampling is the main technique used in small-scale exploratory research surveys. A programme of 'key interviews' might be carried out in order to get some ideas about what the views of members of the population might be with respect to the topic under discussion. This is the sampling basis for the depth interviews described in Section 6.2.1. The manufacturer of a new type of hard-wearing floor covering conducted a depth interview survey among architects working for local authorities. After interviews with only 10 architects about the new material, it seemed that the concept of the material was generally acceptable.

The case quoted is an actual example in which the company went ahead and launched the product on the basis that most of the architects interviewed had expressed an interest in it. Unfortunately that interest was not directly translatable into product sales in the market place. The company is now in the process of improving its sampling procedures for a second attempt to survey the market since its own belief in the product remains unshaken. This time it will not be using a qualitative approach to make a quantitative decision. This highlights the danger of judgement sampling as a form of research. Such research is so small scale and unrepresentative that quite false readings can be obtained.

Judgement sampling is used as the basis for surveys using the method of group discussions. As discussed in Chapter 6, group discussions are a very widely used form of research. They give the decision-maker some insight into and understanding of the attitudes, opinions and feelings of members of his market about his own, or competitive, products. In a survey of housewives about consumer goods it is not unusual for a qualitative survey using group discussions to include only six to eight groups. Eight groups containing eight people is only sixty-four individuals all told and so inevitably the findings cannot be 'representative' in the sense implied by the use of random or quota sampling methods. However, the attempt is made to generate as wide a range of views as possible by using judgement to decide the type of individuals who will be used for each group.

In order to give a breadth of opinion a cake manufacturer commissioning a survey including eight groups spread them as follows: four were held in Northern towns and four in Southern towns. Each group of four interviews was split into two of middle class respondents and two of working class respondents. Each pair of groups included one with respondents aged under thirty and one with respondents aged over thirty. The attempt here was to collect the widest possible range of views from a national, class and age spread of respondents.

Typically, judgement sampling is used in the conduct of smaller surveys. When these are particularly small and qualitative in nature, it is most important not to confuse the attempt to represent a wide range of views with the concept of 'representativeness' implied by random and quota sampling methods. If judgement sampling is used in small-scale surveys the results should never be used in a quantitative way. If half the members of a set of group discussions agree on a particular point, it should not be assumed that 50% of the target population will also agree with that point.

Judgement is used in sampling as a way of overcoming practical difficulties or limitations in using other sampling methods. It is also used for 'toe in the water' exercises and just like using a toe to measure the temperature of water it is equally unreliable if used in place of a thermometer! It produces a 'feel' rather than a measurement. A toe can give some idea of general hotness or coldness but if placed in the edge of the sea or a cold eddy of a river will not give a reliable measure for the whole body of water. In the same way the results of small-scale judgement sample surveys cannot be used as representative of the population as a whole, although they do give some guidance about what that population might be thinking, feeling or doing.

7.5   HOW BIG DOES THE SAMPLE NEED TO BE?

A very commonly held fallacy is that there needs to be some relationship between the size of the sample selected and the size of the population of interest. This is only the case when sampling very small populations. The point has already been made that random sampling has a sound statistical basis which allows the researcher to have confidence in the fact that results from randomly selected samples are truly representative of the population being studied. He can calculate the degree of confidence which he can have in the fact that this is so, and he can calculate a range of accuracy within which the results obtained from the sample would be likely to hold in the population from which the sample was drawn. These factors are linked in a statistical formula which indicates that sample size is dependent on the following three factors.

7.5.1   *VARIABILITY IN THE POPULATION*

The first factor affecting the size of the sample is the proportionate distribution of the characteristics we may be interested in. For example, the proportion who are boat owners or holiday takers. When the proportion is either small, as in the first instance, or very large as in the second instance, the size of sample required in order to measure this accurately is smaller than when the population is more or less equally split between having or not having the attributes under consideration. Thus, predicting the outcome of a general election accurately, when support for the two major parties was more or less equally split, required a larger sample than when support was heavily in favour of one party rather than the other.

7.5.2   *REQUIRED LEVEL OF CONFIDENCE*

In discussing the virtues of random sampling earlier in this chapter, it was pointed out that one of these lies in being able to calculate the level of confidence one can have that the results achieved by the sample are likely to give a true indication of results in the underlying population. Common sense, and the statistical formula, indicate that the higher the level of confidence required in the results then the larger the size of sample necessary. What common sense does not make clear but the formula does, is that to increase the level of confidence from the 68% level (i.e. a one in three risk of the sample not being a good one) to the 95% level more commonly used (i.e. only a one in twenty risk that the sample is not a good one) it is necessary to multiply the sample size by a factor of four. If a survey of 100 respondents indicated that 28% of all households had a separate freezer at the 68% level of confidence, to increase the level of confidence in the results to the 95% level a survey of 400 respondents would be required.

7.5.3 REQUIRED LIMITS OF ACCURACY

It also makes sense at an intuitive level to accept that the larger the size of the sample the more accurate the results are likely to be as a predictor of population values. Once again, the statistical formula of sampling theory makes it possible to quantify this relationship. The relationship is inverse and squared. That piece of statistical jargon simply says that to double the accuracy in the results (i.e. to halve the allowable range in the limits of accuracy) it would be necessary to multiply the size of the sample by four. In the example above, if the sample of 400 respondents indicated that at the 95% level of confidence 28% of all households had a freezer within limits of accuracy of 10%, this would indicate between 25.2% and 30.8% of all homes have separate freezers. For greater precision the limits of accuracy must be reduced. To halve this to + or −5% (i.e. between 26.6% and 29.4%) a sample size of 1600 would be required.

To summarize, then, sampling theory indicates that in random samples there are three factors which should be taken into account in deciding the size of the sample: variability in the population, the level of confidence wanted in the results, and the limits of accuracy acceptable to the decision-maker. All of these can be decided before the survey takes place, and the sample size calculated to meet the requirements for confidence and accuracy in the results.

There are, however, three further factors which need to be considered before the size of the sample can be determined, as follows.

7.5.4   ALLOWANCE FOR NON-RESPONSE

Inevitably some non-response will be experienced in applying any field research method. If this is estimated at say, 10% then if the final number of successfully completed interviews required is 1000 it will be necessary to arrange for 1100 interviews to be attempted.

7.5.5   SUB-GROUP ANALYSIS REQUIREMENTS

The calculations referred to above are concerned with calculating the sample size required for precision in the analysis of the answers to one particular question. The calculation has to be repeated for every question in the questionnaire. In practice this turns out to be a largely unhandleable amount of calculation and is rarely undertaken. The size of a sample needed to meet the requirements of every question on the questionnaire is determined by the smallest proportion of respondents likely to answer any particular question on it.

For example, information may be required from both users and non-users of a product. The questionnaire will be devised to ask all respondents the 'filter' question, 'Do you own a video recorder?' In 1982 it was known that approximately 15% of households had a video recorder. In a random sample, therefore, 15% of the sample were expected to answer 'yes' and go on to give further information about how they decided which one to buy and so on. In a sample of 500 respondents only 75 were expected to give the data we require about video ownership. To expand this number to a more statistically viable level the survey started with a sample of 1000 respondents, anticipating a sub-sample of 150 households with a video recorder. If it were wanted to identify respondents who owned a certain brand of video recorder which accounted for 50% of the video recorder market, it would have been necessary to start with an overall sample size of 2000 respondents in order to end with 150 respondents in this category. It is considerations such as these that determine the overall size of a sample by working upwards from the analysis requirements of particular sub-groups within the sample. As discussed in Section 7.4.1 weighting can also be used in determining sample size when sub-group analysis is required.

7.5.6 *PRACTICAL FACTORS*

As with much else in organizational life it is often the practical considerations that in the end, dominate many decisions. Cost, time and the availability of suitable personnel cannot be ignored. Cost is often the dominant factor in determining how many interviews are undertaken.

For all the reasons given above, cost is not a relevant determinant of sample size, but this ignores practical reality. Some trade-off must be achieved between increased reliability and accuracy in the data arising from a larger size sample and increased cost, so that an optimum level is achieved. If cost is allowed to be the determinant of sample size then the implications for reliability and accuracy must be recognized and not ignored as is so often the case. It cannot be expected that the same quality of results will be achieved from a small sample as from a large sample. However, it is unnecessary to generate a high level of precision in research results when other areas surrounding the problem under consideration are subject to an even higher degree of error. Time is another important element in that the shorter the time in which results are required, then the less time available for field-work and the smaller the size of the sample that can be achieved in the time limits set. Finally, suitably trained interviewers may simply not be available to meet the needs of a very large and widely spread sampling requirement.

A number of factors have been shown to be relevant in determining sample size. This demonstrates that the appropriate sample size must be worked out with respect to the needs of each particular survey. However, most beginners in a subject area like some rough clues as to the order of size which may be usual. As 'rule of thumb' guidelines only, the following points may be helpful. In general for acceptable statistical validity of results generated from quantitative surveys any sub-group containing less than 100 respondents should be treated with extreme caution in statistical analysis. Numbers below 50 respondents should not be subjected to statistical analysis at all. The normal range of sample sizes used in national samples for many consumer goods is 1500 to 2000 respondents. Minimum sample sizes for quantitative consumer surveys are of the order of 300 to 500 respondents. The upper limits of size of sample have been pushed very high by the Government's national housing survey including 100 000 households but this, of course, is most unusual!

The points made above with respect to sample size have been derived from sampling theory which forms the basis for random sampling. In the case of quota sampling, or of variations to the random procedure like multi-stage and random location, it is usual to increase the size of the sample in order to compensate for any inaccuracies introduced by the sampling procedure. Alternatively, a 'design factor' may be used to reduce the confidence level and accuracy in the results, and compensate for the limitations of the non-random sampling techniques in this way.

As a final note on sampling it should be mentioned that the only time when the size of the underlying population need be taken into account in considering the size of the sample to be drawn from it, is when the size of the sample required is likely to account for 10% or more of the population.

7.6   SUMMARY

Sampling is the process of selecting the individuals who will provide the data required in a survey. The term 'sample' is defined and reasons for its use in research given. The main techniques of sample selection are discussed: random sampling and its variants, quota sampling and judgement sampling. The size of the sample needed is shown to be dependent on factors of population variance, required confidence levels and limits of accuracy, allowance for non-response and sub-group analysis requirements.

8 How Do You Ask the Questions?

8.1 INTRODUCTION

Chapter 6 introduced interviews as the most versatile and widely used method of primary data collection. The device used by interviewers for delivering questions to respondents and recording their answers is a questionnaire. This chapter considers the use, design and content of questionnaires. Questionnaires are also used in telephone research and without interviewers in postal research. Some guidelines for questionnaire construction are given, but in large-scale quantitative survey research questionnaires are usually written by research specialists and a framework for vetting questionnaires is suggested at the end of this chapter.

8.2 WHY USE A QUESTIONNAIRE?

Questionnaires have four main purposes in the data collection process: to collect relevant data, to make data comparable, to minimize bias and to motivate the respondent.

8.2.1 TO COLLECT RELEVANT DATA

Since data collection is structured by the questionnaire it is a most important element in the research process. The quality of the data gathered is highly dependent on the design of the questionnaire and the questions it contains. A poorly designed questionnaire will collect inappropriate or inaccurate data and so negate the whole purpose of the research, even though the major costs will have been incurred. No amount of good analysis can retrieve bad data. The first stage in designing a questionnaire is to clarify its objectives. The 'Definition of research required' discussed in Section 5.4, would form the basis for this. The role of the research user is to ensure that research specialists responsible for questionnaire design are fully and adequately briefed. Once the questionnaire objectives are agreed, they form the framework within which all subsequent decisions about the questionnaire structure and question content are made. This mechanism ensures that the data collected is directly relevant to the problem.

The relevance of information produced is also determined by the analysis and interpretation to which it can be subjected. For this reason question design must be clearly linked to schemes for processing and analysing the data. There is no point in including questions that cannot be analysed to produce usable information. A readership study for a local newspaper wanted to measure appeal of various items to different class, age, region and special interest groups. The questions about liking of editorial, sport, women's and motoring sections were made relevant to the purposes of the survey by analysis against the descriptive variables. Both had to be included in the questionnaire.

8.2.2 TO MAKE DATA COMPARABLE

A questionnaire makes it possible to use tens of interviewers and hundreds of respondents, with the main variable being the variation in response. It is then possible to add up similar responses and say, '10% say this'. This requires the questionnaire to be constructed in such a way that the words used have the same meaning for all respondents and all interviewers. To ensure that all interviewers do ask precisely the same question of all respondents it is usual to instruct them to read out the question from the questionnaire exactly as written. If a respondent has difficulty answering, the interviewer is instructed simply to read out the question again and to add no words of clarification or explanation. Clearly, this procedure will only work if questions are well written and use everyday language. If it becomes necessary for the interviewer to assist the respondent in answering, then the questionnaire has failed and the comparability of data is lost. Variations due to different interviewer interpretations will have been introduced, but these will not be known by the data analyst and may result in misleading conclusions being drawn. Questionnaire piloting is an essential procedure in ensuring that questions 'work'.

8.2.3 TO MINIMIZE BIAS

In a research interview 'bias' is defined as the difference between the answers give by respondents and the 'truth'. It is minimized by paying particular attention to the sequence and wording of questions, and to the words themselves. The questionnaire should make it easy for respondents to give true answers and care must be taken to avoid questions or words that may 'lead' respondents into giving answers that do not reflect their true opinions.

8.2.4 TO MOTIVATE THE RESPONDENT

Answering a questionnaire requires a respondent to give time, attention and thought to a subject which, though of great interest to the researcher, may not be of much interest to the respondent. It is important to remember this when designing a questionnaire. The length should be kept to a minimum, although some topics will of themselves maintain the respondent's interest for longer than others. Questions should be as easy for the respondent to understand and answer as possible: an uncertain respondent is more likely to terminate the interview. Explanations should be included to bridge what might appear unconnected changes of question topic: if the respondent feels the overall content makes no sense, he is again more likely to cease co-operation. As much as possible, the format and type of question used should be made varied and interesting for the respondent.

8.3 GETTING THE QUESTIONNAIRE CONTENT RIGHT

For ease of explanation the questionnaire design process is discussed as a staged progression. In practice, like much research procedure, it is an iterative process. Decisions made at one point may affect what has gone before as well as what comes after, so that continual revision and refinement of the questionnaire is going on throughout the process.

In Chapter 5, the first step in the whole research procedure was to define the problem and the data required to solve it. From this statement of general research objectives it is now necessary to specify exactly what information is to be collected using a questionnaire survey. The manager himself should give adequate time and attention to ensure that the objectives set for the questionnaire will result in production of the information required. Faults in questionnaire design commonly occur because this important stage has been completed too hurriedly. What may happen then is that the objectives are never properly clarified. The researchers do what they assume is required, and this can result in expensively produced information, which at best leaves some questions unanswered, and at worst answers none of them. The decision–maker has a prime responsibility for ensuring that if the survey objectives, as defined, are carried out, then this will meet his needs.

Once the survey objectives are agreed, they form the framework within which the rest of the process is set. All subsequent stages are measured against the objectives to see whether they help fulfil them. The next step is to transform the survey objectives into a list of data requirements and then into a list of questions. Each question on the list must be checked against the research objectives: does the information it will generate contribute directly towards meeting those objectives? If the data which will be generated is interesting, but not essential, then the question should be deleted. Asking non-essential questions will only lengthen the questionnaire and potentially reduce the quality of the rest of the data gathered, by increasing interviewer and respondent fatigue. Decision-makers commissioning research will often think, 'Well, while we're out there, let's ask . . .', and so the questionnaire grows. Hence the warning against allowing this to happen. However, it should be noted that the greatest costs in survey research are the field-work costs, so if the basic data required will only take a few minutes of interviewing time, then it may be reasonable to add further questions. For short factual data requirements, the use of an omnibus survey could be a more efficient way of generating the required information (*see* Section 4.4).

After ensuring that every question is essential to the purposes of the survey, and checking that all the purposes of the survey will be met by the questions to be included, the process of questionnaire construction can begin.

8.4   WHAT TYPES OF DATA CAN BE COLLECTED USING A QUESTIONNAIRE?

Three types of information can be gathered using questionnaires.

8.4.1   FACT

This includes what is often termed 'classification data', i.e. facts about respondents which are used to describe them: demographic information like age, sex, social class, geographic location, and so on. It also includes information relevant to the survey, like ownership: of a washing machine, garden, library ticket, credit card, etc. Facts may also refer to behaviour, 'Have you ever bought a book?', 'Have you ever visited an art gallery?', and so on.

Factual information is relatively easy to ask and to

answer, providing the respondent knows and can remember. To be most useful the questions need to be quite specific. For example, a publisher may be more interested in current book buyers than in knowing whether the individual has ever bought a book. In this case the question would be, 'Have you bought any book in the last month?'. Or it may be that he is really interested in people who buy books for their own use rather than for someone else, 'Have you bought any book in the last month for yourself?', and so on until the question quite specifically asks for the information which is required.

Factual information can be described as 'hard' data, because it is data that can be relied upon: people either are or are not in a particular category; have or have not a particular item; have performed or have not performed a particular action. This gives reasonable quantitative estimates for the subject under study, and gives some bases for cross-tabulation of results. In the example, it was possible to look at the ages of book buyers against non-book buyers, and be fairly confident that the findings were relevant, given that the sample was a good one.

8.4.2 OPINION

Included in this category are beliefs, attitudes, feelings and knowledge. Opinion data can be very useful to decision-makers, in giving understanding of the background to behaviour. However, the findings should be treated with rather more caution than factual data. In asking people what their opinions or feelings are about a subject the question itself assumes that they have opinions. This 'cue' will be picked up and answers to the question given. If respondents actually had no opinion before the question was asked, the researcher has collected data which appears to measure something, but does not in fact do so. Also, in answering questions of the form, 'What do you feel about . . . ?', people tend to give answers making only one or two points about their feelings. Feelings and attitudes are generally rather complex, having a number of dimensions, and so this kind of answer is only a limited and sometimes inaccurate reply. It is for this reason that the multi-dimensional scaling techniques, discussed in Section 6.2.2, are commonly used to collect attitudinal data.

The results of opinion questions are described as 'soft' data, because they are far less reliable as a base for decision-making than factual information. Disasters have befallen decision-makers who believed that the sum of the 'yes' answers to the question, 'Would you buy this product?' is the same thing as a demand forecast! Hypothetical responses rarely provide a good indicator of subsequent behaviour. Nevertheless, opinion data is extremely good at suggesting new ideas and approaches which are a valuable input to decision-making.

8.4.3   MOTIVE

Knowing people's reasons for a particular belief or action, can be important to those wishing to influence them. It is quite easy to ask, 'Why do you do that?'—buy slimming aids? read a newspaper? or 'Why do you think this?'—like/dislike your local public house? The difficulty lies in answering this kind of question. It is often hard to explain fully why one does or thinks a particular thing. If asked, 'Why are you reading this particular book?' it is probable that you can give a reason quite readily. It is usual to explain behaviour, when asked, using only one reason. Yet most behaviour has more than one reason. You may be reading the book because you have a particular problem at work, which you hope this book will help to solve, but there will be other, less immediate, reasons. Perhaps you think some knowledge of marketing research techniques will always be useful in any management career. Maybe you are preparing for a job change, or trying to impress your boss. Probably you have reasons relevant only to your own situation.

This illustrates another problem with questions about motive: the answers are likely to be so diverse that they are difficult to compare and analyse. The analysis is inevitably subjective, and the results are impressionistic rather than certain.

To produce quantitative data about motives, possible reasons for behaviour can be explored using small-scale qualitative techniques such as group discussions or depth interviews (discussed in Sections 6.2.1 and 6.2.4). From these, the categories of reason most relevant to the objectives of the survey can be determined. Specific questions, designed to measure how many people share these motives, can then be included in a representative sample survey which will produce quantifiable results.

8.5 WHAT DOES A QUESTIONNAIRE CONTAIN?

There are three parts to a questionnaire:

1 Identification data
2 Classification data
3 Subject data

8.5.1 IDENTIFICATION DATA

This section is usually completed by the interviewer, and identifies one particular interview. It usually contains the name and address of the respondent, perhaps the date, time, length and place of interview, and the name of the interviewer. An example is shown in Figure 8.2. This data is required in case any check back is needed, either to ensure that the interview took place, or if questions are missed out, or completed incorrectly. Usually, these questions are asked right at the end of a personal interview, when sufficient rapport exists between interviewer and respondent for assurance that replies will be treated in confidence is accepted, even though a name is being requested.

RESEARCH SURVEYS OF GREAT BRITAIN LIMITED, RESEARCH CENTRE, WEST GATE, LONDON W5 1EL   TELEPHONE NO. 01-997-5555

| (1) | (2) | (3) | (4) | (5) | (6) | (7) | (8) | | | PUNCHER: PUNCH 9/① | | |
| 0 | 3 | 0 | 7 | | | | | | | | | |

SAMPLING POINT NUMBER

(10)   (11)   (12)   (13)

INFORMANTS NAME & TITLE (MR/MRS/MISS)
(BLOCK CAPITALS)

FULL _____

POSTAL _____

ADDRESS

		(14)
A.	Does the house have a telephone ?	
	IF 'YES' What is the number ?	YES 1
		NO 2

		(15)
B.	SEX OF INFORMANT	MALE 1
		FEMALE 2

		(16)
C.	AGE OF INFORMANT	16 - 19 1
		20 - 24 2
		25 - 29 3
		30 - 34 4
		35 - 44 5
		45 - 54 6
		55 - 64 7
		65 OR MORE 8

		(17)
D.	STATUS OF INFORMANT IN HOUSEHOLD	
	┌─────────┐ ──→ HEAD OF HOUSEHOLD	1
	│BOTH MAY BE│ ──→ FEMALE HOUSEWIFE	2
	│CODED │	
	└─────────┘	

		(20)
G.	ASK ALL WOMEN AGED 16 YEARS OR MORE	
	WOMAN HAS A FULL-TIME PAID JOB (30 HRS+)	1
	WOMAN HAS A PART-TIME PAID JOB (LESS THAN 30 HOURS)	2
	WOMAN HAS NO JOB	3

		(21)
H.	ASK ALL HEADS OF HOUSEHOLD/HOUSEWIVES	
	HOUSEWIFE WITH CHILDREN UNDER 16 IN HOUSE	1
	HOUSEWIFE WITHOUT CHILDREN UNDER 16 IN HOUSE	2

		(22)
I.	ASK ALL	
	How many people are there in	1
	your household altogether,	2
	including any children and yourself ?	3
		4
		5 OR MORE 5

		(23)
J.	DAY OF INTERVIEW	
		MONDAY 1
		TUESDAY 2
		WEDNESDAY 3
		THURSDAY 4
		FRIDAY 5
		SATURDAY 6
		SUNDAY 7

E. MARITAL STATUS

                            (18)

SINGLE/WIDOWED/DIVORCED   1

MARRIED   2

OCCUPATION OF HEAD OF HOUSEHOLD   A   (CODE
OR CHIEF WAGE EARNER   B   WHICH ONE)

WRITE IN FULL DETAILS _____

TYPE OF INDUSTRY _____

IF WIDOW OR RETIRED CLASSIFY BELOW

    WIDOW WITH WIDOW'S PENSION ONLY   C

WIDOW WITH PRIVATE MEANS (E.G. husband's pension)   D
  (SPECIFY HUSBAND'S FORMER OCCUPATION ABOVE)

RETIRED MAN OR WOMAN WITH STATE RETIREMENT
PENSION ONLY   E

RETIRED MAN OR WOMAN WITH STATE RETIREMENT
PENSION AND OCCUPATIONAL PENSION   F
(SPECIFY PREVIOUS OCCUPATION ABOVE)

F. SOCIAL GRADE OF HOUSEHOLD   (19)

    A   1
    B   2
    C1   3
    C2   4
    D   5
    E   6

K. LENGTH OF INTERVIEW   (24)

    UP TO 15 MINS   1
    16 - 20 MINS   2
    21 - 25 MINS   3
    26 - 30 MINS   4
    31 - 35 MINS   5
    36 - 40 MINS   6
    41 - 45 MINS   7
    46 - 50 MINS   8
    51 - 55 MINS   9
    56 MINS OR MORE   0

I certify that this interview has been personally carried
out by me with the informant at his/her address. I further
certify that the informant is not a friend or relative of
mine, and I have not interviewed at his/her address in any
survey in the last 6 months.

SIGNATURE: _____ DATE: _____

AND NAME IN
BLOCK CAPITALS: _____

	INTERVIEWER NUMBER				PUNCHER:
(25)	(26)	(27)	(28)	(29)	SKIP 30-80

Figure 3.1 Identification and classification page from questionnaire

8.5.2   CLASSIFICATION DATA

This is the data required to classify the respondent, and is often used as the basis for analysis of the subject data sought in the body of the questionnaire. It includes data like age, sex, occupation of head of household, income group, marital status, and other data thought relevant, which helps to define the individual for the purposes of analysing responses. In a personal interview this information can be left until the end if the respondent has been selected on a random sampling basis, but if the interviewer must select the respondent for a quota sample, then it is necessary to ask some of the classification questions at the outset. Classification data is also used in checking the representativeness of the sample. (Figure 8.1 shows a typical identification and classification page from a questionnaire.)

8.5.3   SUBJECT DATA

This refers to the information being gathered to meet the survey objectives, and forms the major part of the questionnaire. It is often helpful to begin by constructing a flow-chart diagram. This is useful in planning the sequence of the questionnaire when different questions need to be asked of different respondents, e.g. 'Have you made any journeys by bus in the last week?'

IF 'YES' GO TO Q.2   IF 'NO' GO TO Q.8

The question used in this example is described as a 'filter' question, or 'skip', because it filters respondents into or out of subsequent question sections. Great care must be taken if a number of filter questions are to be used, to ensure that it is quite clear what route the respondent must follow through the questionnaire. Arrows appearing on the questionnaire are sometimes used to aid the interviewer and ensure that sections are not missed completely. Devices to ensure that sections are not missed are particularly important in self-completion questionnaires, and sometimes different coloured pages are used to help respondents identify which sections to complete. Instructions to the interviewer are normally shown in capital letters. Figure 8.2 illustrates the use of 'skips'.

In thinking about the order of questions, it is important to remember that the respondent's reaction to the first few questions will determine whether he decides to continue co-operation throughout the interview. These early questions should therefore be of interest to the respondent and be easy to answer. This latter point is an important one, since many respondents initially regard a research interview as being a test of their knowledge, and on being approached may say, 'I can't help you. I don't know a lot about it.' When they realize from the first couple of questions, that the questions are really quite easy, and well within their experience, then they will relax and the interviewer's task is made easier as the respondent's confidence grows. For opposite reasons, questions that are either uninteresting or rather personal in nature should appear as late as possible in the questionnaire. The assumption is that a good interviewer will have built up sufficient rapport by this time to carry her through less interesting material which might earlier have caused the respondent to terminate the interview.

Another point to bear in mind is the influence of each question on succeeding questions. It is pointless to present a respondent with a show card listing brands and ask about brand attributes, then later in the questionnaire ask what brands the respondent can recall. Obviously, the recall question must come first.

Every attempt should be made to ensure a logical sequence to the questions so that the respondent is aided in his thinking about the subject and is more likely to produce reliable answers.

Figure 8.2 'Filter' questions or 'skips'

On most questionnaires there will be some questions which do not apply to some respondents and will not have to be asked. These questions will be 'skipped'. Instructions will be given either in the margin of the questionnaire or in the body of the questionnaire about the route to be followed.

Example
IF 'NO' TO QUESTION 4, GO TO QUESTION 5.
IF 'YES' TO QUESTION 4, SKIP TO QUESTION 6.
It is normal to write instructions to the interviewer in CAPITAL letters.

	CODE	ROUTE
Q.30 Have you ever received any training, either while you were working or in order to get a job?		
NO –	(48) X	Q.37
YES: ASK: How many periods of training have you done altogether?		
1	1	
2	2	
3	3	Q.31
4	4	
5 OR MORE	5	
(DON'T KNOW/NOT STATED)	A	
IF THE ANSWER IS 'YES' ASK ALL THE FOLLOWING QUESTIONS. IF THE ANSWER IS 'NO' TO Q.30, SKIP TO QUESTION 37.		
Q.31 How useful do you feel this training could be to you now? ASK ABOUT 'LAST TRAINING' IF MORE THAN ONE	(49)	
VERY USEFUL	1	
FAIRLY USEFUL	2	Q.32
NOT VERY USEFUL	3	
NOT AT ALL USEFUL	4	
(DON'T KNOW/NOT STATED)	A	
Q.32 What job or skill was that training for? WRITE IN	(50)	
	(51)	Q.33

Q.33 How long did the training last ?

	(52)	
LESS THAN 2 WEEKS	1	Q.34
2 WEEKS BUT LESS THAN 1 MONTH	2	
1 MONTH BUT LESS THAN 3 MONTHS	3	
3 MONTHS BUT LESS THAN 6 MONTHS	4	
6 MONTHS BUT LESS THAN 1 YEAR	5	
1 YEAR BUT LESS THAN 2 YEARS	6	
2 YEARS OR MORE	7	
(DON'T KNOW/NOT STATED)	A	

Q.34 Was it full-time, or part-time (30 hrs or less, per week) ?

	(53)	
FULL-TIME	1	Q.35
PART-TIME	2	
(DON'T KNOW/NOT STATED)	A	

Q.35 Was it 'on-the-job' training or 'off-the-job' training
(............ away from the normal job situation) ?

CODE ALL THAT APPLY

	(54)	
ON THE JOB	1	Q.36
OFF THE JOB	2	
(DON'T KNOW/NOT STATED)	A	

Q.36 How long ago did you finish it ?

	(55)	
1 YEAR BUT LESS THAN 2 YEARS AGO	1	Q.37
2 YEARS BUT LESS THAN 5 YEARS AGO	2	
5 YEARS BUT LESS THAN 10 YEARS AGO	3	
10 OR MORE YEARS AGO	4	
(DON'T KNOW/NOT STATED)	A	

Q.37 ASK ALL
Now I'd like to ask you a few questions about your health.
Thinking of the present, do you have any handicap or illness
which affects your activities in any way ?

	(56)	
YES - HAVE HANDICAP OR ILLNESS	1	
NO	2	
(DON'T KNOW/NOT STATED)	A	

8.6 WHAT TYPES OF QUESTION CAN BE USED?

There are four main question types: dichotomous (or yes/no), multiple-choice, open-ended and rating scales.

8.6.1 DICHOTOMOUS QUESTIONS

These are questions with only two possible answers, e.g. yes/no questions. For use of these questions to be valid the answer must fall unambiguously into one of the two categories offered e.g. 'Do you buy ready-made biscuits rather than bake your own?' is ambiguous because many women do both and so could not answer 'yes' or 'no'. Similarly, if qualified answers to the question are possible, then the answers may be invalidated. 'Do you intend to invest in new machinery?' is an example of a question which for many companies would be answered, 'It depends'. However, when a straight yes or no is appropriate, dichotomous questions are easy to ask, easy to answer and easy to analyse statistically. For completeness in recording responses, a 'don't know' category is included on the questionnaire. The three possible responses 'yes/no/don't know' can be assigned code numbers which are printed on the questionnaire so that the interviewer just rings the response given. This *pre-coding* saves time, effort and therefore cost in processing responses. Code numbers can be punched directly from the completed questionnaires for computer analysis. Pre-coding is explained further in Section 8.9, and questions 34, 35 and 37 in Figure 8.2 are examples of pre-coded dichotomous questions.

8.6.2 MULTIPLE-CHOICE QUESTIONS

These questions are deceptively easy to ask. In fact, they are one of the most difficult of questions to design, because the question designer not only has to know what to ask, but also all the possible answers. The range of answers provided must be comprehensive (no respondent should want to give an answer that is not offered) and mutually exclusive (no respondent should feel the answer could be in more than one category).

In practice, these requirements are very difficult to meet. One has only to think of the occasions when one has personally been presented with a multiple-choice question for which none of the offered responses exactly matched one's own point of view, to know that this type of question is commonly asked rather badly. The danger is that the researcher gets back nice neat data, where people are tidily classified into boxes, and may not appreciate that respondents have squeezed themselves into boxes, which do not really fit them. To attempt to avoid this problem by offering a category saying, 'Other (please specify)' actually introduces further complications. How many of those who have used one of the classifications offered would have used these additional classifications suggested by some respondents?

Nevertheless, where it is possible to design a valid multiple-choice question, such questions are easy to analyse and are less open to interviewer bias since the respondent selects his own response category. Processing responses is also easy since pre-coding can be used on the questionnaire. In Figure 8.2 questions 31, 33, 36 are examples of pre-coded multiple-choice questions. It is usual to present the alternatives to respondents written on a '*show card*', to avoid the problem of respondents forgetting some of the possible responses. When a number of responses are presented, the order in which they appear can affect their likelihood of being selected. Items which appear at the beginning and end of lists are more likely to be selected. Show cards with the responses listed in different orders are therefore produced so that those 'order effects' are randomized and cancel each other out. Figure 8.3 illustrates interviewer instructions on using show cards, and gives an example of a multiple-choice question with its accompanying show card.

Figure 8.3 Interviewer instructions on the use of show cards.

<u>EXAMPLE</u>

<u>SHOW CARD C</u>

Q.2 **Which of these building materials do you
mainly prefer to see used in the
construction of a building?**

<u>RING ONE ONLY</u>

	CODE
	(13)
STEEL	1
GLASS	2
CONCRETE/CEMENT	3
BRICK	4
TIMBER	5
STONE	6
INDIFFERENT	7

```
           SHOW CARD C

            STEEL

            GLASS

        CONCRETE/CEMENT

            BRICK

            TIMBER

            STONE

          INDIFFERENT
```

Show cards. These are used as visual aids during interviews. They help the respondent to choose a
statement in answer to a question – if the statements are simply read out to him he may not be able
to retain all the alternatives in his memory long enough to make a decision. They *must always be
used* where indicated on the questionnaires.

They should be shown to the respondent and read aloud. (The order of statements on the card may
be different from the order on the questionnaire so care must be taken to ring the correct code.)
Never make the respondent aware of the 'Don't Know' code or he/she may constantly say, 'Don't
Know'.

A respondent may appear to be looking at a show card, but in fact is not reading it at all. People who
cannot read are reluctant to admit it, and it is very important that the card be read aloud to the
respondent in case he has difficulty in reading, or poor eyesight.

8.6.3 OPEN-ENDED QUESTIONS

These are questions in which possible answers are not suggested, as they are by the two previous types of question. The respondent is free to respond in any way at all, and so response variation may be extreme. The interviewer must record all that the respondent says, which can introduce bias if she decides to record only what seems relevant to her. When the completed questionnaires are returned, the responses require manual analysis which is time and labour consuming, and therefore expensive. Since there is likely to be a high degree of variation in response, the results will be qualitative rather than quantitative. These practical limitations usually mean that not more than one or two questions on a questionnaire are open-ended. Wherever possible, qualitative work is carried out before the stage of questionnaire design, so that multiple-choice or attitude scales can be used to quantify qualitative findings and avoid the need for open-ended questions on large-scale surveys. In smaller-scale surveys when statistical validity is not a prime objective, open-ended questions are of great value in exploring complex and variable topics. An example might be, 'What are the things you take into account when buying aircraft components?'

8.6.4 RATING SCALES

In Sections 6.2.2 and 6.2.3, attitude measurement and motivational research were discussed. Commonly, these techniques involve the use of rating scales or projective questions. Where special question techniques are used in a questionnaire, it is important that the interviewers are trained in the application of the technique, and are quite clear about what is required both from them and from the respondent. The great value of rating scales is that they make it possible to quantify complex and multi-dimensional concepts. The dimensions themselves are uncovered in preliminary research using qualitative open-ended question techniques. Analysis of answers to rating scales

Q.14 I am now going to show you some ranges of packs for different
brands of shampoos and read out some comments other people
have made about them. As I do so, I want you to tell me, just
going by the appearance of the packs of each range, to which
of the ranges of packs each comment applies. You may feel a
comment applies to all the ranges or to just some or to none
at all.

<u>ALLOW RESPONDENT TIME TO VIEW ALL BRANDS</u>

Q.15 First of all which of these packs do you personally think look
...(READ OUT)

	A	B	C	D	E	F	All of them
Modern and up-to-date							
Rather ordinary							
Easy to tell for which hair types							
Gimmicky							

Feminine

Not for me

Particularly attractive

Poor value for money

Distinctive

Expensive looking

Easy to handle

Figure 8.4

Q.16 Which of the packs looks as if they would contain a shampoo which would..... (READ OUT BELOW)

	A	B	C	D	E	F	All of them	None of them
Be different from other shampoos								
Be really good for your hair								
Have a fresh and natural perfume								
Be a thin, weak shampoo								
Be a high quality shampoo								
Be made with good ingredients								
Will leave hair looking really nice								

Q.17 Now I am going to read out some descriptions of several different people or personalities all of whom use shampoo. For each description I would like you to tell me, just by looking

at each of the ranges, which ones you think would most likely
be used by .... You may give as many as you like for each
range.
(READ OUT BELOW)

	A	B	C	D	E	F	All of them
A teenage girl							
An older woman							
A lively, youthful person							
A young woman							
A working woman							
Men as well as women							
A natural self-confident woman							
Anyone in the family							
A price-conscious person							

Figure 8.4 (cont)

requires the application of special statistical techniques, and these are discussed in Section 10.3.3. Two kinds of rating scale are commonly used. One is the 'semantic differential' scale discussed in Section 6.2.2 and illustrated in Figure 6.2. This requires respondents to assess each brand separately on a number of dimensions. An alternative approach is shown in Figure 8.4 where all the brands are assessed on one dimension at a time.

8.7　HOW SHOULD QUESTIONS BE WORDED?

8.7.1　MEANING

The key to question wording is to remember that words are not precise descriptive instruments, and so it is necessary to be sure that the words selected have the same meaning for the respondent as they have for the researcher. For example, 'dinner' may be a meal one has in the middle of the day, or in the evening; it may be different for children and adults, and different on Sunday from the rest of the week. 'Supper' and 'tea' are equally imprecise terms. The point of these examples is to illustrate that even the most common of words can be a source of misinterpretation in the context of a questionnaire. In the examples used, the terms most usually applied are, 'midday meal', 'main evening meal', and so on.

When a respondent is being asked about a particular piece of behaviour, the issue must be clearly defined. It is often useful to apply the 'who, what, where, when, and how' checks to what is being asked by the question, and if these questions cannot be answered, then the question needs to be reworded so as to be more specific about exactly what is required. For example, 'How many times have you personally attended an exhibition of industrial equipment, of any kind, in the UK in the last twelve months?'. This question makes it quite clear to whom the question refers, 'you personally'. What information is sought, 'attended an exhibition of industrial equipment of any kind'. Where the relevant behaviour occurred, 'in the UK'. When it took place, 'in the last twelve months', and 'How many times'. In this example 'Why' the individual attended such exhibitions could be a subsequent question.

All questions should be kept as short as possible, and should use everyday language. Every part of the question-naire must communicate effectively with the least-educated member of the sample.

8.7.2 AMBIGUITY

Ambiguous terms should be avoided, or a definition included. 'Do you read a daily newspaper regularly?' What does 'regularly' mean? For some it might mean 'everyday', but a person who regularly buys the paper on Friday could answer 'Yes', and other patterns might be included also. Normally the qualification, 'By regularly, I mean three or more days each week', is added. But what does 'read' mean in this context? 'Looked at?' 'Scanned?' 'Read from cover to cover?' 'Bought, but didn't actually get round to looking at?', and so on. So the qualification, 'by "read" I mean read or look at' is added. Now the question reads, 'Have you read, or looked at, a daily newspaper on three or more days in the past seven days?'.

8.7.3 LEADING

Leading questions and loaded words should be avoided. These are questions or words with meanings which invite particular responses. 'Do you think that the United King-dom should stay in the European Community (the Common Market)?' was the question posed in the 1975 referendum. To ask, 'Do you think the United Kingdom should enter the European Community?' would probably have generated differences in response. The use of the word 'stay' in the actual question invited support for the *status quo*, and received it. Many words are 'loaded' in the sense that they have associative meanings beyond their strict dictionary definition, and individuals tend to respond to the associations the word has for them. The choice of word must therefore be considered from this point of view. 'Bosses', 'managers' and 'administrators' could all be descriptions of the same group of 'workers' (another loaded word). The selection of term used to describe them is likely to affect responses to questions about the group. The problem is that almost all words are loaded in one direction or another. The aim must be to select words least likely to bias response, and also be aware of the possibility and potential direction of bias and treat the results with corresponding caution.

8.7.4   GENERALIZATION

A common problem in question wording is the use of generalizations. 'On average, how often do you buy sweets in a week?' Unless the relevant behaviour is extremely regular, this question is likely to produce bad data, since the respondent is asked to generalize about behaviour. What he is really being asked to do is to calculate his frequency of sweet buying over the last year and compute the arithmetic average per week: a patently unreasonable and probably impossible request. He will either respond using his last week's behaviour, or pluck some hypothetical figure out of the air. It would be better to ask, 'On how many occasions have you bought sweets during the past week?'. An average frequency of purchase can then be calculated from the spread of data generated by the sample.

8.7.5   UNIDIMENSIONALITY

Sometimes it is necessary to ask more than one question. As well as asking, 'What names of airline companies can you recall?', it would be useful to ask first, 'Do you ever travel by air nowadays?'. Analysis of recall among travellers and non-travellers could then be carried out. A check should also be made to ensure that the question is only asking about one dimension. 'Do you think cream cleansers get surfaces clean without scratching them?' In this case a 'No' answer could mean that cream cleansers do not get surfaces clean, or that they do scratch. Most questions of the form, 'Why did you choose a particular product or service?', have two possible lines of reply. One relates to the perceived attributes of the product or service, and the other describes the circumstances leading up to its choice and how the respondent came to hear about the product or service. It might therefore be better to use the two questions, 'How did you first come to use this product or service?', and, 'What do you like about using the product or service?'. Unidimensionality refers to the need for each question to be asking about only a single point.

8.7.6 CUSHION STATEMENTS

When a questionnaire covers a number of different topics, it is helpful to 'cushion' changes of subject with an introductory phrase, like, 'Now I'm going to ask a few questions about leisure facilities in this city . . .', and when the next section comes up, 'Now I'm going to ask a few questions about transport facilities in this city . . .'. This helps the respondent to follow what is going on, and to switch his thinking from one, otherwise unrelated topic to the next, without becoming too confused. In general, a respondent is more likely to co-operate if he feels he understands what is going on in the questionnaire and can appreciate the reason for it. Brief explanations can aid this process, with benefit to respondent, interviewer and researcher.

8.8 WILL THE RESPONDENT ANSWER THE QUESTIONS?

The questionnaire designer must consider whether it is reasonable to ask those questions of respondents. Do they expect too much of the respondent's memory? A travel questionnaire asked, 'How many journeys have you taken by train in the last year?' Obviously an unreasonable time span for most respondents.

Is the respondent likely to have the necessary information? This is particularly a problem when a housewife is asked about the purchasing habits of other members of her family. In general, it is unwise to ask about any behaviour, attitude or opinion other than that of the individual being interviewed.

It is also unwise to ask questions which assume the respondent has experience he may not have, e.g. 'Is this make of industrial machine better than competing machines on the market?' This assumes that the respondent has tried all the brands of machine on the market with sufficient depth to be able to draw valid comparisons with the machine under test.

Will the respondent give the information required? Respondents may be unwilling to answer because they regard a question as too personal. This is often the case for financial questions in both consumer and industrial research. Respondents may be unwilling to admit their behaviour, for example, drinking and smoking are typically under-reported. Respondents may not answer when it is difficult to explain, say, reasons for doing a particular thing. 'What do you feel about mowing the lawn?' In these circumstances the projective techniques mentioned in Section 6.2.3 can be useful.

8.9   ALLOWING FOR METHOD OF ANALYSIS

When preparing a questionnaire, a great deal of time and money at the analysis stage can be saved. One of the major ways of doing this is to use pre-coded questions, as mentioned in Section 8.6.1 and illustrated in Figure 8.2. Not only the question, but also a list of responses appears on the questionnaire. Code numbers for each response appear in the far right-hand column of the questionnaire, and the interviewer simply rings the relevant response. These ringed codes can be input to the computer directly from the questionnaire. This saves the intervening stage of coding original responses when the questionnaires are returned. By pre-coding responses, and deciding beforehand how many codes will be allotted to open-ended questions, the whole questionnaire can be laid out in such a way that as much direct input as possible is facilitated.

The requirements for tabular analysis should also be considered at this stage: which answers will be analysed by which classification categories? This is a very useful discipline at the stage of questionnaire design, because it illustrates whether the data produced will be in the form required for analysis to produce the information needed by the decision-maker. When the actual stage of analysis comes, it is too late to discover that all the data required has not been collected, or that it is in the wrong form for analysis to produce appropriate information to meet the survey objectives.

8.10   WHY DOES PRESENTATION MATTER?

The physical appearance of the questionnaire affects its likelihood of securing a response, and this is particularly so for self-completion questionnaires. Ease of use and analysis are also dependent on good questionnaire layout. The questionnaire should be laid out using adequate space, and reasonable quality paper. If it looks too 'amateurish' the respondent is less likely to co-operate. If the questionnaire looks as though its perpetrators attach little importance to it, then why should respondents give up their time?

Also important at this moment of attracting the potential respondent's attention, is the verbal introduction used by the interviewer. This must be worked out by the researcher, and should be written on the questionnaire. The form of introduction used is a major influence in securing acceptance, and should not be left to the interviewer's own initiative. Where explanations for the purpose of the survey can be given without possibly biasing response, then this should be done. If a specific explanation is undesirable, then

Some precoded questions require that more than one answer be coded, if appropriate. This is called MULTICODING.

	ROUTE

EXAMPLE

SHOW CARD C

Q.11a Please tell me which of these types of people you think would use pastes and spreads?

PROBE: Which others? RECORD BELOW

Q.11b And are there any types of people on this list you think would definitely not use pastes and spreads?

PROBE: Which others? RECORD BELOW

MULTICODE	Q11a WOULD USE (55)	Q11b WOULD NOT USE (56)	
PEOPLE WHO ENTERTAIN A LOT	1	1	
WORKING MAN	2	2	
YOUNG CHILDREN	3	3	
PEOPLE WITH A LARGE FAMILY	4	4	
TEENAGERS	5	5	
MOTHERS AT HOME ALL DAY	6	6	Q.12
PEOPLE ON A TIGHT BUDGET	7	7	
OLDER PEOPLE	8	8	
WORKING MOTHERS	9	9	
BUSY PEOPLE	0	0	
PEOPLE LIKE YOURSELF	X	X	
NONE	A	A	

```
┌─────────────────────────────────────────┐
│                                         │
│            SHOW CARD C                  │
│            ----------                   │
│                                         │
│      PEOPLE WHO ENTERTAIN A LOT         │
│                                         │
│             WORKING MAN                 │
│                                         │
│            YOUNG CHILDREN               │
│                                         │
│       PEOPLE WITH A LARGE FAMILY        │
│                                         │
│              TEENAGERS                  │
│                                         │
│        MOTHERS AT HOME ALL DAY          │
│                                         │
│        PEOPLE ON A TIGHT BUDGET         │
│                                         │
│             OLDER PEOPLE                │
│                                         │
│           WORKING MOTHERS               │
│                                         │
│             BUSY PEOPLE                 │
│                                         │
│         PEOPLE LIKE YOURSELF            │
│                                         │
└─────────────────────────────────────────┘
```

Figure 8.5

a general statement should be made that gives the respondent some good reason for co-operating. 'To help us produce better products, or services' is often an acceptable rationale. Giving the respondent a good reason for co-operating is especially important in interviewing business and professional people, who generally attach more importance to the value of their time.

In considering the form of the questionnaire, the conditions under which the interviewer is expected to use it should be remembered. If a quota sample is being used, when the interviewer will probably be working outside, possibly in wind or rain, then the questionnaire must not disintegrate or fly off in all directions. The explains the wide use made of clipboards, and sometimes of a book format.

As far as layout is concerned, interviewer instructions must be clearly distinguished from questions, usually by using a different type face or capital letters. When filter questions are being used, either the arrows referred to earlier can assist interviewers in following the correct path through the interview, or more easily, the number of the next question for each response can be written on the questionnaire. Examples of these points are shown in Figure 8.2.

Using the questionnaire can be made easier for both interviewer and respondent by providing show cards whenever a choice of responses is available. These ensure that the respondent is not reliant on memory when selecting a response, and as he reads out his answer, the interviewer can ring the appropriate code on the questionnaire. Figure 8.3 gives one example of this, and more complicated examples allowing multiple coding are shown in Figure 8.5 and Figure 9.1.

8.11   WILL THE QUESTIONNAIRE WORK?

It is both easy and dangerous at the point of having designed a questionnaire, to get it out into the field quickly, 'before any more time is wasted'. The danger is that faults in the questionnaire will not be discovered, resulting in unreliable data. It is always worth piloting a questionnaire, even if only a handful of interviews are done. For important pieces of research it is advisable to ask for a pilot survey, even though this will add to the cost.

The process of piloting requires interviewers to conduct the interview in the normal way, and to note any difficulties which they encounter in introducing the questionnaire, asking or recording answers to the questions, following the instructions or coping with the layout. They are also asked to note any difficulties which the respondent has in interpreting or answering the questions. When the interview is complete the interviewer may explain that the questionnaire is actually being tested, and ask the respondent, 'What did you think that question meant?' and, 'What was in your mind when you answered this question?', or 'How did you arrive at your answer?'. This last question is particularly important to test questions involving memory.

The feedback from this process readily indicates any ways in which the questionnaire does not work well, and interviewers can be asked what words they found it necessary to use in order to explain what was required of respondents. It is usually instructive for the manager to try a few interviews for himself, if he really wants to learn about the research process. Hearing how a questionnaire works in the field can lend insight to the way in which the final results are used in decision-making. The interviewers used for piloting should be average rather than good interviewers, so that difficulties they may have can be monitored. When the questionnaire gets into the field the whole range of interviewer abilities will be working on the survey, and all must be able to use the questionnaire easily.

It is also useful to use the results from a pilot survey for a 'dummy-run' of the analysis to check that it, too, will work out. Piloting will lead to revising, modifying and improving the questionnaire until the designer is satisfied that it is a good instrument for collecting the data required in as undistorted a manner as possible.

8.12   SPECIAL TYPES OF QUESTIONNAIRE

Most of the comments about questionnaire design and content made in this chapter apply generally, however the questionnaire is to be applied. However, when questionnaires are presented to respondents for self-completion, often through the post, or are used as the basis for telephone interviewing, there are implications for the number and type of questions which can be asked, the way in which they are phrased, and the order in which they are presented.

8.12.1   *POSTAL QUESTIONNAIRES*

As covered in Section 6.3, when an appropriate mailing list exists, postal questionnaires can be a useful tool for primary data collection. This is particularly true for executives working on a small budget, or in markets where response rates are likely to be good. Industrial researchers often get good response rates from buyers or suppliers. Mail order companies also use this technique to good effect. One of the features of response to postal questionnaires is that they are more likely to come from individuals with an interest in the subject, so if this is the group whose views are required the method is particularly appropriate.

The rate of response to postal questionnaires is influenced by the covering letter introducing and explaining the purposes of the questionnaire, and also by sending reminder letters to non-respondents. At least as much attention should be given to the design of these letters as is given to the questionnaire itself. The letter should be personalized as far as possible, and indicate to the potential respondent the relevance of the enquiry to his personal interests and the importance of his personal response. Small incentives can also be used to encourage response.

As far as length is concerned, if the subject is one of great interest to respondents they may well be prepared to complete a lengthy questionnaire. However, since there is no interviewer present to encourage completion of it, it is probably wisest to assume that less ground can be covered in a postal questionnaire than in a personal interview. The layout should be such that it is easy to answer the questions and easy to follow the sequence, particularly when different questions need to be answered depending on response to a filter question.

In thinking about question sequence, it must be remembered that some of the facilities available in a personally administered questionnaire are not available in a postal questionnaire. For example, it is not possible to ask general questions about a product group and then funnel down to specific questions about a particular brand. Since respondents are able to read through the whole questionnaire before answering any questions, their awareness of the specific brand being researched may influence responses to the earlier questions. However, an advantage is that being able to look through the whole questionnaire, and complete it in their own time, can produce more thoughtful responses than a personal interview.

In general, a postal questionnaire should give the appearance of being relatively quick, easy and interesting to complete. Pre-coded dichotomous or multiple-choice questions should be used as much as possible so that the respondent only has to mark responses. The respondent should think, 'I might as well do that now' rather than, 'That looks as if it needs thinking about – I'll have a go at it tomorrow'. The latter is the questionnaire that probably will not be completed at all.

8.12.2 TELEPHONE QUESTIONNAIRES

Telephone research has, until recently, been more important as a method of industrial research. It is a relatively low cost way of achieving high response rates, which commercial users find invaluable. In consumer research the cost advantage over the personal interview method is not so great, but the speed advantage can be overriding.

The type of questions most appropriate to telephone surveys are brief, and require brief factual answers which the respondent can give accurately without much thought: 'Do you . . . ?' or 'Don't you . . . ?' 'Have you . . . ?' or 'Haven't you . . . ?' This is because the telephone call is going to interrupt the respondent in the middle of some other activity. The difficulty of establishing rapport over the telephone also makes it unusual for a long conversation to be practicable.

Open-ended questions do not work very well over the telephone, because respondents tend to abbreviate responses and so depth of response is lost. Similarly, long and complicated questions offering several categories of response should not be used because the respondent is unlikely to be able to remember the whole question by the time the interviewer gets to the end of it. Questions which would involve the use of a show card in a personal interview, or where the respondent may be required to look at a pack or advertisement before answering are clearly not possible over the telephone. This can be overcome by sending material through the post to respondents and then telephoning to ask questions about it, but this may also not work well if the respondent loses the material or reads directly from it when questioned.

Computer-assisted telephone interviewing (CATI) is a service now offered by a number of research agencies. It gives advantages in questionnaire presentation since the interviewer reads a question from the screen, types in the code appropriate to the respondent's answer, and the next question appears on the screen. This way, quite complicated questionnaires using filter questions can be devised without worrying that the interviewer will get lost in the questionnaire. The possibility of questions being missed out is also eliminated since only one question appears on the screen and an answer must be keyed in before the next question will appear.

8.13   VETTING QUESTIONNAIRES

Whether the questionnaire has been designed by staff

within the company or from a research agency, the individual for whom the research is being conducted should insist on vetting the questionnaire. This is an important control in ensuring that the fieldwork will produce relevant data for the problem needs. Above all, the overall purposes of the research must be borne firmly in mind when vetting a questionnaire, but the subject content and type of respondent will also influence judgements as to whether a questionnaire is a good one. A checklist for vetting a questionnaire is suggested using the points on questionnaire design raised in this chapter.

Questionnaire checklist

Are the objectives right? ☐
Will the data specified meet the objectives? ☐
Will the questions listed collect all the data required? ☐
Is every question essential? ☐
Will the right type of data be collected: fact? ☐
           opinion? ☐
           motive? ☐
Will all the identification data required be collected? ☐
Will all the classification data required be collected? ☐
Is the question sequence logical? ☐
Are the types of question being used appropriate:
  dichotomous? ☐
  multiple-choice? ☐
  open-ended? ☐
  rating scales? ☐
Is the question wording: simple to understand? ☐
        unambiguous? ☐
        clear? ☐
Have cushion statements been used when necessary? ☐
Is it reasonable to expect the respondent to answer every question? ☐
Will the answers be easy to record? ☐
Will the answers be easy to process? ☐
Does the questionnaire look good? ☐
Will it, and any show material, be easy for the interviewers to use? ☐
Has the questionnaire been piloted? ☐
Is the right type of questionnaire being used:
  personal? ☐
  postal? ☐
  telephone? ☐

8.14 SUMMARY

Questionnaires are used to present questions and record answers in quantitative field research surveys, and the quality depends on the design of the questionnaire. Design, content, structure and presentation of questionnaires are discussed. Special aspects of questionnaire design relevant when postal or telephone questionnaires are to be used are mentioned. A checklist for vetting a questionnaire is suggested.

9 Who Asks the Questions?

9.1 INTRODUCTION

An interview is understood as 'a conversation for the purpose of gathering information' and this definition emphasizes the functional nature of the interview situation. Thus, although an interview may have the superficial structure of a conversation it is actually a situation in which one party to the interchange, the interviewer, is required to obtain the answers to a pre-determined set of questions or topics from the other party to the interchange, the respondent. It is this task-related view of the interview situation which is best understood by the researcher using interviews as a method of data-collection. However, a sociological definition of a conversation is 'an inter-personal behaviour event: an inter-action in which the action of one is both a response and a stimulus to the other'. This draws attention to the fact that when people engage in conversation, however purposeful, there is an undercurrent of social and non-verbal inter-play which may affect the nature of their co-operation in the conversation process. It is understanding both the task and social elements of the interview situation which makes interviewing a skilled task.

Good interviewing procedures are of fundamental importance in the data-collection process. No matter how good the planning procedures that go before the field-work or the analysis which follows it, it is in the process of raw data-collection in the field that the quality of research undertaken is determined. The computer acronym 'GIGO' (Garbage in – Garbage out) holds equally true in data-collection. If bad data is collected in the field, bad research information will be produced. For this reason it is necessary to consider who the interviewer should be, the role of the interviewer in different interview situations, the skills and problems surrounding the interviewing process and the characteristics of interviewers themselves.

Since interviewing is a skilled task and since the maintenance of these skills is a lengthy procedure it is usual in large-scale research exercises for the interviewing to be carried out by interviewers from research agencies, although one or two large organizations do operate their own field forces, e.g. ICI, Mars. The processes which agencies use to supervize and control interviewers are therefore reviewed, along with advice on selecting and using an agency for field-work. The chapter concludes with a brief section on 'do-it-yourself' interviewing.

9.2 INTERVIEWERS: 'HORSES FOR COURSES'

Interviewers have two important roles to play in any interview situation. First, they are responsible for delivering the question to respondents and the degree to which they may be required to intervene in the questioning process to help the respondent to answer correctly can vary. Secondly, they are responsible for recording the answer and the degree to which they may be required to intervene in interpreting the respondent's answers can also vary. Therefore, before a decision to use a particular type of interviewer can be made it is necessary to consider what is required from her in both delivering the questions and interpreting and recording the answers. The more that is required in either of these areas then the more skilled, and therefore more expensive, will be the type of interviewer needed. Because interviews vary according to the role demanded of the interviewer, so the amount of error and variability the interviewer can introduce into the data varies also. This is why it is important to consider 'horses for courses' in selecting the type of interviewer to be used according to the type of interview to be conducted.

9.2.1 FULLY STRUCTURED INTERVIEWS

In this type of interview the interviewer must adhere strictly to the questionnaire and the questions themselves are commonly pre-coded so that the respondent too is bound by the confines of the questionnaire structure. This would be the case in a questionnaire using mainly dichotomous and multiple-choice questions. There is very little need for the interviewer to intervene in either asking the questions, apart from reading out what is on the questionnaire, or in interpreting the questions, apart from ringing the appropriate codes. In this situation the least skilled type of interviewer may be used as there is very little the interviewer can do to interfere with the quality of data collected.

9.2.2 USING RATING SCALES

The kind of complex scaling exercises often used in attitude measurement are also fully structured in the sense that both interviewer and respondent are bound by the questionnaire. However, when scaling and attitude battery exercises are used there is a greater need for intervention by the interviewer to ensure that respondents fully understand what they are required to do in order to answer the questions correctly. Once this explanation has been given then recording of respondents' answers is quite straightforward. When using this type of question it is, therefore, sensible to use interviewers who have experience in applying the particular type required.

9.2.3 SEMI-STRUCTURED INTERVIEWS

This type of interview is normally a mixture of pre-coded and open-ended questions combined in a questionnaire. The interviewer is bound by the structure of the questionnaire but the respondent is free to answer the open-ended questions in any way. Open-ended questions are relatively easy for the interviewer to ask but more skill is needed in interpreting the responses. Not least, there is the problem of recording all that a respondent says should he or she speak rapidly. The danger exists that the interviewer will edit the responses to those which seem to her to be most appropriate, or most required. In both these situations the interviewer can distort the quality of data obtained. It is, therefore, necessary for the interviewer to be more aware of the importance of her role in accurately and completely recording the respondent's answers. A higher degree of skill and experience is looked for, and more attention must be paid to interviewer briefing before field-work commences.

9.2.4   *UNSTRUCTURED INTERVIEWS*

Depth interviews
These are usually prolonged interviews in which the interviewer has the freedom to phrase the questions as seems most appropriate and to order them and probe them according to the respondent's responses. In this type of interview the interviewer often has only a checklist of points or topics, and will be using mainly open-ended questions. Depth interviews often use indirect and projective techniques and call on specialized interviewing skills.

Group discussions
These are interviews in which one interviewer or moderator asks questions of a group of respondents usually six to eight persons. The essence of a group discussion is that group dynamics are used to draw out individual beliefs which might not be so freely expressed in a one-to-one interview situation. Once again, an advanced degree of interviewer skill is called upon.

Qualitative techniques of depth interview and group discussion are most demanding from the interviewer's point of view. Often the interviewer will have a degree of psychological training, since it requires considerable skill to manage both depth interviews and group discussions in such a way as to elicit the detail and freedom of response required. In order to do this the interviewer is free to insert questions as seems most appropriate. Since depth interviews are commonly used in industrial, trade or professional research studies, depth interviewers may be required to have some subject qualifications in addition to their research expertise. In group discussions the role of the moderator is often simply to act as a catalyst to the generation of appropriate conversation between members of the group. A good moderator may intervene very little in the discussion process except to keep it on the right lines and to ensure that all required topics are covered.

Interpretation of depth interview and group discussion sessions is also a highly skilled task and is normally carried out by the interviewer or moderator. For this reason, in this type of research, the quality of data obtained is almost entirely in the hands of the interviewer or moderator selected. These are highly specialist individuals often working independently and far better paid than the normal interviewer.

9.3   WHAT DO INTERVIEWERS DO?

Interviewers carry out a number of functions in the fieldwork process. Each function requires the application of skill, and interviewers who lack appropriate skills may introduce error into the data-collection procedure.

9.3.1   SELECTING RESPONDENTS

When random samples are used, unless the interviewer does not do her call-backs as instructed, she can do very little to affect the selection of respondents since she is presented with a list of specific names and addresses to interview. However, in quota samples the selection of actual respondents is in the hands of the interviewers. Quota sampling is often used because it is cheaper than random sampling, since it uses interviewer time more efficiently. In practice, the main difference between respondents obtained through the use of quota sampling and random sampling methods is that when quota samples are used then extreme and unusual types of respondent are less likely to be included. For example, in the AB class category respondents are more likely to be B's than A's and in the DE class category respondents are more likely to be D's than E's in quota sampling. The reason for this is that these are the kinds of respondents that it is easier for the interviewer to identify. If she has to contact a certain number of respondents of a particular occupation type then most experienced interviewers will know where in their area that type of respondent is most likely to be found. This results in middle-class respondents who live in middle-class areas having a greater chance of being included in the sample than middle-class respondents who live in mixed class areas, and so on. Similarly, certain types of manual occupation are more likely to be represented. For example, bus drivers are commonly included because interviewers know that they will be able to find them and interview them easily at their place of work. A gate-keeper in a Newcastle factory admitted having been interviewed sixty times in the preceding month since whenever interviewers in his area required an individual for a quota sample which matched his profile then they knew just where to find him, a warm fire, a friendly welcome and a cup of tea! Random route and random location sampling procedures attempt to overcome some of these problems by restricting interviewers' choice of respondent.

9.3.2   OBTAINING INTERVIEWS

There is evidence to indicate that experienced interviewers are better able to obtain interviews than inexperienced interviewers. This is important, since the higher the percentage of non-respondents in a survey then the greater the probability that some bias will be introduced by the fact that non-respondents are different in some relevant way to those who do respond. For example, in a survey about drinking habits those most likely to be interviewed are those most likely to be found at home and yet the very fact of their being at home means that they differ in important ways from those who are out drinking! Although obtaining co-operation from respondents is thought to be getting harder, it is still true to say that on most consumer type surveys skilled interviewers can obtain response rates of 80% or better. Response rates such as these obviously minimize the potential errors that might be introduced by non-response bias.

In general, industrial, trade and executive interviews are harder to obtain because the respondent is being interviewed in his or her role as a businessperson and there is a need to secure their co-operation using working time. In obtaining industrial and executive interviews, it is usual for an appointment to be made by telephone and this may be preceded by an explanatory letter. When the interviewer keeps the appointment she should be provided with an 'authority letter' which gives the respondent a telephone number to check on the interviewer's credentials. In practice this opportunity is rarely taken up, but it is too minor a detail to lose a valuable interview over if such letters have not been provided.

In certain kinds of highly specialist or technical interviewing it may be necessary for the interviewer to have appropriate educational qualifications, or the ability to absorb knowledge relevant to the interview, in order to comprehend the answers and be able to frame appropriate supplementary questions. There is the danger, however, that if the interviewer is too much of a specialist then his or her expertise in the subject will become evident to the respondent and may inhibit replies. If the interviewer is not sufficiently knowledgeable about the subject the opposite danger exists: that it is a waste of time talking with an interviewer who obviously does not understand the subject, and therefore asks inappropriate questions to which incomprehensible replies are given. In general, the industrial trade or executive respondent should perceive the interviewer as being an informed and intelligent person fully competent to explore the subject of the interview and to comprehend the replies but leaving the respondent feeling the dominant partner to the interchange.

9.3.3   ASKING QUESTIONS

In structured interviewing it is important that interviewers understand the need for them to use exactly the words written on the questionnaire. By changing the words, or even the emphases which they use in reading the questions, it is possible for the interviewer to change the question and therefore to invalidate using the answers in a quantitative analysis. In semi-structured and qualitative interview techniques the way in which questions are asked, and indeed whether they are asked at all, is left to the interviewer and hence her role in determining what data are collected is a fundamental one. In ensuring that interviewers ask questions correctly, the interviewer briefing process is of great importance.

9.3.4   PROBING AND PROMPTING

When open-ended questions are used the interviewer is often required to follow these up in order to get more information. There are two ways in which an interviewer can follow up the question with supplementary questions. The first of these is called probing. *Probing* is a non-directional prompt to the respondent. That is to say that the words used in the probe require the respondent to give additional information without indicating what kind of information that might be. 'What else?' may be used as a probe or just a 'waiting silence'.

Prompting is a directional supplementary question which indicates the kind of answer which the respondent might give. For example a common prompt following the question 'What brands of toothpaste have you ever heard of?' would be to show a prompt card listing the brands of toothpaste and ask the question 'Which of these brands have you ever heard of?'. Where either a probe or prompt is used it should be written down on the questionnaire so that the researcher knows whether the information was volunteered with or without aid from the interviewer. Interviewers vary considerably in their skill and conscientiousness at using probes and prompts and this varies the amount of data which is achieved from each respondent. Where the use of probes and prompts is of importance in gathering the depth of information required then these should be written directly on to the questionnaire to ensure that they are used appropriately by interviewers. Figure 8.5 shows an example of the use of probing, and Figure 9.1 illustrates the use of prompting.

9.3.5 MOTIVATING RESPONDENTS

The interviewer has a role in motivating the respondent to give answers comprehensively, relevantly and accurately. This is achieved through the establishment of 'rapport' between the interviewer and respondent. Rapport is an essential ingredient in conducting and completing an interview but of itself may also be biasing. Interviewers need to be made aware of the effect of their own presence and of the role of rapport in motivating respondents. They should also be made aware that if rapport is too firmly established then the danger exists that the respondent will give answers which, it is believed, will reflect more favourably upon the interviewer. Like any other departure from the respondent's own true feelings, excessively favourable responses are as undesirable as excessively negative responses.

9.3.6 INTERPRETING AND RECORDING RESPONSES

In fully structured interviews the role of the interviewer in

<u>Prompt Cards</u> These are also visual aids and must be shown to the respondent when specified in the questionnaire. Prompt cards must <u>NEVER</u> be shown until the instruction is given as they provide additional information to jog the respondent's memory.

EXAMPLE

Q.1 Good morning/afternoon. I work for a market research company and we are doing a survey about complete meals. What makes of complete meals in cans, packets or frozen can you think of? Any others?

<u>SHOW CARD A</u>

Q.2 Just to remind you, here is a list of complete meals. Which on this list have you heard of including any you have already mentioned?

<u>SHOW CARD A</u>

Q.3 And which of these have you ever bought?

	Q1	Q2	Q3
	(13)	(14)	(15)
CROSSE & BLACKWELL LASAGNE	1	1	1
BIRDS EYE/CHINA DRAGON FROZEN MEALS	2	2	2
FINDUS	3	3	3
VESTA COMPLETE DISHES	4	4	4
CROSSE & BLACKWELL CANNELLONI	5	5	5
FINDUS RIGATONI	6	6	6
WHITWORTHS PIZZA MIX	7	7	7
MARY BAKER FRYPAN PIZZA MIX	8	8	8
OTHER (WRITE IN)_____	9	9	9
	0	0	0
NONE/NEVER	X	X	X
D.K/C.R	A	A	A

```
┌─────────────────────────────────────────────┐
│                                             │
│              SHOW CARD A                    │
│              ─────────                      │
│                                             │
│                                             │
│         CROSSE & BLACKWELL LASAGNE          │
│                                             │
│    BIRDS EYE/CHINA DRAGON FROZEN MEALS      │
│                                             │
│             FINDUS LASAGNE                  │
│                                             │
│          VESTA COMPLETE DISHES              │
│                                             │
│       CROSSE & BLACKWELL CANNELLONI         │
│                                             │
│             FINDUS RIGATONI                 │
│                                             │
│           WHITWORTHS PIZZA MIX              │
│                                             │
│        MARY BAKER FRYPAN PIZZA MIX          │
│                                             │
└─────────────────────────────────────────────┘
```

Figure 9.1 Interviewer instructions on the use of prompt cards

interpreting and recording responses is limited to doing so accurately. However in open-ended and qualitative interviews the interviewer has an important role to play in correct interpretation and accurate and comprehensive recording of responses. In depth interviews and group discussions it is usual for a tape recorder to be employed in order to record responses, but when open-ended questions are used in questionnaires it is more usual for the interviewer to be required to write down exactly what the respondent says. If the respondent speaks fully and quickly this can prove a practical difficulty for the interviewer which may be overcome by editing responses. This may lose some of the quality and detail of information which the researcher would like to acquire. This is one of the reasons why open-ended questions often do not work well when used in fully structured quantitative research surveys. To help overcome this, interviewers are usually instructed to go over the questionnaire as soon as possible after the interview and to record anything remembered but not recorded during the interview.

9.3.7   INTERVIEWER BIAS

Interviewer bias has been defined as 'a uni-directional attitude, opinion or expectation held consistently by an interviewer'. The traditional view is that bias arises through communication to the respondent of the interviewers's own ideology and expectations or through the interviewer's motivation to influence results to conform with his or her own ideology. In practice it seems that interviewer bias is most likely to be a problem when the respondent does not have firmly held opinions or attitudes of his own. It is seen as a problem most seriously in fields of social research but should also be borne in mind when research is being carried out on subjects which may be controversial, for example, drinking, smoking, etc. It is usual when interviewers are recruited for them to be screened for political activity if they are likely to be employed in asking political questions.

9.4   WHO ARE THE INTERVIEWERS?

In the United Kingdom the market research industry depends mainly on freelance interviewers. That is to say, the interviewers like to retain the freedom of when they will work and when they will not. For this reason most agencies need to have a much higher number of interviewers on their books than they will be expecting to use at any one time since some of the interviewers will want to work at a particular time and others will not. Inevitably, there is some degree of lack of control in this type of situation where the interviewer does not see herself as the employee of the company for which she works and indeed she will usually work for more than one research company. The typical characteristics used for selection of interviewers are as follows.

9.4.1   SEX

Most research interviewers are women, particularly for consumer research. Increasingly women are also being used for industrial research. There are a number of reasons why women are more likely to be interviewers than men. First, the work is of a part-time and intermittent nature and is generally rather poorly paid. This may make it an impractical job proposition for a man but a highly suitable occupation for a woman with family commitments. The part-time and intermittent nature of the work enables her to build sufficient flexibility around her work programme to fit in with her domestic commitments. Secondly, the socialization process results in the fact that women generally find it easier to play the neutral listener role then do men and also women are more readily and freely spoken to than men. Increasingly in industrial interviewing where men were used previously, mainly because of the technical knowledge required, it has been found easier for women to obtain interviews and they may obtain fuller information.

Conversely, with increasing levels of violence particularly in inner-city areas and after dark, men are being used for interviewing in these kinds of situations. High levels of unemployment have also led to rather more men being recruited as interviewers.

9.4.2 AGE

The ideal age requirements for entry to consumer interviewing are between 25–45 years. The reasons for these limits are that interviewers below 25 may well have a biasing effect on the information they obtain and interviewers over 45 are less easy to train for a new occupation. A higher level of training and mental agility is required for the more specialist type of industrial interviewing and this may mean recruiting at the lower end of the age range indicated.

9.4.3 SOCIAL BACKGROUND

The ideal requirement for interviewers is that they should not appear to be obviously of any particular social background – i.e. a degree of social neutrality is required. It helps if the interviewer has the ability to be 'chameleon-like' so as to be able to fit in with the respondent. In practice, most interviewers are actually middle-class because of the other requirements for selection.

9.4.4 EDUCATION

For consumer interviewing, applicants are required to have at least 'O' Level GCE qualifications. For specialist interviewing in either industrial or qualitative research then further education qualifications are normally required. In industrial research it helps if the interviewer has some knowledge of the specialist area in which the research will be carried out or is sufficiently well educated to be able to conduct interviews at executive level. For qualitative interviewing the interviewer is often required to have some psychological training.

9.4.5 JOB BACKGROUND

The best interviewers seem to be those whose previous occupations have been people-orientated as, for example, teachers and nurses. Those who have previously held selling occupations tend not to be very good at interviewing but are particularly successful at recruiting respondents for group discussions. In general, research has indicated that it is rather difficult for salesmen particularly, but often other company personnel as well, to conduct interviews in their own product areas.

9.4.6 PERSONALITY

Above all, interviewers need the ability to listen and to record accurately. One agency which uses personality tests in order to select its interviewers requires that on a neuroticism/stability scale they should be just on the stability side of the scale. Too far along the emotional stability scale and they would be such 'suet puddings' that it would be difficult for them to be able to get the interview in the first place. On the extroversion/introversion scale interviewers should be just on the extroverted side of the scale. Too extroverted an individual would not have the sensitivity to listen truly to their respondent, but too introverted an individual would not be able to obtain an interview in the first place. The same agency also finds the use of a lie scale of assistance in selecting appropriate people as interviewers.

9.4.7 TRAINING

Once selected, interviewers should be trained. For most of the leading research agencies interviewer training involves a two or three day programme. The first part of the training is theoretical. In this part of the programme interviewers are lectured on their importance in the research process and in the special skills that they need to acquire. They are fully briefed on the dangers of bias which can be introduced by them. The second part of the training programme is practical. This involves role playing in the classroom situation followed by practice interviews in the field. Finally, for consumer interviewing, trainees accompany the supervisor as she carries out field interviews and then carry out field interviews with the supervisor present. For industrial interviewing the practical training will take the form of listening to and checking off taped interviews before carrying them out personally. The third aspect of interviewer training is that of refresher training. This takes place in three ways. First, when pilot briefings and de-briefings are given. Secondly, when personal briefings on important surveys are given and thirdly through the provision of a handbook for reference and guidance. Once trained and working in the field then maintenance of good interviewing practice is ensured through the system of supervision and checking of work.

9.5   HOW ARE INTERVIEWERS CONTROLLED?

There are a number of ways in which the quality of field-work can be controlled as follows.

9.5.1   MRS INTERVIEWER CARD SCHEME

As good quality field-work is the pivot around which good quality data-collection revolves then it is important that adequate controls be imposed to maintain high quality field-work. As part of its concern about instituting and maintaining good quality field-work the Market Research Society instituted the Interviewer Card Scheme in 1979. By 1983 fifty-four companies were members of the Interview Card Scheme.

The scheme covers the following type of field-work: consumer, social and qualitative research, consumer and retail panels and audits, hall tests and telephone research. In each case the scheme lays down minimum standards for recruitment, office procedures, supervision, training, quality control and survey administration. Each member company is visited annually by an independent Inspector and required to produce documentation and other evidence that it conforms to or exceeds the minimum standards. If accepted as a member of the scheme, this is shown in the Market Research Society listing of 'organizations providing Market Research Services in Great Britain and Northern Ireland'. That booklet and full details of the ICS standards will be sent, on request, by the Market Research Society, 15 Belgrave Square, London SW1X 8PF (Tel: 01 235 4709).

9.5.2   FIELD SUPERVISION

Most agencies with any size of field force will have a supervisory structure starting from a Field Manager in Head Office down to a number of Area Managers or Supervisors each responsible for a number of interviewers. It is usual that the Field Manager is a full-time employee of the agency and that Supervisors work exclusively for one agency. Good practice would require that the Area Manager who is responsible for the quality of work of her team of interviewers supervises their work in the field by spending a day with them from time to time, by attending area briefings and watching mock interviews and generally ensuring that a company's standards are maintained.

9.5.3   POSTAL CHECKING

Under the Interviewer Card Scheme a minimum of 5% of each interviewer's work is followed up with check-backs within 24 hours and up to 25% of these checks will be carried out by post. The follow-up check might contain two questions from the interview, two demographic questions and the questions 'Did you know the interviewer?' 'Did you see a prompt card?' and 'How long did the interview last?'. If any doubt arises as a result of these postal check-backs then the check is followed by a 100% check on all that interviewer's work. An example of a postal check form is shown in Figure 9.2.

RSGB

Research Surveys of Great Britain Limited

A member of the AGB Research Group

Research Centre, West Gate, London W5 1EL
Telephone 01-997 5555 Telex 261978 RSGB G

Dear

I understand that you were kind enough recently to help one of our
interviewers by answering some questions about

Whenever we do surveys such as this we do like to be sure that our
interviewers have left a good impression and that they have recorded
your answers accurately.

I should be very grateful therefore if you would be good enough to help
us further by completing the section below and returning it to me at
your earliest convenience in the enclosed reply-paid envelope.

May I take this opportunity of thanking you for your help.

Yours sincerely,

ASSISTANT FIELD MANAGER

PLEASE TICK THE APPROPRIATE BOX

Q1 Did our interviewer speak to you personally? YES ☐ NO ☐

Q2 Was our interviewer polite and courteous? YES ☐ NO ☐

Q3a Did our interviewer show you an Identity Card? YES ☐ NO ☐

3b Did our interviewer leave you a "Thank You" leaflet? YES ☐ NO ☐

Q4 Were cards shown to you to help you answer some of the questions? YES ☐ NO ☐

Q5 Is the occupation of the head of your household....? YES ☐ NO ☐

Q6 Did you know the interviewer before he/she called on you? YES ☐ NO ☐

Figure 9.2

RESPONDENT NAME AND ADDRESS	INT. DONE	DATE OF INT.	Length of Inter- view	POLITE ---- I.D. CARD SHOWN	SHOW CARDS SHOWN	AGE	SEX	OCCUPATION OF H.O.H.

SUMMARY

SIGNATURE OF CHECKER   DATE(S) OF CHECKS

Figure 9.3

NAME OF BACKCHECKER

Social Grade	WORK FT/PT NOT	CHILD +/-	QU 1	QU 2	QU 3	QU 4	IS THE INT A PERSONAL FRIEND OR ACQUAINTANCE	COMMENTS

9.5.4   TELEPHONE CHECKS

Most checking on the interviewer's work will be done by telephone. This will vary depending on the nature of respondents and the probability of their having telephones.

9.5.5   PERSONAL RECALL CHECKS

As an alternative to telephoning, the interviewer's work may be followed up by personal recall checks usually carried out by the Area Supervisor. Once again a few questions from the interview will be asked, demographics will be checked on and one or two additional questions put to the respondent. It is desirable, although unusual, that field checks should be completed before data analysis so that any errors or mistakes can be corrected or withdrawn from the data analysis process. A personal recall check form is shown in Figure 9.3.

9.5.6   EDITING CHECKS

When completed questionnaires are returned to the office, editing checks will indicate something about the quality of an interviewer's work. They will show, for example, how the amount and calibre of original information varies between interviewers as a result of their probing and prompting skills. They will also indicate the accuracy with which the interviewer works, e.g. sections are properly completed, filter questions are not skipped and the questionnaire is generally completed in an appropriate manner.

9.5.7   COMPUTER CHECKS

Once the data from the questionnaires has been put on to the computer then another range of checks become possible. Once again checks can be made for completeness and accuracy. Where control questions have been used then the computer can check one answer against another. The computer will also check whether the correct sections have been completed following filter questions. Finally, to test the reliability of interviewers then inter/interviewer comparisons are drawn by analysing the results from one interviewer against the results for the whole survey.

9.5.8 MONITORING FIELD-WORK

All these checks are normally carried out by the good research agencies. A manager using an agency for field-work should ask to see the field-work checks on his own survey and agencies who carry out these checks will be only too pleased to show this evidence of the quality of their work. It is also very instructive to spend a day in the field with one of the interviewers while she is working on the survey. It gives the manager far greater insight into interpreting and understanding results if he has seen his surveys actually in the process of raw data-collection. Again, the better agencies would be quite happy to entertain a request to spend a day in the field with one of their interviewers.

9.6 CHOOSING A GOOD FIELD-WORK AGENCY

It is apparent from the preceding sections of this chapter that whether the research being conducted is a quantitative survey involving several hundred respondents or whether it is a qualitative survey requiring specialist qualitative interviewing skills of group moderation, industrial or depth interviewing, then better quality field-work is likely to be achieved using professional and experienced interviewers. This therefore involves the selection of an appropriate agency to carry out the field-work. As with buying most services it makes sense to ask for quotations from two or three companies to give a basis for comparing both procedures and prices. The first step, then, is to determine which two or three companies should be invited to quote. In making the selection a number of other factors must be considered and the procedure suggested should give a pretty clear idea of an agency's ability to handle the work required and of the quality of work they are likely to produce.

9.6.1 FINDING THE AGENCY

Finding an agency to carry out field-work can be quite difficult for a company which has never conducted research before. One starting point is to obtain the Market Research Society's booklet entitled 'Organizations providing Market Research Services in Great Britain and Northern Ireland'. This booklet is up-dated each year. The book is annotated in such a way as to give as much help as possible to the intending purchaser of research services e.g. membership of the Interviewer Card Scheme is shown; an indication is given of the size of turnover of companies, since a small job is likely to be done better by a small agency. The booklet also gives an indication of what services research companies specialize in by showing in bold type those services from which they gain more than 25% or over £100,000 of their income. An initial shortlist can be drawn up by going through the book and noting companies of the right size with the right kind of experience and who have worked in the industry in which the field-work is to be carried out.

Another approach to generating an appropriate shortlist for invitation to quote is to use business contacts. Most managers will know their opposite numbers in competitive organizations or be familiar through the normal network of business contacts with other managers working in their industry. It is always worthwhile asking these people to recommend agencies that they have used. Of course it is not necessarily the case that an agency, which has done a good job for one company, is likely to do a good job for another company, particularly if the nature of the research required is rather different. However, such recommendations do offer a starting point to the inexperienced field-work buyer. It is also often the case that if agencies believe they could not do a good job for a potential client they are likely to hand the enquiry on to an agency better suited to those needs.

9.6.2 ASKING PERTINENT QUESTIONS

Having obtained quotations from two or three companies the next stage in evaluating their ability to do work to the standards required is to visit their premises and ask pertinent questions. These are the kind of questions which will be seen as pertinent and discriminating, and therefore approved of, by the good quality research agency and will be seen as discriminating, and therefore impertinent and disapproved of, by the poor quality research agency. At least that is their objective. The kinds of questions to ask in order to assess the quality of an agency's field-work procedures relate to the structure and organization of its field force. For example, 'Is there a field-work manager?' 'How many interviewers have you?' 'How many supervisors are there?' 'Do the supervisors work exclusively for this agency?' 'What is the agency's supervisory structure, i.e. how many supervisors and how many interviewers per supervisor?' 'How are interviewers selected?' 'How are interviewers trained?' 'On average, how long do interviewers stay with your organization?' 'How many interviewers work exclusively for your agency?' 'What quality control procedures are used?'.

9.6.3 LOOKING AT THE EVIDENCE

From the questions that have already been asked, providing the right kinds of answers have been obtained, then a further check on these would be to look for the evidence which must exist. For example, if the company claims a certain size field force then it should be possible to see the records containing details of the field force – their abilities, their geographical spread and so forth. Similarly, it should be possible to see the documentary evidence of quality control procedures, for example, evidence of postal check-backs. A well managed field force will be supported by a set of administrative records which can be evaluated for quality.

9.6.4 INTERVIEWER CARD SCHEME

It may be helpful to ask whether the agency is a member of the Interviewer Card Scheme of the Market Research Society. If so, then it should be possible to see the report produced by the Society's annual inspectors. Non-membership of the Interviewer Card Scheme does not necessarily imply a poor quality field-work agency. This is particularly true of small agencies, many of which are not yet members of the Scheme. However, for the inexperienced field-work buyer, an agency's membership of the MRS Scheme does offer an independent assessment and control over that company's working procedure.

9.6.5 RELEVANT EXPERIENCE

An important criterion for selecting one field-work agency above another is to look for experience related to the needs of the survey. This experience may be of two kinds. First, it may consist of experience in the industry in which the research will be carried out. Most industries have their special language and problems and an agency familiar with these is more likely to be able to do a good job than one not familiar with them. Secondly, it may be that the particular research method required is one better able to be carried out by one type of agency rather than another, for example, a particular type of quantitative attitude battery scaling exercises, or qualitative research of a particular kind. In both these cases interviewers experienced in the technique are more likely to produce a better job than those who are not. What evidence there is, suggests that interviewers familiar with the industry and technique with which they are working are more likely to produce better quality data than those who are inexperienced. An attempt should therefore be made to identify agencies whose experience is relevant to the particular research problem.

9.6.6 COST

As in other buying areas costs may be a useful indicator in making the buying decision. In the case of field-work there are a number of factors affecting the costs: the type of sample, the penetration of the product, the length of interview, the type of respondent and the type of interviewer to be used. Also relevant will be the method of payment used for interviewers. Interviewers may be paid per interview, per day or per job. With fully structured questionnaires it may make sense for interviewers to be paid per completed interview as this will encourage them to get through the work as quickly as possible. However, when open-ended questions are included in the questionnaire the quality of data is likely to be better if interviewers are paid by the day and have no financial incentive to rush the probing of open-ended questions. The agency will decide the most appropriate method of paying its interviewers, but in comparing costs from different field-work agencies any relevant assumptions should be checked to ensure that like is being compared with like.

9.7 USING AN AGENCY FOR FIELD-WORK

In using agency field-work, the agency and interviewer briefing procedures are the only means by which the intentions of the research initiator are communicated to those responsible for collecting answers to the questions posed. Good briefing is essential to ensure that both agency and interviewers appreciate their role in the research process.

9.7.1 BRIEFING THE AGENCY

The agency should be adequately briefed on the market and marketing background and on the factors which gave rise to the research. They should be told all pertinent facts, like the percentage of product users, and also forewarned of potential difficulties which they may meet. This enables them to develop appropriate strategies for dealing with problems which may arise in the field.

9.7.2   AGREEING THE PROCEDURES

The form of interview to be used must be determined: structured, semi-structured, or depth interview, group discussion, industrial or executive interviewing, and so on. When this has been agreed a check must be made that the agency will be using interviewers capable of doing the job and experienced in the type of interview decided on. Matters of selection and training will have already been discussed. The administrative procedures for handling the project in the field must be agreed, e.g. will the first day's work be checked? how will field-workers be supervised? when will quality checks be undertaken and what type and percentage of checks will be used? What assumptions have been made about the number of interviews to be completed in a day? All matters relevant to conduct of the survey must be agreed and committed to writing in advance of the field-work.

9.7.3   BRIEFING THE INTERVIEWERS

In most routine consumer surveys the interviewers are unlikely to be given a personal briefing. A good explanatory written brief must therefore be developed to be sent to the interviewers with the questionnaires. This may be followed-up by a telephone briefing from the area supervisor. In complex or unusual consumer surveys it may be necessary to hold interviewer briefing meetings, and these will have to be paid for to cover the interviewers' time.

In industrial and executive research, briefing the interviewers is of paramount importance and personal briefing is usually essential. The objectives of the research must be made quite clear to the interviewer. Probes and prompts should be discussed and an indication given of where the areas of greatest potential interest are expected to be. The method of recording the answers must be agreed and this will often involve the use of tape recorders. Possible difficulties and ways in which the interviewer might handle them should be covered. Finally, the importance of establishing rapport in this type of interviewing should be stressed since without the respondent's wholehearted cooperation much of the point of depth interviewing in business situations is lost.

9.8 ASKING THE QUESTIONS YOURSELF

In smaller companies, industrial companies and companies who have not used research previously, there is a strong temptation on the part of the newly-appointed and usually inexperienced research executive to carry out his own research programme. For large-scale research surveys or for group discussions this is unlikely to be viable. In the first case because of the time and expense involved in using himself on a routine and repetitive task, and in the second case because he is unlikely to have the appropriate skills for the method to work to its best advantage. However, for industrial and trade interviewing when only twenty or thirty depth interviews may be required for an exploratory survey it could well be feasible for the manager to carry these out himself. Indeed, there may be good commercial and technical reasons for doing so for a small project with no necessity for confidentiality. A desk research exercise followed by fifteen to twenty personal interviews or by a postal questionnaire could readily be carried out by a manager with enough time and motivation, if the following points are borne in mind.

First, serious thought should be given to the real costs of do-it-yourself interviewing. It is too easy to count one's own time as 'free'. Secondly, the implications for the quality of data to be obtained if the sponsor is identified as personally carrying out the survey must be considered. Thirdly, a manager must objectively decide whether he has, or can acquire, the appropriate skills. A manager used to decision-making, authority and generally playing an assertive role at work may find the role play required to succeed as an interviewer particularly difficult. Essentially, it is necessary to present to the respondent a neutral, empathetic and passively-accepting personality. The questions must be asked in a straightforward manner that gives no clues either verbal or non-verbal as to the kind of answers that would be most acceptable. The interviewer must be aware of his or her own effect upon the respondent, and above all, must resist the temptation to 'correct' the respondent who makes remarks, which the researcher knows to be factually inaccurate.

Whether a manager is able to fulfil successfully the role of industrial or trade researcher is a matter of individual trial and error. It is, nevertheless, a highly salutory experience to attempt to carry out one's own field-work and certainly increases the manager's insight to and understanding of the market in which he operates. It is also a useful learning device which enables managers to appreciate exactly what they are expecting interviewers to accomplish for them. However, if an organization intends to carry out research in any regular way, do-it-yourself interviewing will very quickly become too demanding in terms of time for the manager to carry out all the research himself. Experience suggests that organizations experimenting with the use of research will come quite quickly to realize the need to use professional interviewing services.

A situation in which it may be desirable to ask the questions yourself is if one is involved in questionnaire design. Piloting the questionnaire during the drafting procedure is a very worthwhile experience in producing better questions and better questionnaires. It will give a better feeling for the contribution that questionnaire interviews are able to make to the research problem and for what their limitations might be.

9.9 SUMMARY

Good interviewing procedures are of fundamental importance in producing high quality research information. Different types of interviewer are required for different types of interview. Interviewer skills, characteristics and control procedures are discussed. Selecting and using a research agency for field-work is followed by a brief consideration of 'do-it-yourself' interviewing.

10 What Happens to the Answers?

10.1 INTRODUCTION

Chapter 6 indicated two broad approaches to data collection for made-to-measure research. One is the qualitative approach, where a large amount of data is collected from a relatively small number of people in a fairly unstructured way, usually using group discussions or depth interviews. The quantitative approach is where a smaller amount of data is collected from a large number of people in a structured way, usually using questionnaire surveys often involving 500–1000 or more respondents. What happens to the answers will depend on which approach has been used for data collection. In this chapter the analysis and interpretation of both quantitative and qualitative data are explained. The emphasis in the section on analysis of quantitative data is deliberately confined to a straight-forward description of what various statistical techniques will do. It aims to introduce the non-statistical reader to the usefulness of these techniques, but does not attempt to teach how they can be applied.

10.2 ANALYSIS AND INTERPRETATION OF QUALITATIVE DATA

Group discussions or depth interviews represent the most common ways in which qualitative data is collected. In both cases it is normal for the moderator, in the case of group discussions, or the depth interviewer, to tape-record each data collection session, which normally will last from one and a half to two hours. Group discussions may also be held on premises where they can be watched through a one-way mirror or recorded by closed-circuit television cameras (CCTV), so that behaviour, as well as verbal responses, can be observed. A typical survey involving group discussions might cover six to eight groups and a typical survey involving depth interviews might cover fifteen to twenty depth interviews. In each case it is usual for the individual who was responsible for the collection of the information i.e. the moderator or depth interviewer, to carry out the analysis of the tapes also. The person who was conducting the interviews can bring much greater insight and understanding to bear on their interpretation, since they will have been conscious of the whole range of non-verbal communication going on during the data-collection process.

The tapes of an interview with a doctor on the subject of his use of and attitude towards a number of treatments for bronchial disorders apparently revealed an extremely aggressive respondent. The Field Manager was impressed that the interviewer had managed to complete the whole course of the two hour interview and had doggedly gone on asking questions even after most vehemently expressed negative answers accompanied on the tape by the sounds of violent altercation. In fact, the respondent concerned had leaned forward and thumped the desk close to the microphone in order to emphasize the points he was making. On the tape it sounded quite alarming but the interviewer present was aware from the friendly facial expressions of the respondent that this was just his manner of speech and presentation and not an aggressive response to the interview. If someone else had analysed that tape, quite a different interpretation would have been put on the respondent's approach and attitude to the topic. This illustrates how helpful CCTV recordings can be in improving the analysis of group discussions or depth interviews.

How then does the moderator or depth interviewer go about analysing tape-recorded information? In the first place she (it is most commonly a she although there are many male qualitative and depth interviewers) will listen several times to each tape making notes on points made and categorizing and classifying the answers into the separate topics covered by the respondent.

An alternative method of analysis is to have the tapes transcribed and perform a 'content' analysis of the transcriptions, perhaps by cutting them up into statements and grouping related statements together for analysis and comment.

Since the research is on such a small scale it is important that all responses are considered. One of the aims of this type of research is to collect the range of possible responses, but not to count them. However, when there is a very clear and strong measure of agreement between respondents the researcher will indicate this and also when there is no clear agreement between respondents.

The results of qualitative research should never be expressed in terms of percentages. This is extremely dangerous because it implies that results are somehow representative quantitatively of what a wider sample of respondents might say. Since no statistical procedure has been used in selecting the sample for qualitative research this is not the case. Whilst the researcher and the immediate user of the research may both appreciate this point, the fact of using percentages in interpreting the data will lead to less informed readers of the report talking about market percentages as if they had representative validity.

The outcome of analysis of qualitative data is a report which indicates the range of views expressed on the topics covered and some indication of whether the views were strongly held and widely supported. When proper interpretation takes place by skilled analysts (usually psychologists) the report goes deeper than this and underlying attitudes and motivations are 'interpreted' even though not explicitly verbalized. Hence, this is not a game for amateurs. A characteristic of qualitative research reports is that they contain direct quotations to indicate the way in which respondents express their opinions and the language used. It is this aspect of qualitative research that is often of most use, particularly when considering promotional ways of approaching the market: what to say in advertisements, what environment to use as the background for an advertisement, and so on.

Characteristically, then, analysis of qualitative data is subjective and impressionistic. It conveys to the decision-maker insights into people's feelings about the market, the product, the advertising and their attitudes toward use of competitive products. How good the analysis and interpretation of qualitative data is depends on the individual who undertakes both the conduct of the research and analysis of the tapes produced. This introduces a high risk of bias in both conduct and interpretation of qualitative research. For this reason, once organizations find a qualitative researcher who produces good and useful guidance they will often continue to use the same individual. The advantage of this is that the researcher identifies closely with the organization's interests and is better able to probe areas likely to be of most interest. This also explains why many qualitative research agencies are small one or two person consultancies.

10.3   ANALYSIS OF QUANTITATIVE DATA

From the discussion in Chapter 5 it will be clear that quantitative data is typically produced using a questionnaire which is either interviewer-administered or for self-completion by the respondent. In either case the end result will be a large number (often 500 or more) of completed questionnaires containing both pre-coded and open-ended answers. In order to combine all the answers and thus make a meaningful summary of responses, there are a number of stages in the analysis process: data preparation, data processing, computer and statistical analysis and testing. These are discussed in the following sections.

10.3.1 DATA PREPARATION

This involves ensuring that questionnaires appear to be completed correctly, and that the data they contain are represented in the form of numbers which are suitable for further processing and analysis. The techniques which accomplish this are editing and coding.

Editing

The purpose of editing is to check the returned questionnaires for any errors or omissions. Where possible minor errors are corrected. If this is not possible the error may be sufficiently serious to result in the whole questionnaire being rejected from further analysis. A high proportion of errors being detected at the editing stage may indicate a badly designed questionnaire or poor interviewing techniques. Some feedback system should therefore be introduced to ensure that such avoidable problems are not carried forward into future research undertakings. If an interviewer has skipped a question or series of questions she can be asked to call again on the respondent and complete the questionnaire, or to telephone the respondent if a telephone number is recorded and collect the missing data. Where inconsistencies or other errors are apparent from the editing process these may also be rectified by re-contacting the respondent. Sometimes it is possible to amend data in one question as a result of the answer recorded for another question, but there are obvious dangers in attempting this kind of 'putting answers into respondents' mouths'. Editing is primarily a matter of common sense and experience. At the end of the editing process the editor must decide whether the questionnaire is to be accepted or rejected for further analysis.

Editing may be carried out either manually, by simply reading through each original questionnaire, or mechanically. In this case the data from the original questionnaire is transferred to punch cards and an edit carried out on the punch cards for missing data, inconsistencies and so on. The third possibility is that the editing takes place when the information has been transferred to a computer and a programme is available to edit the data.

Coding

It was pointed out in Section 8.9 on questionnaire design that, for quantitative data, pre-coding should be used wherever possible. In this case the code numbers are printed on to the questionnaire and the interviewer carries out the coding process during the interview by simply ringing the appropriate code. This by-passes the coding stage of analysis and explains why the use of pre-coding reduces the cost of research because coding is a manual procedure, and therefore expensive.

To code open-ended questions, the answers must be analysed for the separate points that they make and each point assigned a code number which must be written on to the questionnaire. The code numbers are allocated from a '*coding frame*'. The coding frame is constructed by a research executive selecting 100, or sometimes 10% of the original questionnaires, writing down all of the separate points made in answer to a particular question on those questionnaires and assigning a code number to each point. Responses which occur infrequently may be grouped together under an 'other' code number. When the coding frame has been derived using this process, a copy of it is given to the coders who then write the appropriate code numbers for answers to that question given on all the other questionnaires. Whenever the coders come across an answer not included on the coding frame these are passed to the research executive who must decide whether they are occurring with sufficient frequency to open a separate code number for them. Figure 10.1 is an example of a coding frame, or 'coding master' drawn up in answer to an openended question, 'which daily or Sunday newspapers do you personally read nowadays?'

Whether answers to questions have been pre-coded or are manually coded as described, this brings the data on the questionnaire to the point where every answer is repre-

ie. Card 2 Column 14

OPEN QUESTION CODING MASTER   *CODE ALL THAT APPLY*

2/14/1	TIMES	Q
2	GUARDIAN	U
3	TELEGRAPH	E
4	MAIL DAILY PAPERS	S
5	EXPRESS	T
6	MIRROR	I
7	SUN	O
8	STAR	N
9	OTHER DAILY PAPER	Q 5.
0	SUNDAY TIMES	Newspapers
X	OBSERVER	read
A	SUNDAY TELEGRAPH	nowadays
	— SUNDAY PAPERS	(national)

2/15/1	MAIL (ON SUNDAY)	Q
2	SUNDAY EXPRESS	U
3	OTHER SUNDAY PAPER	E
4	OTHER PAPER, not elsewhere classified	S
5		T
6		I
7		O
8		N
9		Q 5
0		(cont'd)
X	NONE	
A	DON'T KNOW / NOT STATED	

Figure 10.1

sented by a number in the right-hand column of the questionnaire. The questionnaires are then ready for the next stage of analysis.

10.3.2 DATA PROCESSING

Prior to the widespread use of computers, and still with surveys involving relatively small numbers of questionnaires, data processing was carried out by hand. Simple counts are made of the answers given to questions and numbers and percentages giving each response are calculated. Apart from being time-consuming, hand analysis also prevents any complex interpretation of the data. To analyse one question by the answer to another question, say usage of shampoo by sex, requires that the original questionnaires are first divided into separate piles for male and female, and then counts done within each pile. If it is required to analyse use of shampoo by age then the piles must also be separated into different age groups. It is easy to see that once more than two variables for analysing the data are required, the whole procedure becomes quite complicated from a mechanical point of view.

The introduction of computers as a data-processing tool has therefore been a boon for researchers. Once the data has been fed into the computer it is possible to carry out many checks on the data and to analyse and cross-analyse it in all sorts of ways which just would not be possible using manual procedures. Statistical tests of the data can be carried out easily and weighting to remove bias due to over- or under-representation in the sample is quite straightforward. In addition to giving far greater opportunity for data analysis, computers also reduce the cost of carrying out the analysis. The combination of these factors explains why computers are now the principal method of data processing and analysis in use.

What computers do is to 'read' the data fed into them from punch cards, paper or magnetic tape, process the data and then feed out the answers or store the data in memory

RESEARCH SURVEYS OF GREAT BRITAIN LIMITED, RESEARCH CENTRE, WEST GATE, LONDON W5 1EL   TELEPHONE NO. 01-997-5555

JOB No: — identifies   SERIAL No: — identifies   CARD No: — identifies punch
individual project   individual respondent   card, if questionnaire occupies more
                                                                than one card

(1)	(2)	(3)	(4)		(5)	(6)	(7)	(8)		PUNCHER: PUNCH 9/①
0	3	0	7		5	9	4	1		

	SAMPLING POINT NUMBER
	(10) (11) (12) (13)
	(Left blank in this example)

INFORMANTS NAME & TITLE (MR/MRS/MISS)
(BLOCK CAPITALS)

FULL   MRS T. SMITH

POSTAL   54 ACACIA ROAD
         NEW TOWN
ADDRESS   HALLAMSHIRE

A.	Does the house have a telephone ?		(14)
		YES	1
	IF 'YES' What is the number ?	NO	②

B.	SEX OF INFORMANT		(15)
		MALE	1
		FEMALE	②

C.	AGE OF INFORMANT		(16)
	16 - 19		1
	20 - 24		2
	25 - 29		3
	30 - 34		4
	35 - 44		5
	45 - 54		⑥
	55 - 64		7
	65 OR MORE		8

G.	ASK ALL WOMEN AGED 15 YEARS OR MORE	(20)
	WOMAN HAS A FULL-TIME PAID JOB (30 HRS+)	①
	WOMAN HAS A PART-TIME PAID JOB (LESS THAN 30 HOURS)	2
	WOMAN HAS NO JOB	3

H.	ASK ALL HEADS OF HOUSEHOLD/HOUSEWIVES	(21)
	HOUSEWIFE WITH CHILDREN UNDER 15 IN HOUSE	①
	HOUSEWIFE WITHOUT CHILDREN UNDER 15 IN HOUSE	2

I.	ASK ALL		(22)
	How many people are there in		1
	your household altogether,		2
	including, any children and yourself ?		③
			4
		5 OR MORE	5

D. STATUS OF INFORMANT IN HOUSEHOLD (17)

BOTH MAY BE CODED → HEAD OF HOUSEHOLD ①
→ FEMALE HOUSEWIFE ②

E. MARITAL STATUS (18)

MARRIED ①
SINGLE/WIDOWED/DIVORCED ②

OCCUPATION OF HEAD OF HOUSEHOLD ⓐ (CODE
OR CHIEF WAGE EARNER B WHICH ONE)

WRITE IN FULL DETAILS _MARKET RESEARCH_
MANAGER

TYPE OF INDUSTRY _FOOD MANUFACTURER_

IF WIDOW OR RETIRED CLASSIFY BELOW
WIDOW WITH WIDOW'S PENSION ONLY — C

WIDOW WITH PRIVATE MEANS (E.G. husband's pension)
(SPECIFY HUSBAND'S FORMER OCCUPATION ABOVE) — D

RETIRED MAN OR WOMAN WITH STATE RETIREMENT
PENSION ONLY — E

RETIRED MAN OR WOMAN WITH STATE RETIREMENT
PENSION AND OCCUPATIONAL PENSION
(SPECIFY PREVIOUS OCCUPATION ABOVE) — F

F. SOCIAL GRADE OF HOUSEHOLD (19)

A — 1
B — ②
C1 — 3
C2 — 4
D — 5
E — 6

J. DAY OF INTERVIEW (23)

MONDAY — 1
TUESDAY — 2
WEDNESDAY — 3
THURSDAY — 4
FRIDAY — 5
SATURDAY — ⑥
SUNDAY — 7

K. LENGTH OF INTERVIEW (24)

UP TO 15 MINS — 1
16 – 20 MINS — 2
21 – 25 MINS — 3
26 – 30 MINS — ④
31 – 35 MINS — 5
36 – 40 MINS — 6
41 – 45 MINS — 7
46 – 50 MINS — 8
51 – 55 MINS — 9
56 MINS OR MORE — 0

I certify that this interview has been personally carried
out by me with the informant at his/her address. I further
certify that the informant is not a friend or relative of
mine, and I have not interviewed at his/her address in any
survey in the last 6 months.

SIGNATURE: _K Jones_ DATE: _5/3/83_

AND NAME IN
BLOCK CAPITALS: _K. JONES_

	(25)	(26)	(27)	(28)	(29)
INTERVIEWER NUMBER					
	8	0	2	5	7

PUNCHER:
SKIP 30–80

Figure 10.2

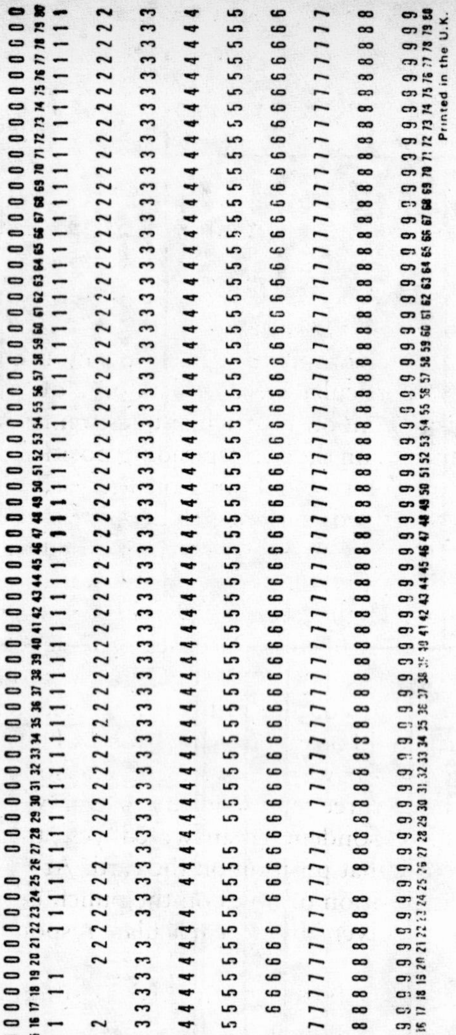

Figure 10.2 (cont)

banks. These, then, represent the requirements for computer processing of data.

Data entry

First, the data must be translated into a form that can be 'read' into the computer. The most common form in which this is done is to punch the codes from the questionnaire on to a punch card. This is a card measuring approximately eleven inches by three inches with eighty columns each containing twelve squares. Each position on the card represents a particular piece of data on a questionnaire. If that item is present on a particular questionnaire then a hole will be punched on the corresponding position on the card. The first one or two columns on the card are normally allocated to coded data which identifies the particular questionnaire: the interviewer who carried out the interview, the day on which the interview was carried out, the location in which the interview was held and any other data relevant for identification purposes. The next column will be allocated for answers to question 1 and the twelve positions in that column will each represent a particular answer that could be given to question 1. The next column will be used for answers to question 2 and so on. If position one on column three represents the answer 'yes' to question 1, and if the respondent has answered 'yes', then a hole will be punched in that position on the card. At the end of this process the position of holes on the punch card represents the answers given by a particular respondent to the questionnaire.

Figure 10.2 illustrates a completed classification page and its accompanying punched card.

When working out the number of answers possible for a questionnaire, the space available on punch cards is usually considered. It would be inefficient to design a questionnaire that required 82 card code columns, since a second card would be required for every respondent using only 2 columns. In this situation it is usual to restrict some of the less important variations of answer possible in questions, so as to bring all the answers on to one punch card. When this cannot be done it could be that additional questions will be added to the questionnaire to increase the efficiency of going on to a second punch card. The computer 'reads' the data from punch cards by identifying where the holes are on each card and reproducing the information electronically.

Thus, the punch card represents the data on the original questionnaire and the computer produces an electronic version of the card. The data can then be stored in three ways: the pile of original questionnaires can be kept, the much smaller pack of punch cards can be kept, and the electronic version of the cards can be stored in the computer's memory. While the data is being actively worked on, it is usual to operate only with the memory store of the computer, without reference back to either punch cards or the original questionnaires. However, since computer storage space is normally at a premium, when a particular survey analysis is complete it is usual to wipe the data off the computer memory bank so that this can be used for current analyses. The punch cards are then kept for a few years in case an organization requires some additional analysis of the data. Then the cards can be used simply to feed the information back into the computer once more. The original questionnaires are also kept for two years in case they are needed. In subsequent analysis of the data, for example, it might be thought useful to identify the actual data coded under an 'Other' code. Respondents may have been asked which brands they used and it would be normal to assign codes to the most frequently mentioned brands and put all infrequently mentioned brands into an 'Other' code. At some later date it may be useful to know which other brands were mentioned. The computer will be used to identify the questionnaires containing an answer under the 'Other' code for that particular question. These questionnaires can then be sorted out and analysed separately.

For some years 'direct entry' computer systems have been available whereby information from the questionnaire can be entered directly into the computer through a keyboard, eliminating the need for punch cards. Optical Character Recognition (OCR) systems are also increasingly used. In this case, the questionnaire is usually pre-coded, and the appropriate codes are marked by the respondent (for self-completion questionnaires) or interviewer (for administered questionnaires). The completed questionnaire pages are fed directly into an electronic scanner which 'reads' the codes directly from the questionnaire and stores them in the computer.

Telling the computer what to do with data

Once the computer has the data, it needs to know what to do with it i.e. what calculations to perform, what tabulations to produce and what statistical manipulations to carry out. This is determined by the research executive often in conjunction with the individual who commissioned the research survey, particularly if the survey is complex or unusual. This is called 'specification writing' because it specifies what the computer must do. The '*specifications*' are a set of written instructions to the computer in whatever computer 'language' is appropriate for the machine being used. A typical set of specifications might instruct the computer to do straight counts and percentages on the answers to all questions and to produce tables of the answer to each question analysed by the demographic characteristics of age, sex, class and region. In addition to this, specifications may instruct the computer to carry out significance tests on any figures which are considered important. 'Spec writing' is an important part of the researcher's art and one with which the research user should become involved. Either at the briefing stage, or after the field-work has been done, the research user should make it plain exactly what analyses he wants to be carried out on the data.

Computer programmes

The computer now has a set of data and a set of instructions

AEROSOL – MEN

	A 195	B 195	C 195	D 97	E 98	F 195	G 195	H 195	ALL 195	NONE 195	DON'T KNOW 195
WOULD HAVE A LIGHT PERFUME	12	15	18	13	8	36	9	40	3	2	3
FOR AN OLDER PERSON	6	59	13	12	10	6	13	4	3	1	—
AN EXPENSIVE SORT OF BRAND	36	7	8	1	—	5	54	23	1	10	1
EQUALLY SUITABLE FOR MEN AND WOMEN	30	43	32	22	31	28	7	24	4	—	—
AN OLD-FASHIONED DEODORANT	3	50	9	25	20	12	6	10	—	11	1
THIS WOULD BE STICKY	7	7	10	13	10	3	9	11	4	34	13
REALLY GOOD AT PREVENTING B.O.	11	35	16	4	7	13	35	12	10	5	8
FOR YOUNGER PEOPLE	28	10	19	6	8	23	58	18	3	3	2
A CHEAP SORT OF BRAND	7	19	16	77	54	12	2	7	1	10	1
A MODERN AND UP-TO-DATE DEODORANT	52	6	13	8	10	16	36	24	5	5	2
REALLY GOOD AT PREVENTING PERSPIRATION	14	33	19	9	10	14	19	15	10	4	11
WOULD DRY QUICKLY	3	23	25	2	3	22	14	16	10	4	13
AN ATTRACTIVE PACK	55	4	16	3	5	24	29	44	3	2	—
MORE SUITABLE FOR WOMEN	15	2	51	1	2	48	2	62	2	—	1

	1	2	3	4	5	6	7	8	9	10	11
MORE SUITABLE FOR MEN	11	61	3	9	11	1	86	1	2	—	1
WOULD LEAVE YOU FEELING FRESH	38	13	6	4	6	23	21	33	4	5	3
LONGER LASTING PROTECTION THAN OTHER DEODORANTS	11	37	13	7	7	8	26	7	3	7	15
MORE LIKE A HOUSEHOLD PRODUCT THAN A DEODERANT	9	41	14	46	61	9	1	6	2	7	1
A GOOD QUALITY PRODUCT	27	31	15	—	3	12	58	17	6	2	4
SOPHISTICATED PRODUCT	33	11	6	1	5	9	36	17	2	13	5
RATHER CLINICAL OR MEDICAL	4	51	7	49	50	5	1	3	1	12	2
RATHER DULL AND BORING	6	36	14	49	46	17	7	12	3	6	1
FRESH AND COOL	39	9	12	3	2	29	16	46	3	4	4
A SOFT DELICATE PRODUCT	12	4	23	2	1	40	5	43	2	5	5
BRIGHT AND COLOURFUL	52	5	28	4	10	12	9	25	2	8	1
A TASTEFUL DESIGN	43	5	16	2	7	17	27	29	3	8	2
A HARSH STRONG PRODUCT	11	28	5	24	27	1	25	3	2	13	9
THESE ARE UNSUITABLE COLOURS FOR A DEODORANT	8	29	19	47	31	19	5	15	1	19	2
WOULD HAVE YOU FEELING FRESH LONGER THAN OTHER DEODORANTS	21	22	9	—	8	16	29	17	4	6	15

Figure 10.3 Q 1 Brand imagery for Deodorant Brands

about what to do with the data. The programme enables the computer to accept and interpret the specifications, to accept the data on the punch cards and to process them as specified. Computer programmes consist of instructions which tell the computer what to do with the data it accepts. They are called 'software' as opposed to the 'hardware' which refers to the machinery itself. Since most surveys have many analysis requirements in common, standard programmes exist which will carry out analysis of research data. These are called 'software packages' and may involve a number of programmes being linked together to do the various things required for all the common types of data analysis. Writing software packages is carried out by computer programmers and many research organizations may themselves contract data processing out to a specialist organization. If this is the case then the research user should know, in order to ensure that his briefing requirements for analysis are adequately communicated.

Getting data out
The major output of results from computer data processing is in the form of tables, or 'computer tabulation'. The tables will indicate the numbers of respondents in each category of answers and percentages. This is usually done for the sample as a whole and for various sub-groups of the sample, particularly the demographic sub-groups. Figure 10.3 shows an example of a computer table. Cross-tabulation is also used, in which answers to one question are tabulated against answers to another question. For example, answers to questions about home ownership or renting might be cross-tabulated against D.I.Y. purchases. Values on one variable are plotted in one direction and the values of a second variable plotted in the other direction, with totals given as the marginal entries. The variables considered might be any two questions on the questionnaire. The major danger in using tabulation and cross-tabulation as a tool of analysis is in asking for too much print-out. Typically, the new research user will ask for everything

tabulated against everything else, and this will result in literally hundreds of pages of computer print-out which the user finds himself unable to handle.

10.3.3 STATISTICAL ANALYSIS

There are three main ways in which statistics are used in the analysis of data: to describe data, to measure its significance, and to indicate relationship between sets of data. These are described in the following sections.

Describing data
The purpose of descriptive statistics is to give the user an impression of the location of the data and its spread. The statistics used are frequency, percentage, average and dispersion.

Frequency The simplest kind of statistical description is a straight frequency count of the number of responses in each category. For example 27 032 000 adults took holidays during 1979/80. These data can also be represented as a 'frequency distribution' which shows how frequencies (i.e. numbers in the category) are distributed across a number of categories (in this case, type of holiday). This is shown as a histogram in Figure 10.4.

Percentage Whilst straight frequency counts are useful to give an idea of the absolute values involved, percentages will indicate what shares of particular markets are concerned, and are useful for making comparisons. In the example in Figure 10.4, the 20.5 million holiday-takers in Great Britain were 48% of all adults. This is obviously of interest to those involved in the holiday business, particularly when compared with other percentage statistics such as: 18% of all adults spent their holidays abroad during the same year; 9% on package tours abroad; and 6% at a holiday camp. 63% of all adults took a holiday at all in that year.

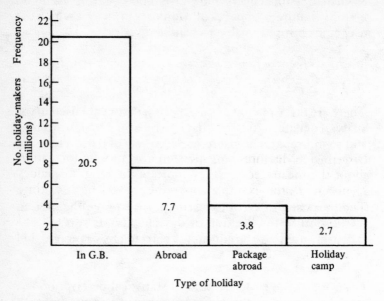

Figure 10.4 Holidays taken by adults during 1979–80. Source: TGI

Averages   Averages are a useful device for indicating with just one number roughly where the data as a whole is located. For example, in October 1982 about 10% of homes owned a VCR and on average watched pre-recorded programmes for 50 minutes per week. Multiplying the number of minutes per week by the number of homes owning sets would give a rough figure for the total weekly market size for pre-recorded programme viewing. The average used in this example is the *arithmetic mean*, which is the most commonly used and colloquially understood measure of average.

Another useful measure of average is called the *mode*. This refers to the most frequently occurring figure. The mode is useful in market studies concerning brand usage, or when it is important to know the most frequently mentioned brand in a brand recall study.

A less frequently used average is the *median*. This is the middle value when all responses are arranged in order. In considering income, the mean average is likely to be a higher value than the median. This is because the mean will be drawn upwards by very high salaries at the top end of the range, whereas the median will indicate what the middle earner is earning.

Dispersion   Measures of dispersion give more information about the mean because they indicate the range of values around it. In the example above the mean length of time spent viewing pre-recorded material on VCRs was 50 minutes per week. What a measure of dispersion would add to this is an idea of how much variation exists around this figure.

The simplest measure of dispersion is called the *range* and is simply the highest minus the lowest value in the data. In the VCR example the range was between 0 and 6 hours pre-recorded material i.e. the range value was 6 hours. This indicates that if the mean was only 50 minutes then most VCR owners are not watching very much pre-recorded material if the top end of the range is as high as 6 hours. However, it could be that only one individual in the sample actually viewed for 6 hours in the week under study and the next nearest length of viewing was 2 hours. If this were the case then our interpretation about the variety of pre-recorded material viewing behaviour would be bad.

To avoid this problem, where the absolute values at each end of the range may be extremely unrepresentative of the actual spread of the data, a standard measure of spread has been calculated. This measure indicates the values within which large proportions of the data lie, and is called the *standard deviation*. The same measure, when calculated from sample data rather than population data, is called the *standard error*. The usefulness of this measure lies in the fact that once it has been calculated it is known that (roughly)

68% of all values lie within 1 standard deviation/standard error of the mean, 95% of all values lie within 2 standard deviation/standard errors of the mean and 99.7% of all values lie within 3 standard deviation/standard errors of the mean. For most business purposes it is common to work at the level of 2 standard deviation/standard errors of the mean, that is to say where 95% of all the values lie. In the VCR pre-recorded material viewing example, the standard error was 10 minutes. This means that 95% of all pre-recorded material viewers were viewing somewhere between 30 minutes and 70 minutes per week. This gives a much better feeling for average viewing behaviour than either the mean on its own or the use of the range.

Measuring significance

Although there are many advantages to using samples rather than collecting data from the whole population under review, one of the disadvantages is that sample statistics only give an approximation of the population statistics within a given range, called *confidence limits* (*see* Section 7.5.3). Often the same measure is taken twice from two different samples. This may be from two different samples at the same time: perhaps a comparison between a sample of men and a sample of women; or between similar samples at two different points of time, say, recall of a brand at one point in time and again six months later after an advertising campaign. In these circumstances it is important to know whether the two figures could have arisen from the same underlying population or whether any difference in the two figures represents a real change in the state of the underlying population. Is there a real difference between men and women in their usage of or attitudes towards a brand? Has recall of the brand name changed over the test period which would indicate the need for more, less or improved advertising?

Significance tests   What *significance tests* do is to measure whether the difference between two percentages is significant or not, or whether the difference between two means from different samples is significant. In each case the calculation will indicate whether the difference is significant at a particular level. A statement of significance will appear in the form. 'This figure is significant at the "5% level", or at the "1% level".' The 5% level of significance means that there is only a 1 in 20 chance that 2 different values could have arisen from the same underlying population. The 1% level of significance indicates that there is only 1 in 100 chance that 2 different values could have arisen from the same underlying population.

Significance, then, is related to *sampling error*. Sampling error is not the same thing as mistake. Sampling error is the variation possible between two samples drawn from the same population simply because a sample was taken and not a complete census. When only 1000 respondents are selected to represent the views of 19 million households, then however well the sample has been selected the estimate of the figure for the 19 million households will not be exact. Because of this, two different 1000-respondent samples could produce two slightly different estimates of the population parameter from the same population. Measures of significance test whether two different values could have arisen from the same population or whether their values are too far apart to have arisen from sampling error.

An important distinction must be drawn between significance of a value and its importance or relevance. All that significance tests indicate is whether there is a real difference or no real difference between two values. They do not indicate that the difference or lack of difference is of any great importance or significance to the decision-maker.

An Insurance Company carried out a piece of research to measure awareness of the company's name. They used an unaided recall question followed by an aided recall question showing a list of company names. The unaided recall question gave a figure of 3.5% respondents who spontaneously recalled the company name. Since the company achieved a much higher figure on aided recall, they decided to carry out an advertising campaign in order to bring their company's name more into the front of the target population's mind.

Six months later, following a £200,000 brand-awareness advertising campaign, the company repeated the piece of research using a similar research methodology. This time unaided recall for the sample was 2%. Immediately, the individual who had commissioned the research became very concerned about significance testing in order to indicate whether the change in levels of recall represented a real fall in awareness following the advertising campaign, or whether both figures could have arisen from an underlying population in which the level of awareness of the company's brand name had not changed.

The significance test showed that there was no significant difference between the two figures i.e. awareness had not fallen during the period of the campaign. However, the important point here, surely, was that the best possible statistical interpretation of the figures was that there had been no change in awareness, yet this followed an expenditure of £200,000 on a campaign with increased awareness as its sole objective. Even without carrying out the significance test the best possible interpretation of the statistical data might still be considered as a measure of the failure of the advertising programme to achieve its objective. Executives in the company concerned, however, were relieved that the results of the significance test indicated no significant difference. They felt it exonerated them from the even worse position that recall might have actually dropped following their advertising programme!

It has already been pointed out that significance testing is only theoretically relevant for use on simple random sample data. In practice, statistical tests are applied to more complicated random sample designs and to quota samples for which they are not really appropriate. When significance tests are carried out on data from other than simple random samples a *design factor* of 1.5 to 2 is applied to the standard error used in carrying out further calculations.

This has the effect of increasing possible variation in the data and therefore reflects the fact that these samples are thought to be slightly less accurate than simple random samples in producing statistical estimates.

Chi-square In the same way that significance tests described in the last section measure the significance of the difference between two means or two percentages, there is a statistical significance test which measures whether differences in cross-tabulated data are statistically significant. This is called the *chi-square test*. For example, purchase of white bread was analysed by social class to indicate any difference in purchase rates among middle class and working class households. Since there were different numbers of buyers and non-buyers in the sample, and different numbers of working class and middle class households in the sample, inevitably each cell in the table had different values. The problem for the decision-maker was to interpret whether those different values represented a real difference. A chi-square test was applied to the data and indicated that working class households were statistically significantly higher purchasers of white bread. Since tables are commonly the output of research surveys, a general purpose computer programme used for obtaining cross-tabulations will normally also indicate significance levels for the data in the table.

Measuring statistical relationships
The importance of statistical tests of relationship between variables is that these measures indicate how various factors operating within a market influence and interact with each other. They can indicate how a market *works* by identifying and quantifying cause-and-effect relationships. These make it possible for a decision-maker to predict the outcomes of particular actions he might take, because they indicate which variables influence the market-place and by how much. Armed with this kind of information the decision-maker becomes a far more informed operator in his market.

He can measure which of the marketing and non-marketing variables have what effects in the market-place. For example, how sales are affected by changes in price, advertising or average daily temperature. It is at this point that marketing decision-making becomes more of a science than an art. These are compelling reasons why any commissioner and user of marketing research data should attempt to understand what measures of relationship a research agency should be asked to provide following a research survey, and should appreciate the importance of their implications for decision making once they are available. As in previous sections, this section will attempt to explain the meaning of statistical measures of relationship without explaining the statistical formulae.

Correlation analysis Correlation analysis is a statistical device which measures the degree of relationship in the movement of two sets of variables. This is expressed as a *correlation co-efficient* which can have a maximum value of +1 and a minumum value of −1. +1 indicates perfect positive correlation between two sets of variables. That is to say, if there is a movement of 10% on one variable it is accompanied by a movement in the same direction of 10% on another variable e.g. when the advertising budget is increased by 10% then sales in the subsequent period also increase by 10%. If this were the case (regrettably it is never that simple!) then the resulting correlation co-efficient calculated for the two variables would be +1. Similarly, if the two variables had a perfect relationship but in opposite directions, say for every 10% increase in price sales volumes decreased by 10% (equally unlikely!), then the correlation co-efficient would be −1. When changes in one variable are not associated with changes in the other variable then the correlation co-efficient will be calculated as zero and this indicates no relationship between the two sets of variables.

The usefulness of correlation analysis lies in the fact that it indicates which variables do appear to have common sets of movement in the market and the strength of association between them. The value taken as significant depends on the sample size but, as a rule-of-thumb, correlation co-efficients above $+0.7$ or below -0.7 are generally thought to indicate an interesting degree of association, and therefore to warrant further investigation of the two variables under consideration, for data derived from large samples.

The usual use of correlation analysis in marketing decision-making is to attempt to measure the degree of association between those variables which the marketing manager would like to see associated. Correlation co-efficients can be calculated for the relationship between company sales volume and variables such as price, level of advertising expenditure, competitive activity, and various consumer variables such as purchase behaviour, income, attitude and so on. Correlation co-efficients can also be calculated for variables which, experience suggests, are relevant to sales volume: seasonal factors, economic factors, competitive activity, and so on.

The simplest form of correlation analysis is *bivariate correlation analysis* in which only two variables are considered. For most practical marketing application *multiple correlation analysis* is more useful, since it indicates association between three or more sets of variables.

It is important for the user of correlation analysis to remember that the statistical technique will simply indicate that there is a statistical relationship in the movement of two sets of data. From this, the assumption is made that there is a cause-and-effect relationship. If a high degree of statistical correlation is found between the amount of money spent on advertising and sales volume, then it is assumed that the high level of advertising support is resulting in high levels of sales. But the statistical technique does not indicate cause-and-effect relationships, it simply indicates related movements in the data. Whether it is appropriate to consider cause-and-effect depends entirely on the subjective application of the user: if a cause-and-effect relationship appears to make sense then it is assumed to be so, if it does not make sense then it is assumed that the correlation is irrelevant. Inevitably, there are dangers in subjective interpretation and common sense is at least as important as statistical technique in interpreting the results.

Regression analysis   Where correlation analysis is concerned with association, regression analysis is concerned with dependence. That is to say, if correlation analysis indicates a number of variables which are associated with sales volume, regression analysis makes it possible to predict sales volumes from knowledge about the other variables. This introduces the concept of *dependent* and *independent* variables. Movement in the dependent variables depends upon movement in the independent variables. The most commonly used dependent variable in practice is sales volume. The independent variables, on which this may depend, are any of the marketing decision variables such as price, advertising, level of distribution, and product quality, and non-marketing external variables such as level of income, changes in the weather, and a whole host of other social and economic variables that may influence sales volume in a particular market. Typically, then, correlation analysis and regression analysis are both carried out on the same set of data. Correlation analysis indicates which variables have a relevant association with, say sales volume. Regression analysis can then be used to predict sales volume given a set of decisions about marketing variables and assumptions about probable movements in external variables.

The most common use of regression analysis in marketing research is for sales forecasting. Since sales volume is normally dependent on a number of variables it is more common to use *multiple regression analysis* than simple bivariate regression analysis. Multiple regression, as with multiple correlation, makes it possible to deal with the effect of a number of variables at once, and therefore to cope with a more realistic analysis of actual market movements.

Multivariate analysis

Multiple correlation and multiple regression analysis form the basis for further complex statistical methods of analysis which can deal with a number of variables at once. These make it possible to cluster respondents who are similar on a number of univariate attributes or to group similar attributes into a smaller number of factors. These techniques are therefore extremely useful in market segmentation studies. They identify and describe market segments, describe and group product attributes, and measure product similarities. The techniques are only briefly introduced here in a non-statistical way. However, readers wishing to obtain the most from use of quantitative marketing research data should equip themselves with sufficient statistical background to find out more about the use of, and application of, these methods.

Multivariate analysis of data is a highly specialized area requiring thorough statistical knowledge of the range of techniques and their appropriate application. The growth in use of computers for analysis of marketing research data has resulted in the increased use of multivariate analysis, but sometimes in inappropriate ways and on unsuitable data. The purpose of this section introducing the idea of multivariate analysis is simply to indicate that some very useful statistical analytical techniques exist which, if applied in the right way to the right type of data, can provide worthwhile operating knowledge to the marketing decision-maker. Research agencies, which carry out quantitative research, will have statisticians on their staff with whom the possibilities for multivariate analysis applied to a specific problem can be discussed. Four techniques are mentioned here: *factor analysis, cluster analysis, multiple discriminant analysis* and *multidimensional scaling*.

Factor analysis This technique reduces a large number of original variables, such as attitude statements, to a smaller number of *factors*. Each 'factor' consists of a group of related statements that form a broad dimension of attitude. In a research survey on television programme assessment, 750 viewers used 58 rating statements to describe 61 different programmes. Factor analysis reduced the 58 statements to 9 factors. One factor was called 'information' and contained attitude statements about the degree of scientific interest in the programme, whether it made the viewer think, whether it contained education information or whether it was meant to entertain. The value of this exercise lay in the fact that 58 possible comments about television programmes were reduced to 9 main dimensions of thought, which allow viewers to give a rating to any programme.

Cluster analysis   This technique analyses responses on a large number of variables, say attitude statements, from a large number of respondents and groups together or *clusters* respondents who are similar in the pattern of their responses. This technique can therefore be used as the basis for identifying segments in the market who exhibit similarities to each other and differences from other clusters in the market. Identification of market clusters and knowledge of the ways in which they are similar can lead to changes in the product or marketing methods used to reach this group.

Multiple discriminant analysis   The objective of this technique is to classify respondents into two or more groups on the basis of a number of items of information about them. Once respondents are discriminated into one group or another it may become possible to predict or explain their response to a given marketing situation. The major discriminating factor between shoppers and non-shoppers in a particular department store was found, through discriminant analysis, to be the perceived price level within the store. Subsequent advertising of lower-priced lines resulted in an increase in the number of shoppers. A variant of this technique growing in popularity is called '*automatic inter-action detection*' (AID), and is commonly used for market segmentation studies.

Multidimensional scaling This technique is used for producing 'perceptual maps'. Consumers rate brands or products by their attributes, by the degree to which brands are seen as similar or by the degree to which one brand of product is preferred to another. These rating questions usually include a rating for the consumer's 'ideal' brand. Multidimensional scaling is applied to the responses, resulting in 'perceptual maps'. An example is shown on page 96.

These can be used to change product attributes to be nearer the 'ideal' brand, or to suggest advertising messages which will stress the brand attributes most near to the ideal brand. They indicate the real competitors in a market-place from the consumer's point of view and so can be used to determine market positioning strategies.

10.4 INTERPRETATION OF QUANTITATIVE DATA

Interpretation of quantitative research data is an area in which a systematic method of approaching data and a great deal of common sense are the two most useful attributes. The first step is to go through all the tables one by one looking at the statistics. What do the descriptive statistics indicate about the characteristics of the market: frequencies, percentages, averages, dispersion? When differences are seen between two related statistics, is it a significant difference? Do men differ from women? Older people from younger? Users from non-users? When there is no difference, is that significant? If it is statistically different, will it matter anyway? What relationships exist within the data using techniques of correlation and regression?

The purpose of the analysis is to uncover whatever is relevant and significant in the data. To isolate trends, tendencies or new factors in such things as competition, market structure, consumer habits or external variables. Interpretation should draw out implications of the data for management policy and action in the present and in the future. It should also highlight indicators based on this survey by which to monitor and assess results of any action proposed. Interpretation of the data should also identify any weaknesses in the data base and point these out if real assistance is to be given to the decision-maker.

Within the marketing research industry there are two schools of thought about interpretation of marketing research data. One school suggests that the role of the marketing researcher is simply to collect, analyse and report on the data without drawing interpretation for management policy and action. Only in this way can objectivity as a researcher be preserved and freedom be left for management to act on data as it sees fit. The other school of thought suggests that the researcher who has been involved in deciding what data is to be collected, with its actual collection and with subsequent analysis of it, will have developed ideas about the implications of the data for decisions to be made. Those ideas should be transmitted to the research user as recommendations. It is up to the research buyer to indicate at the outset whether or not he is looking for guidance on possible action as part of the interpretative process.

10.5   REPORTING

The final stage of the marketing research process, from the researcher's point of view, lies in the report. This can take a number of forms. It may be written, and a written report can be either brief comment on tables or a full report. For research data of sufficient significance to the organization, the report may be given in the form of a personal presentation, often using a variety of sophisticated audiovisual devices.

For the research user the form in which the research report is presented has some significance. First, in terms of cost: a full written report is far more expensive than brief comment on tables, since it involves a considerable amount of senior research executive time. For the same reason, a personal presentation by members of the research agency will normally be charged to the client. Whether these additional costs are justified will depend on the type of research, the sophistication of the client in handling research data and the degree of importance attached to the research survey in question.

Research users unfamiliar with research reports, or who may be presented with raw data from a research survey and have to compile their own report, may find the following brief section on research reports useful. It discusses report objectives, and suggests a convention for report writing.

10.5.1 THE RESEARCH REPORT

Objectives
The research report has two equally important objectives. First, to *communicate* the findings and their *significance* to decision-makers. This has implications for the lay-out, style of writing, content and analysis of the data. Secondly, to gain *acceptance* of the findings. This has implications for the manner in which the report is presented. A short report is more likely to be read and assimilated than a long one. The key elements in a research report are listed below, although variations may be required for specific reports. A concise communication of the nature and outcome of the research programme is contained in sections 1–4. Sections 5–9 provide the detailed evidence from which conclusions and recommendations are derived.

1 *Title Page*
   Lists: title, client, research organization, date.
2 *List of Contents*
   Gives a detailed numbered guide to report sections, followed by a list of graphs and statistical tables.
3 *Preface*
   Outline of agreed research brief, followed by statement of objectives, scope and methods of research undertaken.
4 *Summary of Conclusions/Recommendations*
   Summary of main findings, sometimes accompanied by

some creative interpretation in the form of recommendations.

5 *Previous Related Research*
It is sometimes useful to show how previous knowledge may have had a bearing on the research undertaken.

6 *Research Method*
Procedures used to collect information. Where, how and from whom, and techniques used in analysis. The characteristics and size of samples should be recorded.

7 *Research Findings*
The main body of the report commenting on the findings in detail. Emphasis should be on ease of understanding and logical presentation for the reader.

8 *Conclusions*
Even though the findings may speak for themselves, it is helpful to bring them together in a conclusion related to the terms of reference stated in the preface.

9 *Appendixes*
Any detailed or technical matter that is essential to a full understanding of the research report e.g. copy of the questionnaire.

Whether the findings of a research report are read, noted and acted upon, should properly be a concern of the individual commissioning the research. If the findings are of such significance that the power to implement any recommendations lies outside his area of authority, then it is a useful device to call a meeting of appropriate personnel to receive and consider the main findings of a research study. This ensures that the findings can be effectively communicated, and that they will be considered and action decided upon as part of the agenda of the meeting.

If report findings are not noted and acted upon, then the whole research procedure represents an area of waste resources for the organization and the position of research expenditure within the organization must be questioned.

10.6 SUMMARY

Analysis and interpretation of qualitative data are subjective and impressionistic. They are usually carried out by the individual who conducted the field-work, and the report contains direct quotes from respondents. Analysis of quantitative data involves the processes of: data preparation, data processing, computer and statistical analysis, and interpretation. Each of these is discussed and statistical procedures for analysis are described. The chapter concludes with a brief section on reporting research findings.

11 How Do You Buy Good Research?

11.1 INTRODUCTION

'Good' research is research whose findings are directly useful to the manager, and help him to make a better decision. The research answers the questions it was designed to answer and those questions were directly relevant to the problem. The research design was appropriate and it was well conducted, analysed and reported.

The art of buying good research is very much like buying anything else. The buyer who knows why he needs research, what he needs, what he will use if for, when he needs it by and how much he is willing to pay for it, is more likely to make a good buy. It also makes sense to 'shop around' a bit in order to find a good supplier, and having found one to check that they are doing a good job. After the event one can learn from experience and so get better still at buying good research in future. This chapter suggests a systematic approach to buying research, which should increase the chances of making a good buy when commissioning an agency to carry out 'made-to-measure' research surveys. It also looks briefly at buying 'off-the-peg' syndicated services, and at judging how good, and therefore reliable, a piece of research is when one is presented with the report without having been involved in commissioning the survey.

11.2 GET THE RESEARCH REQUIREMENT RIGHT

It is very easy to waste money on research which is

'interesting' rather than necessary. The difference lies in having a clear idea of why the research is needed, what research is required, what it will be used for, when it is needed by and how much should be spent on it. Working out the answers to these questions will clarify the research requirement and form the basis for a good research brief.

11.2.1 IS RESEARCH REALLY NECESSARY?

It is just as important to know when not to use research as to know when it should be used. Almost all research is of some value to an organization, even if only at the level of general interest. It is all too easy for the manager facing a decision to decide that research will help him make a better decision without really thinking it through. 'What would happen if the research were not carried out?' is the most basic, yet most challenging and most often overlooked question. It involves analysing the action alternatives available, and may highlight the fact that with or without research the options are so limited that research cannot materially influence any subsequent action by the organization. It is also possible that the manager will discover that his organization is already fairly heavily committed to what it wants to do and the moment for decision-making research has effectively already passed. In that case it would be more efficient to decide not to carry out a research programme however desirable it may seem. Research may also be unnecessary if the costs or risk involved in taking action are small. The only research that should survive this question is that which can be clearly identified as being essential for the organization because it is relevant to an important, costly or high-risk decision and has the power to influence its outcome.

11.2.2 WHAT TYPE OF RESEARCH IS NEEDED?

As with a lamp post to a drunken man, research can be used in two ways: for illumination or for support. The type of research needed will be affected the purpose for which it is used. A decision-maker may want research in order to generate new ideas or to help him understand a situation better. In this case he is using research for illumination and will probably need to use qualitative research, often before undertaking a quantitative study. Using research for support implies the need for some factual base on which to rest a decision, and usually indicates quantitative research.

It may be that the organization is considering entering a new field of operation with which it is unfamiliar, or dealing with a new group of customers whose requirements are unknown. In these examples the most appropriate research approach is an exploratory study. More commonly, an organization may wish to make decisions in an area with which it is already familiar, but where some market data is necessary to direct the decisions to be made. For this purpose descriptive information will be most useful: a descriptive profile of customers in terms of age, sex, social group, geographical location and so on. A third possibility is the organization which has been operating in its market for some years and now wishes to understand more about cause-and-effect relationships in its markets. In this case the requirement will be for causal research, using experimental approaches to uncover the relevant variables in the market-place and measure the ways in which they influence it. Analysing the purpose for which the research is required will suggest the type of research needed: qualitative or quantitative; exploratory, descriptive or causal.

11.2.3 WHAT WILL THE RESEARCH BE USED FOR?

The particular reason for which research will be used and who will be using it, is also relevant in deciding the type of research required. A manager deciding which new products to introduce may be at the early stage of the new product-development process looking for possible new product ideas. In this case qualitative research methods will be useful. When the new product idea is further along the development process, the decision to be made is a quantitative one about production and distribution levels. This will require a large-scale research survey producing hard quantitative data.

For the creative team deciding what message to use in a new advertising campaign there are also two possibilities. A range of ideas for them to work on may be generated by group discussions, and the same method could be used to test initial response to creative ideas. A decision about what kind of background to use in advertisement illustrations, or what kind of activities to show individuals in an advertisement being engaged in, could come from quantitative research. Large-scale surveys would show the kind of activities which members of the target audience are most likely to be involved in, and these can be used in advertising.

11.2.4 WHEN IS THE RESEARCH NEEDED BY?

Most business decisions have deadlines and this should be taken into account before any research is undertaken, to allow for the fact that some research methods take longer to complete than others. However good a piece of research may be, if its findings are produced after the deadline for a decision, then the whole exercise has been a waste of time and money. The decision deadline may mean that the most appropriate research method cannot be completed in the time available. If this is so a choice must be made between delaying the decision until the research findings are available, carrying out no research at all, or deciding that a less than ideal method of research can be used within the timescale and still be valid for the purposes of the decision. The most common mistake made in this situation is to carry out rushed research and then not allow for this in using the findings.

11.2.5   HOW MUCH IS THE RESEARCH INFORMATION WORTH?

Gathering information is a costly procedure and so some attempt at evaluating the worth of information needs to be carried out before deciding on the level of research expenditure. Common sense indicates that there is no point in spending more on marketing research than the costs of making a wrong decision and so an attempt must be made to estimate costs of the decision. Sometimes this is easy. If a new product is to be launched then the costs of this include all the development costs associated with the product plus the marketing costs associated with its launch. This generally indicates a large cost and therefore a rationale for considering an expensive research programme. It is more difficult when a decision concerns whether to ´use one message or another in an advertising campaign. In this case the costs of a wrong decision are extremely hard to quantify, as are the costs of making a right decision.

One approach for deciding how much research information is worth is simply to take a subjective view which attempts to relate the overall amount involved in the project costs to the amount to be set aside for research. Marketing research expenditure can be looked upon rather like insurance in that its aim is to reduce risk. Its value is therefore related to the level of risk likely to be incurred: the higher the level of risk then the higher the level of research appropriate to guard against that risk. In assessing the value of research information most people operate at this subjective and intuitive level. However there are more formal devices which offer a framework for putting a money value on to information costs.

One technique uses theoretical calculations of expected profit from the project with and without availability of prior research information. The basic assumption of the technique is that research information increases the certainty of a particular outcome being achieved and the outcome can be evaluated in terms of expected profit.

Expected profit without the benefits of research information is likely to be less than the expected profit after buying research information. The difference in the two calculations puts a money value on the reduction of uncertainty produced by the research findings. The implication is that research information is worth the difference in money values and therefore a research project costing up to that amount would represent a worthwhile investment for the organization.

This technique requires the decison-maker to quantify subjective assessments of possible outcome i.e. he is required to quantify factors which might otherwise be called 'hunch' or 'intuition' or simply 'experience'. This is an advantage because it allows other members of the organization to evaluate and perhaps challenge what might otherwise remain as implicit decision-making processes. The disadvantage of this technique is that it puts a superficial air of elegance and sophistication on to what is, in effect, guesswork. However, it does form a useful framework for those who would simply like to work out the numbers as just one way of estimating how much to spend on research. A simplified version of the calculation is shown below.★

Example
A manufacturer wishes to decide whether to improve the quality of his product. The improved product will cost more, but it is likely that sales and profitability will increase. If sales increase by 25%, then the product's contribution to profit will increase by £100,000. The manufacturer therefore needs to assess the chances of achieving that 25% sales increase. He calls a meeting of his experienced senior management team and asks them to assess subjectively the probability of achieving the sales increase, i.e. to make a joint 'guesstimate'. The outcome of

★ Boyd, H. W. and Massy, W. F. *Marketing Management*, Harcourt, Brace, Jovanovich, Inc. (1972) pp. 247–53 give a fuller explanation of this.

the meeting is that the management team assess the probability of achieving the sales increase at 0.4. Expected Profit can therefore be calculated at: £100,000 (profit estimate)×0.4 (chance of making it) = £40,000. However the company has used research in the past to assist in making sales forecasts, and in its experience has found that, if a particular value is forecast by research, then there is a 75% probability of the value being achieved. In this case, then, if the research forecasts a sales increase of 25%, then the probability of its being achieved would be 0.75. Expected Profit following the research can therefore be calculated at: £100,000 (profit estimate)×0.75 (chance of making it, following research)=£75,000.

This calculation indicates that Expected Profit after research is £35,000 greater than Expected Profit before research and assumes (oversimplistically) that the sales increase would be maintained for only one year. A research programme costing less than £35,000 would therefore be a worthwhile undertaking i.e. what this reduction in un-certainty is 'worth'. The two factors in the equation, then, are the value of the decision outcome (in this case profit) and the degree of certainty with which that outcome can be anticipated without conducting research. The higher the outcome value and the higher the level of uncertainty within the organization about achieving it, then the greater the need for, and worth of, research.

11.3   PREPARE THE BRIEF

Armed with answers to the questions posed in the last section, the decision-maker must produce a specific written definition of the research requirements. This forms the basis for briefing the research agency, so the clearer and the more specific it is then the better able the agency will be to meet the needs identified.

Preparing the brief will involve a consideration of the environment in which the decision is to be made and the resources available. It is usually helpful at this stage to involve other managers within the organization. The aim should be to agree the objectives for the research programme and these should be distinguished from marketing objectives. An adhesives manufacturer with the marketing objective of attracting new users to a product set the research objective 'to identify groups who might have a use for the product and the attributes which appeal to them most'.

The second point to agree internally is the limitations of the research programme. What is it reasonable to expect the research to accomplish? Research does not make decisions for managers, it gives them more information which enables them to make better decisions. For example, research cannot directly predict sales of a new product. What it can do is to measure the new product's acceptability, performance in blind trials against competitive products, and so on. Increasing use of research in mathematical market modelling is, however, improving predictive ability and is a major area of current development.

A third point for internal agreement is the action standards required of the research programme. Research prior to the launch of a new product may be measuring factors such as rate of trial, intent to purchase, or preference. In these cases it is necessary to decide beforehand what figures will be acceptable for the launch to go ahead. A chocolate manufacturer sets a minimum score of 40% preference for the launch decision to be taken. The reason for deciding action standards prior to the research programme is that if these are left until later it is always possible to persuade oneself that the results are good enough, whereas before the research is carried out a greater degree of objectivity is possible in determining what requirements must be met for the project to go ahead.

Internal agreement on all these points in the course of preparing the brief will ensure that the eventual research programme takes account of all essential information needs. This is generally better decided by a group rather than an individual. The other reason for obtaining internal agreement at this stage is that organizations which hold their first meeting about proposed research projects with would-be research agencies in attendance may find themselves disagreeing about what is exactly required. Apart from presenting a rather poor view of the organization to the research agency before any working relationship has been established with them, this will probably result in a very poor brief being given.

Confusion and lack of clarity in the brief tends to produce confusing and unclear research. Adequate time and thought must be given to this process of preparing the brief before any research agencies are approached. The outcome of the process should be a clear definition of the research requirement committed to paper and approved by all the appropriate people within the organization.

11.4 CHOOSING THE RIGHT AGENCY

11.4.1 DRAWING UP THE SHORTLIST

The first step in buying research from an outside agency is to draw up a shortlist of agencies who might be appropriate. A set of guidelines for doing this is outlined in Section 9.6.1. The same rules apply here. A good starting point is to obtain the Market Research Society's booklet 'Organizations providing Market Research Services in Great Britain and Northern Ireland'. The details given in this make it possible to match the agency to the job: large job – large agency; small job – small agency; industrial job – industrial agency, etc. The booklet also identifies agencies with appropriate specialist services, say in travel and tourism, in motoring research, industrial research, financial research, and so on. Another useful source is to ask colleagues, friends and business acquaintances to recommend agencies with whom they have had good experience. From this selection procedure a shortlist of two or three agencies should be drawn up and a meeting arranged to discuss the research.

11.4.2   BRIEFING THE AGENCIES

The purpose of a briefing is to enable the research organization, which is going to carry out the research, to know
exactly what it is required to do. The brief should contain all
that is necessary to accomplish this. The following
suggestions come 'straight from the horse's mouth' having
been made by the Managing Director of one of the largest
and most successful research agencies in the UK. He
suggests that the research brief should contain the following.

Background and objectives of the research
This section should indicate to the agency why the research
is being carried out, the competitive situation of the product
concerned, any preconceptions which the organization may
have about possible outcomes of the research and as much
relevant information about the history of the product as it is
possible to provide. The research organization can draw
more useful conclusions from their interpretation of the
research material if they have a thorough understanding of
the background to the product situation.

Data on the relevant population group
If the population group of interest is entirely male it
obviously makes sense to tell the agency, because that will
prevent them wasting research money on collecting data
from females. The same thing holds for special age,
occupation, interest, industry, service or any other specific
group. It is also helpful to give an indication of the probable
rate of occurrence of the population group of interest as this
will affect the sampling method used.

Example   A car component manufacturer wanted to learn
more about the growing phenomenon of the motorist who
has his car serviced at home by someone else. In particular,

the component manufacturer wanted to know where these individuals who service other people's cars obtain the spare parts they need. It was known that some of the people carrying on this trade did so openly, but many more did this kind of work on an 'unofficial' basis. The manufacturer suspected that they accounted for something like one-tenth of all servicing done. If so, they would represent a useful source of business if some method of distributing parts into this unofficial trade could be devised. The first step was to undertake a research survey to confirm the number of people who had their cars serviced in this way and learn more about it. By indicating to the research agency their suspicion that this represented approximately one in ten of all motor car owners, the agency knew that to generate a sample of 500 relevant respondents it would be necessary to contact 5000 motorists. This obviously would mean a more time-consuming and expensive sample identification procedure than would be necessary, say, for the manufacturer of a food product used by 80% of all households. In this case to generate a sample of 500 respondents only 625 would need to be contacted in the first place.

Giving as much information as is available about the characteristics and occurrence of the target group will enable the agency to suggest the most appropriate method for contacting the sample, and be more precise in estimating the cost of doing so.

The type of research envisaged

The agency should be informed about the thinking that has gone into suggesting the kind of research that might be required. If it is felt internally that the most appropriate kind of data would be qualitative, perhaps involving group discussions, then the agency should be told this. If a quantitative decision, based on hard data, is to be made then a quantitative survey will be needed and the agency should be informed. This will guide them in deciding on an appropriate sample size. Of course it is likely that the research buyer is looking for the agency's advice on the most appropriate type of research for the problem and it is perfectly reasonable to expect this. Any agency worth its salt will tell a client if they believe an inappropriate type of research is being suggested. However, it also makes sense to give the agency clues as to the sort of work that is being expected from them. This will avoid the aggravation of receiving a detailed proposal from the research agency for a major survey when all the client really wanted was a few group discussions.

The question areas to be covered

The agency will do a better job the more specific the client is about exactly what is required. This can be accomplished by indicating in some detail the question areas to be covered. This does not mean writing a questionnaire, because that is part of the expertise for which the agency is needed. A detailed list of question areas identifies for the agency exactly what it is required to find out about. It is their responsibility to obtain answers to the questions in as technically correct a manner as they can. It is the commissioner's responsibility to ensure that the agency is adequately briefed with the areas of questioning to be used.

A realistic timetable

In briefing a research agency it is essential to indicate the date by which answers are required. This has implications for the type of method which can be used and for the factors which the agency will need to take into account in planning its field-work programme. The first date to be included in the timetable will be an indication of by when the research proposal is required. This will be followed by the amount of time available for research from the date on which the research is commissioned. Research agency experience is that clients are at least as likely as agencies to create delays in the research timetable either by taking too long to decide to commission the survey or by taking too long to agree the questionnaire. Any such delays cut down the time available for carrying out the research. Giving an agency an impossible deadline for a research survey to be completed in is bound to produce poor work. As in any other area, rushed work is likely to suffer from lack of attention to detail and general inaccuracy. The commissioning organization should be sure that it is itself able to meet any obligations required by the timetable: if a product test is under consideration it must be able to produce the product for test in the quantities required and by the dates specified.

An invitation to discuss the research

A research brief, particularly for a new, important, unusual or complicated survey, should always include an invitation to the research agency to discuss the research. During these discussions the research agency will be asking questions to clarify all the points they need to know to carry out a good job. The discussion will be useful in identifying different, and perhaps more effective, or cheaper, ways of under-taking the research than those which occurred to the client. Discussions with research agencies will be especially helpful to those organizations who have not used a great deal of research in the past. They will learn whether their original written brief has proved adequate in communicating to the research agency exactly what is required. From the questions which the agency personnel will ask, the client will learn more about possible technical problems which will arise and more about what the research will actually be able to produce in the way of answers to questions. Probably, during these discussions the original brief will be improved upon. Any changes are best recorded in writing in a revised brief including the changes which have taken place.

The less familiar the client is with research, the more time he should be prepared to devote personally to enabling the agency to brief itself through comprehensive discussions with him. At the conclusion of these discussions it is important for both parties to agree in writing exactly what it is the agency is being asked to do. Client–agency discussions are useful not only in producing a good final brief, but also because the client has an extended opportunity to assess the ability of the personnel from the research agency to understand the requirements. These discussions are the basis for any subsequent working relationship and from them it should be possible to determine whether the client and the agency personnel are on each others' wavelength. It is important to ensure that good two-way communication can be established at this stage. If the client does not feel that the agency has a clear idea of what is expected of it, then it is quite probable that the work produced will produce only approximate answers to the questions set.

In discussions with agency personnel the overriding principles, particularly for the new research user, should be to provide as much relevant marketing information as is available and to be as technically specific about the survey as possible.

The budget

There is some disagreement about whether or not the budget available for the research programme should be disclosed to the research agency at the briefing stage. The argument for disclosing the budget available is that the type and scale of research which can be carried out is clearly limited by its size. If the agency does not know what this working limit is, then it may well produce a proposal which is rejected simply because it cannot be carried out within the budget available. This is a waste of time for both parties to the exercise. The argument against disclosing the size of the research budget to the research agency is that if the agency knows how much money there is to be spent then they will find a way of spending it!

On balance the author believes that the weight of the arguments lies in favour of giving some indication of the funds available to the research agency before a proposal is received from them. This avoids the time-wasting exercise of the agency producing an inappropriate scale of research to that envisaged. Sufficient protection is available from an agency being tempted to do an unnecessarily large and expensive survey by the fact that three agencies will be invited to submit proposals. If the agencies know of this competitive element in the situation then they are not likely to produce a proposal that is certain to lose them the job on cost grounds.

11.4.3   THE RESEARCH PROPOSAL

Having briefed three research agencies, what can be expected from them by way of a research proposal? In the first instance, the proposal itself should arrive by the agreed deadline. The proposal should be in writing, so that it is absolutely clear both to the client and to the agency what is being promised. It should demonstrate that the quoting agency has a good understanding of the problem. Most importantly, the research proposal should be a detailed specification of exactly what the agency is planning to do for the money it is asking.

Generally speaking, it is unreasonable to expect that the research agency will have done a great deal of work on the problem at this stage because they do not know whether or not they are going to get the job. However, if the agency is worth its salt (and the client's money!) it should have put in enough work to demonstrate in the proposal that it is quite clear about what is expected and is competent to deliver that efficiently.

It is not usual for agencies to charge clients for producing research proposals, but the Association of Market Survey Organisations (AMSO) agreed in 1979 that clients should be asked how many agencies were being asked to write proposals. If it is more than three agencies then AMSO members agreed that they may charge the offending organizations for each proposal produced. This is an attempt to control the activities of client companies who waste time and money by asking for an unreasonably large number of research proposals as a means of obtaining free research advice.

What are the points to look for in a research agency's proposal?

Statement of the objectives

The first thing to look for is a clearly defined statement of the objectives of the survey. They should reflect those agreed as a result of the briefing procedure and be no more and no less than required by the client. The objectives should be checked for their relevance to the needs of the problem.

Description of how the research will be done

The sample   The proposal should contain a precise and relevant definition of the sample to be selected. It should explain the method to be used in selecting the sample and indicate the size of sample to be used, with reasons for this.

The field-work   The proposal should indicate clearly the research method to be used: group discussions, personal interviews, telephone research, postal research, and so on. It should indicate how the field-work is to be organized, how the quality of the field-work is to be controlled and checked. This section will also be used to indicate if the agency is a member of the Market Research Society Interviewer Card Scheme. If so, then this can be taken as an indicator of the quality standards maintained by the company concerned. Its absence, of course, does not necessarily indicate poor quality of field-work, but the client must form his own judgement of this.

The questionnaire   It would be unreasonable to expect to see a final questionnaire included in a research proposal. What should be shown are comments indicating what the agency believes should be included in the questionnaire. This will be partly as a result of the briefing they received and partly as a result of their own analysis of the requirements of the problem. There will be suggestions from the agency as to what topics might be included and what type of question might be used. There should also be an indication of the expected length of the questionnaire and its composition.

Data handling   The proposals should contain details of the work to be undertaken in editing, coding, punching and processing the data produced if it is a quantitative survey. If tables are to be produced then the proposal should indicate how many tables there will be and whether any cross-tabulation is to be produced. For a qualitative survey an indication should be given of how the data produced will be handled. Will the tapes be transcribed, or will analysis be conducted straight from the original tapes by the moderator?

Reporting

Proposals should make it clear whether or not a written report is included in the costs. This is particularly important nowadays, since, for a large report on an important survey written by a senior research executive, it is not unusual for a charge of up to £1000 to be made. Often a full report is not required, particularly by the client who is a regular user of research and perfectly able to write the report himself. If a report is included in the cost then the number of copies to be provided should be shown. This may seem a trivial point, but faced with a large report it can be very irritating and time-consuming to have to run off additional copies. It is as well to have these matters clearly specified at the outset.

The proposal should also show whether a verbal presentation of the results will be made. Once again this is not always required or provided. If a personal presentation is required this will be costed to cover the time and presentation preparation required of agency personnel.

Research timetable

The proposal should contain a detailed schedule of start dates for each phase of the research procedure. From the date of commissioning, when will the draft questionnaire be produced? When will field-work begin and end? When will data processing begin? When will top-line results be available? When will the final report and verbal present-ation, if these are included, be available?

The timetable should be one that it is reasonable to expect the research agency to meet and that the commissioning organization can also meet for its input into the research procedure. If the timetable allows one week for approval of the questionnaire, then is the client company able to involve all those who need to be involved and reach agreement within five working days? If the product is required in special packaging for testing is it feasible that the amount required in the test packaging can be produced by the date indicated?

Costs
The proposal should give a clear indication of the cost of the research being proposed and of how those costs are derived. When comparing costs of a number of different proposals against each other, the cost-related assumptions should be checked. Is the length suggested for the questionnaire reasonable for the data required of it? If a 10-minute questionnaire is indicated in the research proposal and the questionnaire finally approved turns out to be 20-minutes long, then additional costs will be incurred. If the number of tabulations indicated in the proposal turn out to have been unrealistic and further tabulations are required, then once again additional costs will be incurred.

Are the costs all-inclusive? Check whether or not a report with the number of copies required and a verbal present-ation are included or excluded in the cost quoted. Is VAT included or an extra? For how long is the proposal cost valid? It is unusual nowadays for a research agency to offer open-dated cost proposals. Like all other businesses, re-search agencies' costs rise, so it is unreasonable to expect the price to remain the same for a research proposal quoted this year and commissioned next.

Justification

As we have seen from the foregoing sections the research proposal is a detailed specification of exactly what the research agency proposes should be done to solve the research problem. This specification of the research method should be accompanied by an explanation and discussion of what it is proposed to do and why. For example, why the sample selection procedure indicated? And why the size of sample indicated? Why the personal interview technique rather than group discussion? Why a twenty minute questionnaire and not a thirty minute questionnaire? Why are open-ended questions requiring expensive coding and analysis being included in a large-scale quantitative survey? Why is a written report or verbal presentation included, or why not? Why the timetable indicated? Why the cost indicated? At each stage of the research proposal, the agency should make clear *why* they are proposing what they are proposing, and the client should find their arguments convincing.

Supporting evidence

It is sometimes useful to be aware of any evidence the agency may have in support of their particular qualifications to undertake the research. For example, they may have particular experience in this marketing area. The problem may be to do with new product development and the agency is particularly well known for the quality of its new product development studies. It could be an advertising problem and the agency is particularly well known for its expertise in the area of advertising research, and so on.

The agency may have particular experience of the kind of techniques involved. Perhaps the research problem demands the application of complicated scaling exercises. It would be reassuring to know that the agency, or more particularly its interviewers, are well practised in the use of these techniques and will not be experimenting with a new and complicated system on this survey.

It is sometimes helpful to read brief and relevant curriculum vitae of the personnel who will be working on the research project and involved in the day-to-day matters of organizing and controlling it. This is particularly so when agency personnel have relevant industry experience. A point to note here, as with most service agencies, is which personnel will actually be working on the job, as opposed to those who have been involved in selling it! A good job is more likely to be done if the people involved in day-to-day running of the research have also been involved in the briefings and proposals.

Points to watch
In assessing a research proposal it is wisest to assume that anything not specified will not be provided or will have to be paid for in addition. If no mention is made of a report then assume one will have to be paid for, if required. If a verbal presentation is not mentioned then assume that it would have to be paid for, and so on. Check every point of assumption about what will be provided and ask the agency quite specifically whether or not it is included in their costing.

Beware of vagueness in a research proposal. If the proposal does not make it quite clear exactly what is going to be done, why it is going to be done, who is going to do it, and when they are going to do it by, then assume that the agency itself is not perfectly clear on these points otherwise they would have communicated it. Beware, too, of research 'mumbo jumbo'. The point of a research proposal is to explain to the client what he is getting for his money. Research jargon and techniques can be used to confuse and impress the client rather than to explain and reassure him of the agency's ability to answer his problems, starting from where he himself is. Suspect that an agency will be no more concerned to make the findings clear than it is to make its proposals clear. So if the proposals are not given straightforward explanations where necessary, then select another agency.

11.4.4   SELECTING THE RESEARCH AGENCY

It will be clear from the preceding sections of this chapter that a fair amount of contact with all the research agencies invited to produce proposals will already have taken place. Also, if research proposals are produced in the form suggested in the last section then there should be a good basis for comparison, although not necessarily a straight-forward one. There are a number of points to take into account when deciding which agency should be given the job. As with buying most things, the cheapest is not necessarily the best. Five criteria for determining to which agency to award the job are considered.

Approach
An assessment should be made of the agencies' approaches to solving the problem. Have they been imaginative or creative? Have they followed precisely the brief given to them? Have they improved upon it? Is the approach the one which the agency was instructed to take and, if not, have they given convincing reasons for changing it? If three different agencies have been asked to quote and three different approaches to solving the problems have turned up in the proposals, then which approach actually seems most likely to produce a good and cost-effective answer to the problem?

Perceived quality
As in buying all services, it is impossible to test the quality, measure the length, or feel the width, before agreeing to purchase. However, some clues as to the potential quality of the services to be offered are provided by the proposal and by contact with the agency personnel. Do the agency personnel seem to know what they are talking about? How many actual interviews are you being offered for your money? Does the organization field-work impress you with its adequacy and efficiency? Is the company a member of the Market Research Society Interviewer Card Scheme? What proportion of quality check-backs are done on the

field-work? Does the procedure for handling the data appear to be efficient and well organized? Was the proposal itself a good quality piece of work?

Relevant expertise
Did the agency produce any convincing evidence to support their particular suitability for the work? Do they have relevant expertise? How many years of appropriate research or marketing experience do they have? Have their field-workers used the sampling and questionnaire techniques before? Have their data processors used the statistical techniques before?

Communication
This is a most important aspect of determining which agency to select. If the proposal is well explained then it is more likely that the final report will be. If the agency personnel have clearly demonstrated their understanding of the problem, then it is far more likely that they will produce a sensible answer to it. The client should feel 'on the same wave-length' as the agency personnel with whom he is dealing. If the client and agency personnel have communicated easily over briefing and proposals then it is far more likely that they will work effectively together in handling any problems that may arise during the research. Feeling that a particular group of people are the right people for the job should not be underestimated as a criterion for awarding the job to them.

Cost
Now to tackle this most important criterion in deciding from which agency to buy the research. How useful is cost as an indicator of good value? As will be seen from the foregoing points it is important to check any differences in the cost-associated variables like sample definition, size of sample, number of interviewing points, length of interview, composition of questionnaire, number of open-ended questions included, data processing techniques to be

applied, provision of a written or verbal report, and so on. Differences in these variables will quite naturally lead to differences in cost. What then has to be decided is to what extent differences in the variables are justified by the quality of research required. That depends on the importance of the problem and can only be judged by the individual commissioning the research.

There are two circumstances in which it may make good sense to go for the cheapest research proposal. The first is when the research brief is 'tight', i.e. when the research agency has no discretion over the cost-associated variables. All agencies are quoting to exactly the same specification and hence the only variation will be in cost. The second case is when the research agencies are in a competitive business situation. There are times of the year, and years, when research work is comparatively short. Since the major area of cost for research agencies is their personnel, if these are relatively under-employed it represents a very high level of fixed cost. This can best be defrayed by offering research 'bargains' when the agency is short of work. If comparison of the cost-associated variables indicates no real reason for variations in cost, and yet variations exist, then suspect that one agency is pricing high. It probably already has sufficient work and additional work will impose an extra burden of cost. The agency therefore feels that the client adding to their costs should pay for them. A research agency pricing low is signalling that it wants the job, and providing all the other criteria are satisfied, then it makes sense to respond to that signal!

The commissioning letter
Using the criteria outlined in this section, one of the agencies invited to submit a research proposal will be judged as most capable of producing research of an acceptably high standard at an acceptable cost. When the selection has been made, the research buyer should write a commissioning letter, authorizing the agency to begin the work, and restating all the points of agreement. This letter

then provides the basic specification for the work and its costs, by which both parties to the agreement are bound. The importance of ensuring that a detailed commissioning letter is written occurs when the actual research design and costs agreed on differ from both the original research brief and from the agency's original research proposal. At some stage an agreed set of rules for the conduct of the research must be laid down to govern the conduct of the research programme, and to avoid the possibility of later disagreement over exactly what the rules were.

11.5 CHECK THAT THE AGENCY DOES A GOOD JOB

Having agreed to buy the research, the buyer will want to know that he gets good value for his organization's money. There are two stages to checking the quality of research bought. The first is monitoring during the progress of the research programme, and the second is evaluation when the final results are delivered. It should perhaps be emphasized that, if the research has been bought in the manner suggested in this chapter, then the evaluation of its quality should be straightforward and the risk of poor quality research low. Choosing the right agency in the first place is the best way to get a good job done.

11.5.1 *MONITORING WHILE IN PROGRESS*

Questionnaire and field-work
Once the research is in progress it becomes the responsibility of the research agency. However, the wise buyer will keep himself informed. The first opportunity occurs when the questionnaire arrives for approval. Does it arrive in the time allowed for this in the research timetable? Has it been piloted? How satisfactory does it seem to be generally? Arrival of the draft questionnaire for approval is also the first opportunity the agency has of working with its new

client. Do they introduce delays by taking too long to approve the questionnaire? Do they suddenly decide to introduce different topics from those agreed in the final brief? For an effective working relationship to develop, both parties to the research should keep to the agreements laid down in the commissioning letter.

A second opportunity to monitor the research in progress arises at the field-work stage. The buyer should ask to spend the day with one of the interviewers, and should himself suggest the day and area to be used, rather than allow the agency to select their best interviewer. Particularly for the new research user, this experience gives great insight to and understanding of the real situation in which the questionnaire is applied and how consumers respond to it. This greatly enhances the client's understanding of the final research report when it is presented to him, and the insights gained are likely to influence the quality of his own interpretation of the data and use of the findings.

Data preparation and processing
It is useful to discuss data preparation and processing with the agency after the field-work has been completed and before data preparation and processing is begun. This will ensure that any modification which it would be sensible to implement as a result of discoveries made during the field-work can be applied and agreed. It can also be helpful from the agency's point of view. A discussion at this stage can be useful in deciding code frames and will focus on what might be useful in terms of analysis and emphasis in the final report. This will lead to a more useful report being presented to the client.

Timing
A simple way of monitoring research in progress is to check that timings agreed are adhered to. This will indicate whether the agency has been able to meet the objectives which it set for itself in its proposal, in the time-scale which it designed for itself in the same document. If nothing else,

it indicates something about the agency's realism and efficiency.

11.5.2 EVALUATING THE FINAL RESULTS

Once the final results have been delivered then there are a number of indicators as to the quality of the research.

Was the research to specification?
Stress has already been laid on the importance of a detailed research proposal being agreed and confirmed in writing in the commissioning letter. Since this commissioning letter contained the agreed specification for the research then it can be used to check that the research was to specification. The technical aspects of the survey should be checked e.g. sample, definition, method of selection, size, interviewing method, organization, questionnaires, data handling procedures, and so on. Are the tabulations as agreed, with the correct number of tables and the correct cross-tabulations? Is the report as agreed, and with the number of copies required?

Field-work quality checks
If a quantitative survey has been undertaken then the research agency will have indicated in its specification the percentage of back-checks to be done. 'Back-checks' is the term researchers use to refer to the field-work quality-control checks described in Section 9.5.1. The client could ask to see the back-check results of his own survey. This will give an indication of the quality of the field-work undertaken on his behalf.

Tabulations
Tabulations nowadays are likely to be copies of computer print-outs and this, of itself, can create problems. Check that the tabulations are legible, simply from the point of view of print quality. Check that they are comprehensible. Original tabulations are likely to have abbreviated headings

which may not be immediately understandable. It is important that either a key to the headings is provided or that the headings are shown typed in full. If a large number of computer tabulations are included with the report it is helpful if these are indexed. Reams of computer print-out with no clear means of identifying the answers to one question from the answers to another are of little help to the report user.

The report

If there is a written report, then it is an important indicator of the quality of the research since it gives clues to the clarity of the researcher's mind. The first thing to check is whether the findings have been presented in a logical order, i.e. not necessarily in the order that questions come off the questionnaire. A logical order is either one in which the report presents relevant data and draws conclusions from it, or where the report draws conclusions and offers supporting data for them. Topics will be sequenced in such a way that the report draws the reader along a well-structured argument to the point of conviction. A jumble of ill-organized facts is not an indicator of good quality research. The report should be clear and readable and written in good English. It should include a meaningful summary, and should reach sensible and well-argued conclusions, if appropriate.

The research buyer must be convinced that he asked quite specifically for something sensible; that he got what he paid for; and that it was of good quality. He will then have more confidence in relying on and using the results.

11.6   LEARN FROM EXPERIENCE

Even research that has been done to specification, and in which the agency did all that could be reasonably expected of it, may not turn out to be good research. Good research is that which influences a decision to be better than it would have been without the research. This can only be judged after the event. To become an intelligent and informed research user, taking the time to learn from experience is very worthwhile. The following questions can help to do this.

11.6.1   WERE THE OBJECTIVES RIGHT?

A common fault of research is that the objectives were not defined with sufficient precision. This results in a research report which, whilst interesting, turns out to have no real practical value. The more precisely the objectives can be defined then the more specific the research can be to meet the requirements made of it. Responsibility for getting the objectives right must lie largely with the research buyer. He has most to learn if he believes that he fell down in this area, but the agency input should also be questioned.

11.6.2   WAS THE RESEARCH PROGRAMME RIGHT?

An assessment should be made of whether the research programme was adequate for meeting the research object-ives. It may well be felt on reflection that the research programme went astray from the objectives set for it, resulting in information not suited to the decision-maker's real need. Responsibility for adequate translation of the research objectives into an appropriate research design must lie largely with the research agency.

11.6.3   WAS TOO MUCH OR TOO LITTLE INFORMATION PRODUCED?

The most common fault at the end of research programmes is that they produce more information than the decision-maker can deal with. This is probably a fault in research since it means that the research buyer has paid for more information than he can use, and the information not used represents waste. Although the defence can be made that information is always useful, in practice it does not turn out to be so. When someone actually comes to make the decision for which that information might be useful, it is probably out-dated.

The problem of providing too little information from a research programme is also of concern since it also means that money has been unwisely spent. In this case better value might have been achieved through spending a little more money.

11.6.4 DID IT HELP PROVIDE A SOLUTION?

The 'acid test' for research results must be whether the findings assisted in solving the original problem. If they did then that is fine and indicates an appropriate use of research. A similar approach might be used in the future. If the results did not help in solving the original problem then this may indicate a poor use of research or inappropriate research design. An attempt should be made to assess why the research failed so that the same mistakes will not be made again.

11.6.5 USING FEED-BACK

As the items discussed so far indicate, both the research buyer and the research doer have something to learn from their joint experience. It is therefore a wise move to feedback to the research agency any points which they could learn from the outcome of the research programme. A client may be genuinely satisfied with the quality of research that he has received from the agency, but still feel that lessons could be learned from it. It makes sense to share these with the agency, as in working together on a second project both parties are likely to produce a better result.

11.6.6 WHAT ACTION RESULTED FROM THE RESEARCH?

The point of doing research is in order to change or

influence some action to be taken or decision to be made. This holds true even when the results indicate no certain outcome or perhaps that the right decision is to do nothing. If nothing occurs as a result of the research then this must be considered bad research. It was either unnecessary or undertaken for the wrong reasons. The individual responsible for buying this piece of research needs to question why it influenced nothing. Was it a fault of the buying, commissioning, or conduct of the research programme?

If some decision or action did result from the research then the outcome of the decision or action needs to be analysed for its correctness. If it turns out that a wrong decision or wrong action was taken as a result of the research programme, then the research buyer must assess why this was so. Was the research poorly applied, or poorly conducted? If so, what can be learned from that?

The value of learning from experience cannot be under-estimated. It involves thoughtful and intelligent analysis so that good experience may be learned from and built upon, and bad experience may be used as the basis for future improvement.

11.7   BUYING SYNDICATED SERVICES

Buying syndicated services is 'the same, but different' from buying made-to-measure research surveys. The difference is that the results or the design of the service already exist, and this makes buying easier. The similarity is that it is still necessary to ensure that the service is specifically appropriate to the real information need, and that it is of good quality and offers good value for money. The buying procedure is therefore as follows.

11.7.1   DEFINE THE REQUIREMENT

First identify exactly what information is needed. This is an essential first step in all research buying.

11.7.2 DOES THE SERVICE MEET THE REQUIREMENT?

It is important to judge the service offered specifically against the research requirement. The danger in buying syndicated services lies in bending the information requirement to meet the service provided, and therefore buying inappropriate data.

11.7.3 DOES THE SERVICE PROVIDE ADEQUATE FLEXIBILITY?

Is the timing and frequency of reporting appropriate, or can it be varied? Can relevant groups and sub-groups be analysed from the data provided? Is it possible to add supplementary questions to the existing format, or to influence the wording of existing questions to make them more appropriate?

11.7.4 IS THE MONEY WORTH SPENDING?

Most syndicated services produce good quality data and represent good value for money. The key question for the buyer is whether the money is worth spending from his organization's point of view, i.e. will the information influence decision-making in a cost-effective way? The prospective buyer should be able to produce specific instances to support the answer 'yes' to that question.

11.8 EVALUATING OTHER RESEARCH REPORTS

It will often be the case that a manager is presented with a research report and asked to apply its findings when he was not himself responsible for commissioning the research programme. In this case the research must be assessed for its quality before its findings can be used with confidence. The following checklist can be used to judge research quality when only the report is available for assessment.

11.8.1 A SCHEME FOR JUDGING RESEARCH QUALITY

1 What were the objectives of the research?
   Are they appropriate to the problem to which the findings are now to be applied?
2 What method was used to collect the information?
   Was it appropriate to the information need?
3 Who was asked the questions?
   Is the sample definition appropriate?
4 How many people were asked?
   Is the sample size adequate?
5 What were the actual questions?
   Check the copy of the questionnaire in the technical appendix. Do they seem to be good questions, well framed and appropriate to the objectives?
6 Who did the field-work?
   Is there a basis for judging the quality of the field-work? Were professional interviewers used? What checking procedures were used?
7 When was the field-work carried out?
   Was the timing sufficiently recent for the results still to hold? Was the time of year/time of day appropriate?
8 Are the tabulations comprehensible?
   Are they legible, with clear headings, and indexed?
9 Would further cross-tabulations produce useful information?
   Are these possible?
10 Is the report in a logical order and readable?
   Does it make sense?
11 Is there a meaningful summary?
   Is it easy to grasp the main points being made?
12 Are there conclusions? (if appropriate)
   Are they supported by the data?
13 Did the research meet its objectives, and if not, why not?
   Does this invalidate the research?

A satisfactory answer to all these questions should reassure the decision-maker that the report he is being asked to use is actually of real relevance to the current problem, and is of sufficiently good quality for its findings to be applied with some confidence. An unsatisfactory answer to some or all of the questions would indicate the use of appropriate caution in applying the findings of such research.

11.9 SUMMARY

Most organizations requiring research commission it to be carried out by research agencies. A systematic approach for buying 'made-to-measure' research is suggested covering five stages: get the research requirement right; prepare the brief; choose the right agency; check that the agency does a good job; learn from experience. Buying and evaluating syndicated services is also discussed. A checklist for judging research quality is suggested.

12 Using Research in Industrial Markets

12.1 INTRODUCTION

The use of research in industrial markets differs from its use in consumer markets mainly in application and degree, rather than in technique. This is because industrial organizations have tended to lag behind consumer organizations in the sophistication of their approach to marketing generally. Recent years have seen considerable growth in the use of marketing research techniques in industrial markets and the full range of research techniques and applications discussed in this book are increasingly being applied. In this chapter differences of emphasis in industrial marketing research are considered for each of the chapter topics in the book.

12.2 GETTING STARTED

An industrial organization will need to answer the same questions as those which are presented in Chapter 2. There must be an organizational commitment to the need for marketing research and an allocation of resources in order to carry it out. In the first instance, this may mean recruiting an individual with the title of 'Statistical Assistant' and allowing that person to build up an in-house marketing department, or giving responsibility to a senior executive already within the organization. Which of these, or other possible strategies, is most appropriate will depend on the size of the organization and its level of marketing sophistication.

12.3   MARKETING RESEARCH BEGINS AT HOME

This is certainly true for industrial marketing research. Industrial organizations are likely to put far more reliance on the use of internal staff and internal records as a major source of research information. Market intelligence will also form a more significant aspect of the marketing information system than in consumer organizations. This is because industrial organizations, by their very nature, are more directly in touch with their market than is usual in consumer markets, where the nature of the distribution system creates a physical separation between the manufacturer and consumers. It is therefore both more feasible and more productive for an industrial organization to organize a market intelligence system utilizing feedback from the sales force as a mechanism for reporting customer views.

12.4   'OFF-THE-PEG' RESEARCH

Desk research generally is again of far greater significance in industrial marketing than in consumer marketing. Government publications, trade information, published sources and so on, form a very important part of the data input for marketing decision-making and planning. Setting up an in-house information service to handle relevant information in such a way that it is collected, classified and retrievable is well worthwhile. This may be concerned mainly with abstracting relevant statistics on a regular basis from appropriate secondary sources, or with generating an original cuttings or abstracting service from appropriate publications. A well-organized information officer might be expected to provide both these services for the company, its markets and its industry. Advice on searching for secondary sources is largely the same as indicated in Chapter 4. The main difference will be in the types of publication found to be useful. Where the consumer researcher is interested in the census of population, for example, the industrial researcher is more likely to be interested in the census of production, and so on.

As far as syndicated and omnibus research services are concerned these are unlikely to be available in any but the largest and most sophisticated industrial markets. Some off-the-peg information is available, for example, the Businessman Readership Survey, and specialist research services discussed in Section 4.5.1.

12.5 'MADE-TO-MEASURE' RESEARCH

In carrying out quantitative surveys, industrial marketing researchers are more likely to make use of postal research and telephone research. Postal research presents itself as a fairly obvious first step for an organization new to using research. It has the attraction of economy and may be seen as particularly appropriate when address lists of the population to be sampled are readily available, such as, lists of customers. It is also particularly suitable for gathering basic market data and very often in industrial marketing research this is what is required. Its limitations as to representativeness of respondents when response rates are low must, however, be considered. There is some evidence to suggest that as industrial organizations become more regular users of research they are less likely to be users of postal research methods.

Telephone research has traditionally been an important technique for industrial marketing research and has only in the past few years been applied in consumer marketing research in the United Kingdom. Its major advantage over the use of personal interviewing in industrial marketing research is that a geographically dispersed sample can be more economically contacted. It can produce better response rates than postal research, and many industrial repondents will give a brief telephone interview where they would be unwilling to see a personal interviewer.

The most frequently used technique of qualitative research in industrial marketing research is depth interviews, rather than group discussions. This is a result of the simple practical difficulty involved in getting eight industrialists in the same room at the same time for the purpose of a research group discussion. This is not to say that group discussions in industrial marketing research are not used or are not useful, but simply that depth interviews are more readily obtained. Also in industrial marketing research, expert informants in particular fields of industrial marketing are more likely to be of value in providing information than is the case in most consumer markets. For this reason, too, depth interviews at the exploratory stage of research study are of particular significance in industrial marketing.

12.6   HOW ARE THE DATA COLLECTED?

The last section indicated that the research techniques more heavily used in industrial markets than in consumer markets are postal research, telephone research and depth interviews. Having said this, the manner in which these and other research techniques are applied in industrial markets is similar to that in consumer markets and is covered in Chapter 6.

12.7   WHO PROVIDES THE INFORMATION?

Sampling methods discussed in Chapter 7 are also used in industrial marketing. Random probability sampling is only possible when a comprehensive sampling frame (or list of all members of the population to be sampled) exists. In some industrial markets such lists do exist and are used as the basis of random probability sampling. Business direct-ories are often used for this purpose, or internal lists such as customer lists or business mailing lists. Stratification as a sophistication of random sampling and to some extent quota sampling are also practised in industrial marketing research. In this case the allocation of sample segments would be based on appropriate industrial criteria like SIC (standard industrial classification) or size of organization in terms of turnover, or number of employees, and so on. When applied to customer lists, stratification is used in order to ensure appropriate representation of large, medium and small customers.

A difficulty that exists in industrial sampling, which is not apparent in consumer sampling, is who is actually to be asked the questions. The sampling procedures described above may produce the name of the firms to be sampled, but the industrial marketing researcher has also to be concerned with which individual in the firm should be asked the questions or to whom should a postal or telephone enquiry be addressed? It is often a problem in industrial marketing research to know who might be the correct individual for any particular enquiry. This is further complicated by the fact that in different organizations the same functional responsibility may be held by individuals with different job titles. Only experience in a particular market area can suggest who the most likely prospects might be. Even so, problems in this area are notoriously difficult to resolve. Some filtering or screening questions at the start of a questionnaire may help to identify the qualifications of the respondent in terms of their appropriateness to complete the interview. If a postal questionnaire is sent to the firm, the covering letter should make it very clear who the ideal respondent in the firm would be.

12.8 HOW ARE THE QUESTIONS ASKED?

Problems of question and questionnaire design discussed in Chapter 8 hold equally for industrial marketing research.

12.9 WHO ASKS THE QUESTIONS?

Here industrial marketing research differs from consumer research in that it is more likely that the researcher will be a member of the organization's own staff. This is particularly so when the interviews are depth interviews with expert respondents, as in an exploratory market survey. In this case, the company researcher may wish to carry out these interviews personally as a briefing background in order to acquire greater insight into the market being studied.

Some industrial organizations have used sales personnel in order to carry out research interviews, but there are dangers in doing this. The first is that sales personnel are rarely sufficiently objective to make good researchers. The second, that although the use of sales personnel makes the research appear very cheap, once the opportunity cost of loss of selling time is costed into the procedure, then specialist industrial marketing research interviewers appear to be a more economical and effective means of gathering the required information.

There are a number of research organizations which specialize in industrial marketing research and these carry special teams of industrial interviewers who are generally more qualified than consumer research interviewers and better able to obtain co-operation from industrial respondents. For certain technical enquiries it may be necessary for interviewers to have particular specialist background qualifications, and these are often available from specialist industrial research organizations. When this is not the case a more comprehensive briefing should be given to interviewers than would be usual in consumer research surveys.

12.10   WHAT HAPPENS TO THE ANSWERS?

Techniques for analysis of both qualitative and quantitative data are as described in Chapter 10 and hold equally well for the results of industrial marketing research surveys.

12.11   HOW DO YOU BUY GOOD RESEARCH?

Systematic procedures for identifying, evaluating and selecting a marketing research agency are equally applicable in industrial markets as described in Chapter 11. The main differences are that in many technical industrial markets characterized by relatively few and highly specialized potential customers it may be more likely that the company's own research department will handle any depth interviewing required. It is also more likely that industrial companies will make use of industrial marketing research consultants for guidance on specific 'made-to-measure' projects, rather than establish an in-house research department. The search for appropriate industrial researchers can be extended from the Market Research Society book of 'Organisations providing market research services' to the Industrial Marketing Research Association (IMRA) directory 'European Guide to Industrial Marketing Consultancy' which is published every two years. Organizations interested in industrial marketing research should consider joining IMRA as an appropriate specialist body which is a source of useful information and relevant training courses. They can be contacted at 11 Bird Street, Lichfield, Staffordshire WS13 6PW (Tel: 054 32 23448).

12.12   USING RESEARCH IN INDUSTRIAL MARKETS

A study published by the Industrial Marketing Research Association in 1966 indicated that the following industries were most active in their use of marketing research, ranked by rate of use: chemicals and allied industries, vehicles, engineering and electrical goods, construction, food drink and tobacco, metal manufacturers. The same report indicated that companies using marketing research are those characterized by financial and capital intensity rather than by numbers of employees. Uses to which industrial marketing research was most likely to be put were, again in order of importance:

sales forecasting
analysis of market size
trends in market size
estimating demand for new products
competitive position of company products
determining characteristics of markets

determining present uses of existing products
studying economic factors affecting sales volume
general business forecasting
evaluating proposed new products and services.

This list indicates the relatively limited range of applications for marketing research in industrial markets as compared to consumer markets. In the years since that survey was published, the use of marketing research in industrial markets has grown and its range of applications gradually spread. Nevertheless marketers in industrial organizations are still less likely to be using marketing research data than their counterparts in consumer product and service industries.

12.13   SUMMARY

The use of marketing research in industrial markets is growing, but there are some differences in emphasis in the way in which techniques outlined in this book are applied. This chapter considers each of the previous chapter topics in turn and points out ways in which there are similarities or differences for using research in industrial markets.

13 Using Research in Experiments

13.1 INTRODUCTION

Experiments are used when some decision is under consideration and the results cannot be predicted from existing experience either of the organization itself, or of the activity of other organizations within the market-place. Experiments attempt to measure change under, as far as possible, normal market-place conditions. The problem is that they are expensive and can disclose plans to competitors. It may also be difficult to achieve normal market-place conditions on a sufficiently small scale for the exercise to be considered an experiment rather than a 'suck-it-and-see' trial. Experiments should normally be confined to situations where the expense and effort involved is calculated to be more than compensated by the outcome of the experiment. This should be estimated beforehand. It should also be determined that the information could not be gained any other way. For example, by monitoring similar approaches by other companies, comparison with other markets, re-analysing existing data from past or syndicated surveys. Given that experiments are thought to be worthwhile, a number of approaches are possible.

Two types of market experiment can be used prior to new product launching: *experimental launching* or *pilot launching*. For existing products, market tests may be either *specific* or *exploratory*. If an experiment is to be carried out, then the type of experimental design to be used must be decided, and this may be: *ex post facto, split-run, before-and-after with or without control*, or a *formal experimental design* based on statistical theory. Some factors to be considered in setting up research experiments are discussed, and two syndicated research services available for testing purposes are described. This chapter draws on the work of two good, but statistically based books in this area, and both are fully referenced in the list of further reading for those wishing for further guidance in particular areas. They are *Experimental Marketing* by E. J. Davis, and *Experimentation for Marketing Decisions* by K. K. Cox and B. M. Enis.

13.2   TYPES OF RESEARCH EXPERIMENT

13.2.1   *EXPERIMENTAL LAUNCHING*

This can also be called the 'projectable test launch'. It represents the most demanding type of market experiment because it is used to project the results from those achieved in the test area to what might be expected following national launch. In order for such projections to be made with any degree of accuracy it is necessary that the experimental procedure be statistically designed and rigorously controlled. Validity of the test procedure and accuracy in measurement are essential if usable projections are to be achieved. The difficulty and expense involved in carrying out a projectable test launch has led to a situation in which this kind of major test launch procedure is used less commonly than it was. Its main objective was to produce a sales projection with sufficient accuracy for a go/no go decision to be made for the product, based on sales profitability forecasts. In practice, inadequacies in procedure, or simply changes in the market-place, made statistical calculations very difficult. An absolute measure of the product's likely success in the market-place cannot necessarily be achieved.

13.2.2   *PILOT LAUNCHING*

This has a less demanding, and therefore more easily achievable, objective than experimental launching. In this case, the decision to launch the new product has already been made. The aim of the pilot launch is to introduce the product into a limited area in order to test various aspects of the marketing approach, such as the price, the advertising, the distribution method, and so on. A pilot launch is often the first stage in a 'rolling launch'. In this case, the new product is launched into one area, measurements are taken about its performance in that area, and the marketing strategy modified accordingly. The product is then launched into a neighbouring area, and so on, rolling out to cover the whole country. Decisions about whether this product form is better than that, whether this package is more successful than that, whether this price commands higher sales volume than that, can quite reasonably be made as the launch is under way.

13.2.3 SPECIFIC MARKET TEST

This is used for market testing of some aspect of an existing product's marketing mix. Some specific decision is to be made, and the experiment is required to predict the outcome of that decision. Once again, when prediction is involved, the need for rigorous control of the experimental situation, experimental validity, and accurate measurement, are demanded.

13.2.4 EXPLORATORY MARKET TEST

This type of market test is more exploratory. It involves testing a number of possible variations in the mix in order to discover which alternatives might produce better results. This kind of comparative testing is more amenable to experiment than the predictive type.

13.3 TYPES OF EXPERIMENTAL DESIGN

13.3.1 INFORMAL EXPERIMENTAL DESIGNS

These designs are termed 'informal' because no statistical

control is exercised over the variables under test, and no calculation can be made of experimental error.

Ex post facto measurement (after-the-event measurement)
This approach can hardly be called an experimental design since it involves measurement of a situation only after a decision has been made and implemented. For example, awareness might be measured using omnibus survey questions following an advertising campaign. The difficulty with this approach is that although the level of awareness at the end of the campaign is known, the prior level of awareness is not known, and therefore the results of the advertising campaign cannot be assessed. This is not the case, of course, when some new activity has been undertaken and an 'after-the-event' measure of awareness is, in itself, indicative of the results of the action. A measure of the awareness of a product name after its launch will evaluate the success of the product in penetrating market consciousness. It will not indicate what aspect of the marketing plan has been successful in doing this, for example, whether it was through the advertising or distribution or sales activity.

Split run (side-by-side) measurement
In this approach half the sample gets one treatment and the other half another, perhaps different prices, or different advertising messages. At the end of the experiment, measurement is taken of both halves of the sample and any differences between them are assumed to be the result of differences in treatment. Difficulties can arise in interpreting data from this type of experiment when, for example, sales increases are observed of a similar order yet the price levels being tested were different. This is usually because some other, more relevant, factor in the market-place has changed over the period of the test. It might be a change in weather, or change in general economic circumstances of consumers.

Before-and-after without control
This involves commencing the experiment with a 'bench mark' measurement survey. The test treatment is then applied, for example, perhaps an advertising campaign or change in distribution. The measurement survey is repeated at the end of the period. The advantage of the before-and-after measurement is that change during the period of the test is measured. However, the same difficulty as in the last example exists, that the change could be due to the operation of variables not part of the test.

After only with control
In marketing experiments the difficulty always exists that variables not under the control of the marketing manager will often affect results of any marketing activity. The use of control areas in marketing experiments will give an indication of the effect of these other, or exogenous, variables. The test is applied in only one area, but measurements are taken in two areas. The assumption then is that any difference between results in the control and experimental areas is due to the effect of the experiment. The problem remains that no base-line measurement is available.

Before-and-after with control
This is the most sophisticated of the informal experimental designs. It measures change only during the period of the test and takes into account both test variables and exogenous variables by the use of a control area.

13.3.2 FORMAL EXPERIMENTAL DESIGNS

These designs are research methods based on statistical principles. This means that in analysing the results not only the result of the experiment can be calculated, but also an estimate can be made of the degree of experimental error in the procedure. Formal experimental designs therefore do for market experimentation what random probability sampling does for sample selection. It allows the experimenter not only to calculate the results of his experiments but also to calculate the probability that the results are good within specified limits of accuracy, at a given confidence level. Since the declared aim of this book is to explain marketing research procedures without going into statistical detail, it would not be appropriate to explain how the formal experimental designs are constructed. This is explained well in Cox and Enis, referenced in Chapter 15. The non-statistical research user should simply take note of the fact that the use of appropriate statistical techniques in the design of market experiments can increase the number of variables that can be tested in one experiment, allow for calculation of experimental error, and assess the interaction effects. The price which must be paid for these benefits, is in terms of design complexity and, of course, cost. Four designs are introduced:

Completely Randomized Design

This allows experimental error to be calculated for the treatment effect only.

Randomized Blocks

This technique allows for experimental error to be calculated for the treatment effect and one other variable.

Latin Square Design

Conducting an experiment using this system allows two different treatment effects to be measured at the same time.

Factorial Design

This is the most complex of the formal experimental design methods. It allows the effect of a number of different treatment factors to be measured, and it also measures the interaction effects between them. Since there is considerable interaction in the market-place between marketing variables and exogenous variables, this type of research design comes closest to representing the real-life situation which the product will face in the market-place.

13.4   SETTING UP RESEARCH EXPERIMENTS

13.4.1   *SELECTING THE EXPERIMENTAL DESIGN*

Three factors must be taken into account in selecting the appropriate experimental design. First, there is the need to measure the change generated by the test; secondly, the need to assess the reliability of the results; and thirdly, the need to be able to project results with sufficient accuracy to meet the experimental objective. The greater the need for each of these to be achieved, then the more complex the experimental design must be.

13.4.2   *THE SCALE OF THE EXPERIMENT*

In determining how big the experiment must be, there is a trade-off between smallness, which equates with cheapness, and largeness, which equates with increasing reliability. Whether cost or reliability of data is the more compelling criterion will be decided by the nature of the experiment and its significance to the organization.

The scale of the experiment may also be influenced by the size necessary to produce a representative experimental area. Sometimes this can be done by simply using a group of shops or outlets for the product, or by using test towns. On a larger scale, ITV areas are used for experimenting with consumer products, and sales districts may be used for experiments with industrial products.

The size of the test area will also be influenced by its need to be representative in ways appropriate to the experiment. This may mean representative of characteristics of users, (whether they be consumer or industrial), distribution channels, sales of the product group, sales force capacity, or representative in terms of media coverage.

13.4.3 CHOOSING THE TEST AREA

Area selection is influenced by most of the considerations discussed in the last section. The area selected should be of sufficient size to achieve the test objectives. It should also be representative in appropriate ways as described in Section 13.4.2. It is helpful if the test area is not too popular as a test market, since this can result in unrepresentative behaviour in the market–place. Generally speaking, test areas must be selected in such a way as to give a reasonable representation of what might be expected of the product from a national launch.

If control areas are to be used, these should match the test areas as closely as possible. The same measurements are taken in both areas, and this makes it possible to isolate effeccs of the test from the general effect due to market change in both areas during the period of the test. Multi-area testing is more efficient than single-area testing in detecting change due to the experiment, but has the disadvantage of increasing cost.

13.4.4 TIMING

The longer a market experiment is continued, then the greater the probability that it will give a correct prediction of results. Set against this is the fact that the longer a product is in test market the greater the risks of disclosure to competitors. This raises the possibility that they may copy the product, and launch it nationally, before, or not very long after, its originator. Also, the longer the product is in test, the greater is the cost of the experiment. The question must be asked whether the additional information generated by increasing the length of test is worth the additional cost. It is usually necessary to stay in test for long enough to be able to calculate initial penetration data for the brand and repeat purchasing rates. The length of time will therefore be indicated by the normal pattern of repeat purchase of the product under test. Both items of data are necessary for an ultimate brand share to be estimated.

13.4.5 TEST CONDITIONS

One of the difficulties in marketing experimentation is being able to scale down all aspects of the marketing plan. There may be a particular problem in replicating the advertising support a brand would get on national launch, particularly if a mini-test procedure is being used. Some allowance therefore needs to be made for what difference this would make in acceptance of the product. When company, and particularly sales, personnel are involved in market tests then there is sometimes a problem in persuading them of the need to conduct a test under normal conditions. There is a very human tendency to give extra effort to support the product under test, particularly when it is known that the results of those efforts are being carefully monitored! There is also rarely such a thing as 'a fully representative test market'. To the extent that the test does not replicate the normal marketing conditions for the product then allowance must be made for differences between test performance and what would actually happen in the market-place. It is this area of subjectivity in extrapolating potential market outcome from experimental procedures that has led to a growth in smaller testing procedures, rather than the large scale, expensive and often unreliable projectable test launches.

13.4.6 TEST VARIABLES

In any research experiment there are three types of variable, as follows.

Independent variables
These are the subject of the experiment. They must be held at known levels in order for response to them to be measured. Examples are price, advertising, distribution

level, and so on.

Dependent variables
These are the factors which are measured in assessing the outcome of the experiment. Commonly they are sales measures such as factory shipments, retail store audit data, consumer panel data, levels of awareness, trial, repeat purchase, distribution levels. It is helpful to collect more than one type of data in evaluating the outcome of the experiment, since this will not only increase confidence in the measures but may also prove diagnostic. For example, if both product penetration and advertising awareness are collected it may be that a high level of awareness is associated with a low level of penetration. This would indicate that the advertising is not communicating a desirable message. Alternatively, a low level of awareness may be accompanied by a low level of penetration and here the problem may simply be insufficient advertising. If repeat purchasing levels are also taken then this adds further insight into performance. High levels of penetration accompanied by low levels of repeat purchase suggest the advertising is communicating desirable messages, raising expectations which the product in practice is not delivering. Alternatively, low levels of penetration accompanied by high levels of repeat purchase would indicate that the advertising is probably insufficient, but that once individuals are persuaded to try the product they like it sufficiently to buy it again.

Data is likely to come from one of three sources. Sales data, such as factory shipments and retail audits. Generally factory shipments are not a very satisfactory measure of sales response since they are separated from actual market behaviour by the length of the distribution chain and this can mask actual market movements. Retail audits are a better indicator of actual consumer take-off of the product. The second source of data is consumer panel data. This provides cumulative penetration data, and repeat purchasing rates. From these two measures an estimate of ultimate brand share can be calculated. The third type of data is that from 'usage and attitude' studies. These are consumer surveys which measure awareness of the product and its advertising, the extent of purchase and usage of the product, repeat purchase, frequency of purchase, amounts purchased, and opinion of and attitudes towards the product.

Exogenous Variables
These are the factors which effect the experiment but are not part of it. For example, the effects of competitive activity during the period of the experiment is bound to affect sales, as will changes in the economic environment, the weather, and other exogenous (outside) variables. In most markets the exogenous variables are more influential on sales than those that can be controlled by the marketeer. For this reason control areas are used in market testing to allow an estimate to be made of the influence of exogenous variables.

13.4.7 COST

In calculating the cost of marketing experiments an estimate must be made not only of the research costs involved but also of the costs of preparing appropriate product samples or samples of other test material. A possibly more important factor involved in calculating the cost of marketing experiments, and one often overlooked, is the opportunity cost of delay whilst the product or change is under test. The point of experimenting is in order to minimize losses if the experiment turns out to be a failure. The larger costs which would be incurred on a national scale are reduced. However, if the experiment turns out to be successful and the new product or product change is subsequently introduced to the market, there will be an opportunity cost in the sales, which have been foregone on a national scale for the period for which the product has been under test. This opportunity cost may also be reflected in the fact that competitors may hear of the test and be in a position to copy a successful product prior to its national launch.

13.4.8　SYNDICATED TEST PROCEDURES

In the fast moving consumer goods market, two standardized procedures are available for brand share prediction prior to product launch.

The Mini test market

This is a consumer panel of 1000 housewives split between two areas of the country, and selected to be representative of households in the North and the South of the United Kingdom. Panel members agree to do their regular weekly shopping in a mobile van carrying some 1500 lines representative of supermarket stock and priced accordingly. Members of the panel are sent a monthly catalogue featuring the items that are available and an order form is completed each week with items delivered from stock held in the van. This system can be used to test any aspect of the marketing mix proposed for the launch of a new product, together with some measurement of likely penetration and repeat usage of the product.

Area Marketing Test Evaluation System (AMTES)

This system uses multiple regression analysis (discussed in Section 10.3.3), to identify variables which show an association with changing sales levels. The most commonly used inputs are retail selling price, weight of advertising, and percentage distribution for a test brand and its competitors. The significance of these variables is calculated by analysing past panel data. Once these relationships are known they can be used to forecast the next period's expected sales in the test area. For that period a test is run. Actual sales achieved in the test area are then compared with forecast sales. Any difference can be assumed to be the result of the test treatment and this can then be used to predict the effect on national sales if the change is launched on a national basis.

13.5 SUMMARY

Research experiments can be used to predict the outcome of marketing decisions, or to test the effects of changes made in a product or its marketing mix. Four types of research experiment are described. Informal experimental designs are not statistically based, and a range of approaches from simple to more complex are discussed, with brief mention being made of the statistically-based formal experimental designs. The chapter concludes with a discussion of factors to be considered in setting up research experiments.

14 Using Research in Marketing Decision-Making

14.1 INTRODUCTION

This chapter consists of a set of 'guides' for research users. The purpose of these guides is to introduce the new research user to some of the common marketing problems to which research is applied, and in each case to suggest a data requirement and data sources. To use the guide, read down the following list and if one of the problems shown is close to your needs then look up the data requirement suggested. If this also meets your needs, then the problem could be tackled using the research approaches suggested under 'data sources'. Each data source mentioned is referenced back to its description elsewhere in the book. Some specific terms and techniques used in this section are explained in notes which follow the guides at the end of the chapter.

RESEARCH USERS' GUIDES

GUIDE 1

Using research for market analysis (section 14.2)
Where do our products/services stand in the market?
Should we enter a market?
Should we withdraw from a market?
What different market segments exist and how do they
    differ?
What different needs, motives, satisfactions could my
    product/service gratify?

GUIDE 2

Using research to develop new products and services (section 14.3)

Generating ideas for possible new products or services

Selecting the most promising ideas for further development

Identifying target market segments and appropriate appeals

Developing product attributes, design and formulation

Testing the marketing plan

Testing different marketing strategies

Predicting market sales

GUIDE 3

Using research to select brand names and pack designs (section 14.4)

Which name to choose for a new product or service?

Which pack and pack design to use for a product?

GUIDE 4

Using research for pricing decisions (section 14.5)

What price to charge for a new product or service?

What is the actual selling price for our product in retail outlets?

What is the actual selling price for competitive products in retail outlets?

GUIDE 5

Using research for decisions about advertising
Before an advertising campaign (section 14.6)

Who would the advertising be aimed at?

What should the advertising be saying?

How much should we spend on advertising?

Which media should the advertisements go in?

How much should we spend in the media?
How much space and time should be bought?
How much should we spend in the media?
Which advertisements to use?
After an advertising campaign
Were our advertisements seen?
Has the advertising worked?

Notes for Guides 1–5 appear at the end of Chapter 14.

14.2   GUIDE 1: USING RESEARCH FOR MARKET ANALYSIS

PROBLEM

Where do our products/services stand in the market?
Should we enter a market?
Should we withdraw from a market?

Data requirement (Market size and structure)
How big is the market?
How profitable is the market generally?
Is the market growing or declining?
What are the main products in the market?
Who are the major competing firms in the market?
What is the distribution pattern?
What marketing strategies are used in the market?

Data sources
Secondary desk research; Government and other published statistics, information services (*see* Section 4.2).
Syndicated research services: if available for this market. Consult index and MRS (*see* Section 4.3).
Omnibus survey: to collect basic market data. Only possible for markets in which this service operates. Consult index and MRS (*see* Section 4.4).

PROBLEM

What different market segments exist and how do they differ?

Data requirement
Market characteristics

Data sources
Secondary desk research: *see* 'Information about markets' (Section 4.2.3) for sources like Mintel, Retail business, etc.

Syndicated research services: TGI, Retail Audits, etc. (Section 4.3).

Omnibus survey: for basic data on market characteristics related to product attributes. Only possible if this service operates in the market. Consult index and MRS (*see* Section 4.4).

PROBLEM

What differing needs, motives, satisfactions could my product/service gratify?

Data requirement
Characteristics and attitudes of users and potential users.

Data source
'Made-to-measure': market segmentation study (*see* Notes for Guide 1, Section 14.7) psychographic market analysis (*see* Notes for Guide 1, Section 14.7).

14.3 GUIDE 2: USING RESEARCH TO DEVELOP NEW PRODUCTS AND SERVICES

PROBLEM

Generating ideas for possible new products or services.

Data requirement
New and creative ideas and suggestions.
Identify areas of unfilled customer need.
Brand mapping to identify possible market gaps (gap analysis).

Data sources
Synectics: (*see* Section 6.2.4).
Group discussions: (*see* Section 6.2.4).
Depth interviews: (*see* Section 6.2.1).
'Made-to-measure' market survey: usage and attitude study (*see* Notes for Guide 2, Section 14.8).

PROBLEM

Selecting most promising ideas for further development.

Data requirement
Need to identify big, growing, profitable, not-too-competitive, relatively easy-to-enter markets.
i.e: market size, structure, characteristics, trends, profitability, competitors, basic market facts.

Data sources
(*See* 'using research for market analysis', Guide 1.)
Secondary desk research (Section 4.2).
Syndicated research services (Section 4.3).
Omnibus survey (Section 4.4).

PROBLEM

Identifying target market segments and appropriate appeals.

Data requirement
Reaction of different consumer groups to product appeals.
General consumer response and characteristics.
Identification of market segments.

Data sources
Made-to-measure research surveys.
Concept tests (*see* Notes for Guide 2, Section 14.8).
Group discussions (*see* Section 6.2.4).
Quantitative attitude survey using factor and cluster analysis (*see* 'psychographic market analysis' in Notes for Guide 1, Section 14.7).

PROBLEM

Developing product attributes, design and formulation.

Data requirement
Consumer response to product attributes.
Data on product quality and attributes in use.
Product performance tests.
Comparative product performance.

Data sources
Specialist research services for product testing (*see* Section 4.5).
'Made-to-measure' research surveys for product testing.
Test centres, hall tests, mobile vans, using monadic tests, or paired comparisons, blind testing (*see* Notes for Guide 2; Section 14.8).
In-home placement tests (*see* Notes for Guide 2; Section 14.8).
Test panels (*see* Notes for Guide 2; Section 14.8).

PROBLEM

To test marketing plan.
To test different marketing strategies
To predict market sales.

Data requirement
Consumer reactions to elements of marketing mix: product, price, promotion.

Rate of purchase of product (penetration level).
Pattern of repurchase of product.
Pattern of retail sales.
Consumer reactions to different marketing strategies.

Data sources
Research experiments using:
Specialist research services for market testing (*see* Sections 4.5 and 13.4.8).
Consumer panels (*see* Sections 4.3 and 6.4).
Mobile shop/van purchasing panels (*see* Notes for Guide 2; Section 14.8 and Section 13.4.8).
Matched area/town tests (*see* Notes for Guide 2; Section 14.8).
Retail outlet test stores (*see* Section 4.5).
'Made-to-measure' research surveys with users, buyers (*see* Chapter 5).

14.4 GUIDE 3: USING RESEARCH TO SELECT BRAND NAMES AND PACK DESIGNS

PROBLEM

Which name to choose for a new product or service?

Data requirement
Is the name easy to pronounce?
Does the name suggest any associations or expectations?
Does the name carry any, and/or appropriate, imagery?
Is the name easily recognized?
Is the name easily recalled?

Data sources
Specialist research services (*see* Section 4.5.1).
'Made-to-measure' research surveys, usually small scale, using pronunciation, name association, name imagery, recognition and recall tests (*see* Notes for Guide 3; Section 14.9).

PROBLEM

Which pack and pack design to use for a product?

Data requirment

Does the pack 'stand out' in a display?
Is the pack easily recognized?
Is the pack easy to open, use, and close if necessary?
Does the pack design communicate positive messages?

Data sources

Specialist research services (*see* Section 4.5.1).
Consumer surveys to measure:
'Attention' value (*see* Notes for Guide 3; Section 14.9).
'Identification' score (*see* Notes for Guide 3; Section 14.9).
Test centres, hall tests or mobile van tests: for functional performance e.g. ease of opening, understanding of pack instructions, (*see* Notes for Guides 2 and 3; Sections 14.8 and 14.9).
In-home placement tests: for performance in normal use (*see* Notes for Guides 2 and 3; Sections 14.8 and 14.9).
Group discussions, depth interviews: for package concept association tests.
Consumer survey using attitude rating scales for pack designs (*see* Notes for Guide 3; Section 14.9).
Pseudo product-test: to uncover pack communication value (*see* Notes for Guide 3; Section 14.9).

14.5   GUIDE 4: USING RESEARCH FOR PRICING DECISIONS

PROBLEM

What price to charge for a new product or service?

Data requirement

What prices are competing products selling for?
What price would consumers expect to pay?

What price would consumers be prepared to pay?
What quantities are likely to be sold at different price levels?

Data sources

Secondary desk research: recent market reports, or trade sources, may provide information on the price structure of a market (*see* Section 4.2).

Observation research: a simple DIY exercise on price range and 'ruling prices' (*see* Notes for Guide 4; Section 14.10).

Syndicated research services: retail audits provide price and quantity of sales in the markets they cover (*see* Section 4.3, and Notes for Guide 4; Section 14.10).

Specialist research services: pricing is offered as a research specialism by some agencies (*see* Section 4.5.1).

'Made-to-measure' research surveys: using 'buy-response' method, and/or 'propensity to purchase' (*see* Notes for Guide 4; Section 14.10).

PROBLEM

What is the actual selling price for our products in retail outlets?
What is the actual selling price for competitive products in retail outlets?

Data requirement

Prices charged for our product in different retail outlets.
Prices charged for competitive products in different retail outlets.

Data sources

Observation research: a simple, but limited, DIY exercise in local retail outlets (*see* Notes for Guide 4; Section 14.10).

Syndicated research services: retail audit data for markets covered by this service (*see* Section 4.3).

14.6 GUIDE 5: USING RESEARCH FOR DECISIONS ABOUT ADVERTISING

1 Using research before an advertising campaign

PROBLEM

Who should the advertising be aimed at?
What should the advertising be saying?
How much should we spend on advertising?

Data requirement

How big is the market/potential market?
What are the demographic characteristics of users/potential users?
What are the demographic profiles of different market segments?
What are the behaviour and attitudes of different market segments?
What language do consumers use in talking about the product field?
Are we under-represented in particular market segments or geographic areas compared to our competitors?

Data sources

Secondary desk research; especially market reports and trade press data (*see* Section 4.2).
Syndicated research services: e.g. MEAL, (*see below*) consult index and MRS (*see* Section 4.3).
Omnibus research: for basic market data (*see* Section 4.4).
'Made-to-measure' research surveys: group discussions (Section 6.2.4), quantitative 'usage and attitude' surveys (*see* Notes for Guide 2; Section 14.8).

PROBLEM

Which media should the advertisements go in?
How much space and time should be bought?
How much should we spend in the media?

Data requirement

How big are the media audiences?

What are the demographic characteristics of the media audiences?

Which media do our market targets use?

How much do advertisements cost to place?

Which media do our competitors use?

How much are our competitors spending?

Data sources

Secondary desk research: BRAD (British Rate and Data) 76 Oxford Street, London W1N 0HN. Publishes three directories giving comprehensive information on media, annuals, advertisers and agencies.

Syndicated research services: BARB, JICMARS, JIC-NARS, JICRAR, TCA, TGI (*see* Section 4.3) Businessman Readership Survey (from Research Services Ltd, Wembley. Tel: 01 903 8511)

MEAL (Media Expenditure Analysis Ltd), London (Tel: 01 240 1903) Continuous information on advertising expenditure (at rate card costs) for individual brands. Includes national advertising in press, magazines, television and regional newspapers. Covers 350 product groups in 22 industry categories.

PROBLEM

Which advertisement to use?

Data requirement

Consumer response to advertisement ideas/roughs:

Do they understand the advertisement correctly?

Can they recognize it easily?

Can they remember it easily?

Do they like the advertisement?

Does it give positive associations and imagery to the product?

Does it make them want to buy the product?

Data sources

Specialist research services: some research agencies specialize in advertisement testing (*see* Section 4.5.1).

'Made-to-measure' research surveys: usually small-scale
qualititative research using recall tests, recognition tests
(*see* Notes for Guide 5, Section 14.11) group discussions
or depth interviews for comprehension, liking, positive
associations and imagery. Projective techniques may be
used. (*see* Sections 6.2.3 and 6.2.4, and Notes for Guide 5;
Section 14.11).

'Hardware' techniques occasionally used for advertisement testing are 'eye-camera', 'tachistoscope', 'psychogalvanometer' (*see* Notes for Guide 5; Section 14.11) area
testing using quantitative techniques (*see* Chapter 13).

2 Using research after an advertising campaign

PROBLEM

Were our advertisements seen?
Has the advertising worked?

Data requirement

Did the media chosen reach the target audience?
Did we get good value for our media expenditure?
Are more of our target audience aware of the brand name?
Can more of the target audience remember the brand name?
Does the target audience have more favourable attitudes
toward the brand?
Do more of the target audience intend to buy the product?
Have more of the target audience bought the product?
Have more of the target audience used the product?

Data sources

Syndicated research services: *see* under 'advertising' and
'media' (*see* Section 4.3) for relevant syndicated services:
advertising measurement services e.g. TABS; product
panel data, retail audits; media measurement services e.g.

BARB, JICNARS.

Omnibus research surveys: for advertising 'tracking' studies (*see* Notes for Guide 5; Section 14.11). Repeated measurement of brand recognition, recall.

Specialist research services: for measuring advertising effectiveness (*see* Section 4.5.1).

'Made-to-measure' research surveys: measuring recall, recognition, attitude, pre- and post-advertising to detect shifts, (*see* Notes for Guide 5; Section 14.11), coupon enquiry counts from keyed advertisements, sales enquiry counts post-advertising, point-of-purchase research to measure intent-to-buy, area testing (*see* Chapter 13).

14.7   NOTES FOR GUIDE 1

MARKET SEGMENTATION STUDIES

These are research surveys designed to discriminate between consumers and identify different market patterns, or segments. Segmentation criteria should predict or explain market differences and be exploitable in practice. The traditional segmentation criteria are geographic (North/South), demographic (sex, age, social grade, income, marital status, number and ages of children) and product usage (heavy *v*. light buyers). In each case, collecting data using the criteria listed will increase understanding of relevant characteristics of buyers.

A more complex, but very revealing type of segmentation analysis is termed 'psychographics'. This term distinguishes the approach from 'demographics' which use general 'people' characteristics. 'Psychographics' are concerned with people's subjective attitudes to, and feeling about, specific products or services. It produces multi-dimensional groupings which are often highly explanatory of actual market behaviour.

PSYCHOGRAPHIC MARKET ANALYSIS

Background

To carry out this type of study, some background knowledge of the market is needed, including purchasing profiles and ways in which the brands are used. From this a topic guide can be developed for use in qualitative research.

Qualitative Research
Group discussions or depth interviews are used to develop ideas about different market groupings, indicate the language consumers use about the market and brands in it, and suggest attitude statements for developing measuring instruments.

Developing Measuring Instruments
To quantify market segments large-scale questionnaire surveys are necessary. The long list of attitude statements from qualitative research must be reduced to those which are most discriminatory. A quantitative survey with factor analysis of the results will reduce the list of specific attitude statements to more general 'factors' relevant in the market place. Alternatively, the list may be reduced through piloting and subjective analysis.

Identifying Customer Groupings
The developed questionnaire containing the final short list of relevant attitude statements is administered to a statistically significant representative sample. The statistical technique of cluster analysis is then applied to the results, and this will identify sub-groups of consumers with shared attitudes in the market-place. Psychographic analysis indicates target groups in the market, and may suggest new products which would appeal to them. Alternatively, it can suggest which appeals would be most attractive to different groups in the market.

14.8   NOTES FOR GUIDE 2

DECISIONS ABOUT PRODUCTS AND SERVICES

Major decisions about the nature of products or services to

be offered by an organization are normally taken prior to development. After the product has been launched on to the market, modifications may be made to the product/service attribute mix to appeal to different market segments or for different applications. Guide 2 concentrates on the uses of research in new product development but the techniques suggested are, of course, also used to test product modifications during its market life. The scheme outlined suggests a theoretically ideal approach to the process of new product development. Not all products or services do, or should, go through all stages using the research techniques suggested in the Guide. This format is intended to offer an outline approach, which may be of value to the new research user, and should certainly be adapted to meet any specific requirements of the product, service or market under consideration. Notes explaining some of the specific techniques referred to in the Guide follow.

Usage and attitude study

The typical 'U and A' study is a quantitative survey involving around 1500 respondents to allow for analysis of sub-groups of the sample. The questionnaire will include general questions on use of brands in the product group, attitudes towards the product group and one or two brands within it. Usually, the brand leader and the brand being researched.

Test centres

These are used for product testing when the product is too large, too expensive or too complicated to be taken to consumers for testing. One or more test centres will be set up and a representative sample of consumers brought to the test centre for exposure to the product and questioning about their reaction to it.

Hall tests

These are commonly used for product testing or testing other aspects of the marketing mix such as advertising, price, name and package testing. A representative sample of target consumers are recruited, usually in a shopping centre, and brought into a conveniently located hall. Here they are exposed to the test material and asked questions about it.

Mobile vans
These are used for similar purposes to hall tests, but employ a motorized caravan which can be parked in a shopping centre.

Monadic tests
The respondents are given only one product to try, and asked their opinion of it. This is the normal situation in real life when a consumer tries a new product and draws on recent experience with the product they usually use, to judge the test product. The method is not very sensitive in comparing the test brand with other brands because of this.

Paired comparisons
A respondent is asked to try two or more products in pairs and asked, with each pair, to say which they prefer. This is less 'real' in terms of the way consumers normally use products, but does allow products to be deliberately tested against each other.

Blind testing
Refers to testing products in plain packages and without brand names. The package and brand name heavily influence product perceptions. Blind testing is used when factors such as taste, smell, texture, preference are to be measured comparatively without this brand influence e.g. in testing a new brand against the brand leader. However, a 'dressed' test must be made at some stage since this will be an important factor in the market-place.

In-home placement test
Used when an impression of how the product performs in

normal use is required. The product (or products if a comparative test is being carried out) are placed with respondents who are asked to use the product in the normal way and complete a questionnaire about it, which is collected or posted back after the test. Products may be tested 'comparatively' i.e. two or more products are left at the same time, and respondents asked to compare them; or 'sequentially' where first one product is left and after testing replaced with another.

Test panels
Representative panels are recruited (*see* Section 6.4) and used for product testing. Many companies who carry out a lot of new product development and testing use panels for this purpose. Once the panel is recruited, test materials and questionnaires can be sent through the post, which cuts down the cost of conducting in-home placement tests. Industrial and service firms may also have test panels of customers or intermediaries with whom new product or service ideas or prototypes can be tested.

Concept tests
Qualitative techniques, especially group discussions, are used to obtain target customer reactions to a new idea or product. Question areas would cover: understanding and believability of the concept, ideas about what it would be like, how it might be used, when and by whom. This would suggest the most promising appeals of the new product, and groups to whom it might appeal.

Matched area/town tests
The marketing strategy or tactic under test is applied in two or more areas or town. The areas or town are selected to be representative of the target market and similar to each other. Differences in test treatment can then be applied and the results measured, e.g. different advertising, price, pack, etc. Area/town test facilities may be offered by media owners (e.g. ACE listed in Section 4.3) or by specialist

research services (*see* Section 4.5.1).

14.9   NOTES FOR GUIDE 3

DECISIONS ABOUT NAME AND PACKAGING: NAME TESTING

Debate continues in the marketing world about just how important the 'right' name is in contributing to the success of a product or service. Both sides can point to names which have been a help or a hindrance to marketing appeal. Some argue that with sufficient advertising support any name can be made to work for the product or service. Others, that if a name is to be given advertising support, then it surely makes sense to ensure that the name has at least no readily uncovered negative associations. Out of this debate, some generalizations about choosing the name for a product or service can be made.

First, the name should be consistent with the overall marketing strategy for the product. This implies that any research about names should start with a clear statement of the marketing objective for the brand.

Secondly, the name should be easy for its target market to read and pronounce in a consistent way. (How *do* you pronounce 'Lancôme' or 'Meux' in Friary Meux?)

Thirdly, the name should project desirable associations for the product, and have no negative associations.

Fourthly, any imagery associated with the name should be appropriate for the product, its use and its target users.

Finally, it helps if the name is easily recognized and recalled. These aspects of naming are amenable to research testing, as listed in Users' Research Guide 3, and explained in the following notes.

Ease and consistency of pronunciation

A short list of possible names is produced, which repondents read aloud, often on to a tape recorder. Ease of, and variations in, pronunciation can be observed.

Name associations

Following the use of a few practice words, the respondent is required to freely associate with the test name by giving all the thoughts and ideas that occur after hearing the name. Time for response and verbatim response are both recorded. The length of time taken to respond is thought to indicate blocking or emotional response to the name. Content analysis of verbatim responses indicates positive or negative associations, related or unrelated imagery, and any spontaneous expectations about the product, arising from the use of a particular name.

Further product expectations which might be associated with the name can be generated by reading the test names and asking respondents to suggest what kind of products they might be names for.

Name imagery

Respondents are given a card listing the test brand names. The interviewer reads out a series of attribute statements – (e.g. 'would be a luxury product') and respondents say to which names on the list they feel the statement most applies.

Name recognition and recall

The extent to which a brand name is easily recognized in a pack display, and its name recalled, is best tested as part of the overall packaging for the product, since that is how it will be seen by consumers. Package testing is considered in the next section.

PACKAGE TESTING

Package design has grown in importance with the growth of self-service shopping. Increasingly, the pack has to do the job the sales assistant used to do in terms of drawing attention to the product, communicating its salient features and presenting it in its most favourable light to the target buyer and user. In addition to these new functions, the package also has to fulfil its traditional role of containing, protecting, and sometimes storing the product, yet allowing it to be extracted by the user with the minimum of frustration. The need for all these functions to be performed effectively in more and more markets is increased as the self-service concept has extended from consumer-goods supermarkets to consumer durables, builders merchants, cash and carry wholesalers, office suppliers, travel agents and many other market areas. The three aspects of package design described above are tested in the following ways.

Attention Value　The degree to which a pack is able to draw attention to itself and communicate its salient features when surrounded by competing packs is tested on two factors: 'stand out' and 'identification'.

'*Stand out*' is defined as the attention-getting value or impact of the pack when seen in a competing display, and is measured by 'find time'. Respondents are shown usually six realistic-looking product displays with the test pack present and three in which it is absent, the order of presentation and test item being varied for different respondents. Minimum average time in seconds taken to identify the test item is used as the criteria for 'stand out' or 'attention' value.

'*Identification*' is related to the respondents' ability to recognize the brand and the readiness with which salient messages on the package are absorbed. This is measured using a 'tachistoscope': a device which displays a picture for a specific length of time, which can be varied. The respondent is shown a picture of the pack for time periods of, say, 1/100 of a second up to 2 seconds. After each exposure the respondent reports what has been seen. This indicates the readiness with which various aspects of the pack, including the brand name, are identified. The technique can be used to test different pack designs, colours, brand names, messages and so on.

Functional Performance　The ability of the packaging to contain, protect and store the product is obviously testable without the need for consumer research. Where consumers' views are relevant in pack design is in ease of opening, convenience in use, and suitability for closing and re-opening if the product is used in that way. For this reason functional performance tests must attempt to replicate in-use conditions.

Products which are opened and consumed only once can be tested in the *test centres, hall tests* or *mobile vans*. Ring-pull cans were tested against tear-off tag cans by inviting consumers into mobile vans to try the two opening devices. Film cameras recorded the manner in which respondents handled and opened cans. A similar approach might be used to test whether package instructions are read, and how readily they are followed.

Products which are used over time must be tested by *in-home placement tests*. The packaging is usually plain or 'blind' to eliminate 'symbolic interference' from the brand name or pack design. The now familiar 'flip-top' packaging of cigarettes was developed in this way. The product is left with the respondent to use under normal conditions. Often two packs will be tested: either two test-pack variants, or test-pack against the current pack, or competitor's pack. At the end of the period the respondent is asked which packaging is preferred, and why.

Communication Value   The introduction to this section on package testing pointed out that an important function for packaging, particularly if sold in a self-service context, is to communicate positive messages about the product to the buyer or user. This is measured in two ways: package concept association tests and pseudo-product tests.

Package concept associations are generated using small-scale qualitative research procedures such as group discussions or depth interviews. Respondents are shown the packet and asked what thoughts come to mind as they look at it, what kind of product might be in it, who might use the product, and how, and what type of shop they would expect such a product to be sold in. This exploratory research may be used to generate a range of attitude statements about the product, its attributes and its appeal to users. These statements could then form the basis for rating scales to be applied in a quantitative questionnaire survey with respondents being asked their degree of agreement with each statement related to a particular pack design.

The pseudo product – test procedure measures the degree to which the communication value of the package affects respondents' perceptions of the product it contains. A representative sample, often 200–400 consumers will be given two packs of the product to use, either side-by-side or one after the other. Respondents are asked to compare the products inside and rate them for various attributes like taste, quality, strength, etc. In fact, the only difference lies in the packaging. In a beverage test 75% respondents reported one version of the 'product' to be more acceptable than the other on taste, when the only difference lay in the packaging. Both these types of communication value tests demonstrate the high level of influence which packaging may exert over physical perception of contents. In the first case, consumers form quite well-developed expectations about the product and its attributes from looking at packaging, and this must be expected to have an influence on their decision to purchase. The second goes one stage further in demonstrating that liking or disliking of the product in use may be modified by the pack it comes in.

14.10   NOTES FOR GUIDE 4

DECISIONS ABOUT PRICE

Research is only one input into a company's decision about the price of its products. Other important factors will relate to the cost of production, profit objectives set by the organization for its products, and perhaps the overall financial health of the organization. However, price is an important determinant of whether, and how much of, a product can be sold. For this reason most organizations will want information on the price of products in the market-place and on consumers' response to different price levels.

Observation research
Market price can be determined using desk research or straightforward observation. This will indicate the highest and lowest market prices at which the product is sold and the range of pricing in between. The 'ruling' price for a market is not necessarily calculated by a straight arithmetic average of the prices available. It is usual to take into account the fact that the ruling price in a market may be determined by the brand leader, particularly when the brand leader has a high level of market dominance. Ruling price may be calculated by multiplying market share by price, to produce a weighted average.

Syndicated research services
Another source of information about price, including different pricing for different packs in different outlets, is by buying syndicated data. Most retail audits provide information of this type. These sources of data will give a clear indication about competitive pricing in the market-place and will therefore suggest guide-lines appropriate to pursuing different marketing tactics. It will indicate the price levels relevant to pursuing a premium policy or a cut-price strategy.

Consumer price responsiveness
This is useful when attempting to estimate a sales forecast, or to indicate the effect on sales volume of a possible change in price. Two techniques can be applied in attempting to determine consumer propensity-to-purchase products at different prices.

Buy-response research
The 'buy-response method' embodies the idea of price as an indicator of quality. It recognizes that there is a price below which consumers would not be prepared to buy the

product, because they would distrust its quality, and that there is a price above which consumers would not be prepared to buy the product, because they would believe it to be too expensive for its worth. This results in 'buy response curves', which map the probability that respondents will buy the product in the range of prices between the minimum and the maximum. This is discovered using a quantitative survey in which respondents are asked whether they would buy the product at up to ten different prices, which cover the range between the minimum and the maximum. A curve is then drawn of probability of purchase against price. For products entering into existing markets, respondents could also be asked the 'price last paid' and this too would be charted. Analysis of the charts produced from this procedure is thought to indicate optimum price levels.

Propensity-to-purchase research
Attempts to calculate consumers' propensity to purchase a product at different price levels have used mock selling situations. At the end of product tests, and sometimes at the end of concept tests, the interviewer may offer to sell a pack of product to the respondent. Different respondents are offered packs at different price levels. The frequency with which they agree to buy at different price levels is recorded and this is thought to give some indication of the product's worth to relevant consumers.

14.11 NOTES FOR GUIDE 5

Research about advertising may be used before, during, or after an advertising campaign, and if the campaign is of sufficient significance it may be worthwhile using all three.

PRE-CAMPAIGN RESEARCH

This is useful to assist in defining the problem which the advertising campaign may seek to solve, to guide creative strategy development and indicate the type and level of advertising which might be required. The objectives for research before a campaign are to increase the effectiveness of the campaign when it does run, to screen out any negatives in ideas being considered, and to select the best of those possible. Those who argue against pre-campaign research do so on the grounds that it is generally artificial and limited in nature.

RESEARCH DURING CAMPAIGN

This is most likely to be carried out for a long running and important campaign in which specific objectives for levels of awareness have been set. The use of 'tracking studies' during the campaign monitors performance and allows fine tuning if, say, objectives are being achieved in one area and not in another. Resources can be re-allocated to compensate for this.

POST-CAMPAIGN RESEARCH

This measures the degree to which advertising objectives set for the campaign have been achieved. The argument for post-campaign research is that feedback from one campaign becomes input for improving the next. The argument against it is that spending research money after the media money has been spent is futile. Research money is more constructively spent in guiding decision-making prior to advertising campaigns rather than assessing performance afterwards.

FACTORS TO CONSIDER

Which research technique will be appropriate for any particular advertising problem will depend on: the objective and significance of the campaign under consideration, the amount of uncertainty about the brand and the market segment, and the possible outcomes of advertising expenditure. Also relevant will be the purpose for which the research is being used. Research for creative development is typically small scale. It uses qualitative methods which are relatively quick and inexpensive but rich in insight, ideas and depth. For targeting, media planning and campaign evaluation, large-scale quantitative surveys or syndicated data are more commonly used.

At a more sophisticated level, when attempts to measure or predict the effects of particular advertising approaches are required, then some form of research experiment is normally indicated.

The use of experimentation in research may employ any of the data–collection methods discussed. The key feature lies in the approach, structure and design of the research procedure. Experiments are normally used when the decision-maker has more than one option open to him, and requires data on the possible outcomes of alternative strategies. The implication of this is that the research design must be sufficiently rigorous to ensure that valid comparisons can be made. Using research in experiments was discussed more fully in Chapter 13.

RECALL TESTS

Respondents are exposed to test or actual advertisements for a specific period of time and then asked what they remember from the advertisement. Used in both pre- and post-testing of advertising.

Unaided recall
Respondent spontaneously recalls advertisements and their content from a test selection, or from memory of actual advertising or product classes. Thought to measure levels of awareness and brand salience of advertising.

Aided recall
Respondent is shown a selection of advertisements or cards with brand names on (usually after a campaign has been

run) and asked which advertisements they have seen. Thought to measure campaign penetration. Problems exist in using recall as a measure of advertising effectiveness because brand leaders have higher levels of recall, advertising seen in one medium may be reported as having been seen in another, and effects of earlier advertising campaigns may be difficult to distinguish from effects of current campaigns. Respondent variability in memory may also influence results. Generally, recall is best used as a comparative measure ie. repeat same test on different occasions and measure differences.

Recognition

Mainly used in post-testing advertising. For print media, respondents are taken through a current issue of a magazine or newspaper they report having read and asked to say which articles and advertisements they looked at. Items are 'scored' for their degree of readership: 'noted', 'seen-associated' (saw advertisement and associated it with correct brand name), 'read most' (read advertisement in some detail). These are called 'Starch scores' after the man who invented the method, now used as the basis for the Gallup Field Readership Index. For television, respondents are shown pictures from television commercials which may or may not have been shown in their areas, and are asked whether they saw the commercials. Recognition scores are thought to measure campaign penetration.

Comprehension

Respondents are asked what they feel the main points, which an advertisement was trying to make, are.

ADVERTISING 'HARDWARE' TESTS

A few experimental measuring devices have been applied in communications or advertising research. The method involves connecting the respondent to the appropriate piece of hardware which measures the degree of reaction.

Inevitably, such experiments can only be conducted on a small scale, and the artificiality of the laboratory type of situation under which the experiment is conducted, gives rise to the concern that the results cannot be validly generalized to the real-world situation under which advertisements are normally seen. However, given the very high levels of media expenditure necessary for mass-advertised products, it seems reasonable to attempt what experiments are possible to ensure that the layout and content of the advertisement selected should be as effective as possible. These techniques are most useful in a minor diagnostic way, and are generally applied on a very small scale, if at all.

Eye camera

This device records the passage of the eye as it looks at a test advertisement. It indicates where the eye falls first, the path it takes around the advertisement, where it lingers, and what it misses altogether. The combination of this technique with subsequent recall questioning indicates how effective parts of the advertisement have been in communicating with the respondent.

Tachistoscope

This device exposes test material such as an advertisement logo, brand name, or pack design, to the respondent for a period of time measured in one-hundredths of a second. The amount of time for which the respondent can observe the test material is gradually increased, and after each exposure the respondent is asked to report what has been seen. It is assumed that the most effective advertisements are those in which the respondent most quickly reports perceiving the name of the product, the pack in a competing display, and so on. This is a useful technique for improving advertisement and display design if its basic assumption is accepted. There is some evidence that advertisements which are not rapidly perceived but are studied in detail can also be effective, so the decision-maker must decide whether this device is relevant to the objectives of his communication.

Psychogalvanometer
This is the same device used as a lie-detector. It is attached to the hand, and measures electrical skin resistance. Skin resistance varies with the amount of moisture, (sweat) present on the skin, and this varies with the degree of emotional arousal in the individual. When used to test advertisements, the psychogalvanometer is therefore measuring the degree to which the advertisement affects the individual emotionally. Since an important objective of some advertisements is to create the emotion of liking for the product, this can be a useful test, particularly when combined with the individual's self-report of whether or not the advertisement was liked.

Advertising 'tracking' studies
Measurement of awareness, penetration or liking are taken regularly using a quantitative survey to 'track' changes over time. A special syndicated service may be used (e.g. British Market Research Bureau's (BMRB) 'Advertising Planning Index' (API), Market and Opinion Research International's (MORI) 'Corporate Image Survey, Television Advertising Bureau (Surveys) Ltd (TABS) 'On-Air' Panel. Alternatively, the same questions may be regularly added to an Omnibus Survey. If sufficiently important, an organization may decide to commission a regular 'made-to-measure' survey to track advertising performance. This would normally be combined with research into other aspects of the product.

14.12 SUMMARY

Research applications in marketing decision-making are considered by identifying marketing problems and suggesting data requirements and sources used in providing research data to help solve them. Five areas are covered:

market analysis, developing new products and services, selecting brand names and pack designs, pricing decisions and advertising decisions. The research approaches suggested are referenced back to explanations given earlier in the book, or to the Notes which accompany each Guide, and appear at the end of the chapter.

15 Where Do You Go From Here?

15.1 INTRODUCTION

This book introduces marketing research:

	Chapter
What marketing research is	1
Why an organization needs it	2
What research can be carried out within an organization	3
What research data is already available	4
How research surveys are carried out	5–10
How research services are bought	11
How research is used	12–14

Where you go from here depends on:

15.2 WHO YOU ARE, AND IN WHICH DIRECTION YOU WANT TO GO

15.2.1 WHO YOU ARE

You may be a manager in some specialist area of marketing, or a manager in some other functional area working for a consumer organization, a service organization, an industrial organization or local or central government. Your motivation for buying *Marketing Research for Managers* is your desire to use marketing research techniques appropriately and intelligently in improving your decision-making.

A second possibility is that you are a junior manager or aspiring junior manager, perhaps a management trainee.

You have been assigned some responsibility in the research area in your organization and feel that you would like to do some marketing research yourself on behalf of your organization.

A third possibility is that you are pursuing studies in the business area and wish to know more about marketing research, either because of its value as a managerial tool, or because you wish to pass the marketing research component of your examination system.

15.2.2   IN WHICH DIRECTION DO YOU WANT TO GO?

A title like *Marketing Research for Managers* implies the first step in the development of your knowledge and expertise in this area. There are two directions in which that development might go. Either you may concentrate on developing your use of marketing research techniques for decision-making in whatever area you may operate managerially (i.e. develop as a research user), or you may wish to concentrate on marketing research and become a specialist in that area of management (i.e. develop as a research practitioner). Let us look at the implications of both these possibilities. These are shown in Figure 15.1, and discussed in the following sections.

15.3   DEVELOPING SKILLS AS A RESEARCH USER

STEP 1

Decide whether you already have sufficient background information and experience to use market research intelligently. If the answer is 'no' then you need more information and/or experience. More information can be gained about the subject by going on to read books which deal with the topics introduced in this one, in more detail and in more depth.

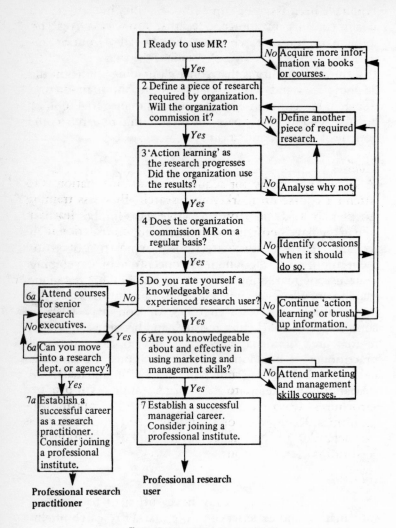

Figure 15.1 Where do you go from here?

Further reading
Using books as a basis for acquiring more information is cheap and time-efficient, in the sense that you can acquire the information at your convenience. However, they suffer from being only a one-way source of communication and impose the self-discipline and lack of interaction of learning alone. The booklist shown at the end of this chapter suggests further reading which follows on from this introduction to the subject.

Courses
A second possibility for acquiring more information is to attend a course on marketing research. Business training courses provide a more effective 'hot-house' learning situation than is possible when acquiring information from books. They are also two-way communication systems, in which it is possible to tailor the information to meet precise requirements by the simple expedient of asking questions of the lecturer. Another advantage of attending courses is the enormous amount of learning which goes on from inter-actions with other delegates to the course.

The Institute of Marketing, The Market Research Society and The Industrial Marketing Research Association all run courses and seminars on aspects of marketing research. An enquiry to these organizations will produce brochures describing their course and seminar pro-grammes. Keep an eye on the business and marketing press for details of other management training organizations and institutions, and the courses they offer.

STEP 2

If and when the answer to step 1 is 'yes' then the next stage is to define a piece of research required by your organization which will be of indisputable value to it. Chapter 2 should assist in this process. Indentify an important decision that has to be made by the organization and indicate in writing exactly how the use of marketing research will improve the decision-making situation. Use this as a basis for lobbying the purse-string holders above you, in favour of commissioning a marketing research survey. Repeat the process on appropriate occasions, as suitable decisions arise within the organization for which you believe marketing research could provide a valuable input, until you are successful.

STEP 3

Once your organization has approved the commissioning of a marketing research survey you are in a position to design an 'action learning' programme for yourself. This is done by using Chapter 11 to ensure that a good research organization is commissioned for the survey. As each stage of the survey in action unfolds, practice your new found research skills by making 'shadow' decisions and comparing them with those which the research agency advocates. For example, you will set out in writing your research objectives and survey objectives drawn from that. In commissioning the research programme from two or three agencies, discussions with research professionals may cause you to revise your list of objectives. As you do so, take note of your reasons for the revision and what you can learn from that.

The next stage will be the choice of research method. Prepare a research design plan independently from the agency and, when they return with their research proposals, compare them with your own. Did you suggest the same research design as the professionals are suggesting to you? If not, why not? Whose are more likely to achieve the stated research objectives most effectively and most efficiently? You may feel that the research agency's suggestions are better than your own, in which case you will have learnt why in analysing the basis for your feeling. The possibility exists, however, that you may believe your own suggestions would improve upon the research design suggested by the agency. In this case you have the basis for an extremely constructive discussion with the research agency.

The next stage is questionnaire design – repeat the process. In either case you win. Either the agency's questionnaire is better than yours and you can learn from that, or you have suggestions which would improve the questionnaire produced by the agency, and your company gains better research from that.

When it comes to field-work, spend a day or two in the field with interviewers to get the feel of the raw data-gathering process. You will learn something about interviewing techniques, but you will learn even more in terms of insight and understanding which will be of great value to you in interpreting findings at the end of the research survey. At the data analysis stage visit the agency and talk with them about their systems for data preparation, processing, editing, coding, tabulating and statistical analysis. Talk through with the researcher what tables and statistical analysis will be most appropriate and most helpful in dealing with the data they have generated.

Finally, sketch out for yourself how you would write the report on the research and, before the actual report is written, discuss with the research agency executive his own approach to report writing. Once again, you will either learn from his experience or be in the position to improve what the research agency is about to do for you.

STEP 4

If you took enough care at the outset to ensure that the research being conducted was going to be of real value to decision-making in the organization, then the outcome will be that your organization will find that research has a positive, constructive and cost-effective role to play in its decision-making procedures. Once this idea is accepted within an organization, then commissioning a research survey the next time around becomes normal operating procedure.

STEP 5

By repeating the same action learning programme suggested above on subsequent surveys you will eventually get to the point where you are either coming up with the same recommendations which research professionals would make, or better. At this point you are ready to bring in other individuals to work for you and to establish a research department in your own organization simply by buying in field-work, data processing, and other research 'commodities' as you require them.

STEP 6

Once you are a confident, experienced and knowledgeable research user, the next step is to develop and improve your analytical and decision-making skills by attending senior management courses dealing with any of the particular problems you may have or skills you may wish to acquire. For example, new product decision-making, advertising, pricing, and so on. As your analytical and decision-making business skills improve, so will your confidence and career prospects.

STEP 7

As a last stage in being a marketing professional you may decide to join a professional institute such as the Institute of Marketing. Information about the costs and benefits of this organization can be obtained from them.

15.4   DEVELOPING SKILLS AS A RESEARCH PRACTITIONER

Follow Steps 1–5 as in Section 15.3.

STEP 6a

Develop and improve your research skills by attending

courses for senior researchers on techniques and applications. The more sophisticated your professional development as a researcher becomes, the more likely it is that you will be interested in building up and heading your own research department within an organization. Alternatively, you may wish to switch into a research agency and become a professional researcher.

STEP 7a

The professional institute for marketing researchers is the Market Research Society or the Industrial Marketing Research Association and you should consider joining one of these organizations in order to pursue your interests in this area.

15.5   PASSING EXAMINATIONS

This book has been approved by both the Institute of Marketing and the CAM (Communications, Advertising and Marketing) Foundation as being appropriate for students of their examinations. It should also prove helpful to students following degree courses, BEC courses or other general courses in business or management. For students taking a specific marketing research examination, it is unlikely that, from the technical point of view, reading this book alone will prove sufficient preparation. Particularly, the subjects of sampling and data analysis have not been treated in the statistical manner required for most examination courses. Marketing research students are therefore strongly advised to do more specific statistical studying in these areas, using the recommendations given in the booklist at the end of this chapter.

15.6   FURTHER READING

BIASED TOWARDS RESEARCH IN CONSUMER MARKETS

Crimp, M. *The Marketing Research Process* (Prentice/Hall International, Hemel Hempstead, 1981).

Worcester, R. M. and Downham, J. (eds.) *Consumer Market Research Handbook*, 2nd edition (Van Nostrand Reinhold, Scarborough, CA, 1978).

BIASED TOWARDS RESEARCH IN INDUSTRIAL MARKETS

Rawnsley, A. (ed.) *Manual of Industrial Marketing Research* (Wiley: Chichester, 1978).

ON SPECIFIC ASPECTS OF RESEARCH TECHNIQUE

Hoinville, G., Jowell, R. and Associates *Survey Research Practice* (Heinemann Educational Books, London, 1978).

Oppenheim, A. N. *Questionnaire design and attitude measurements* (Heinemann Educational Books, London, 1966) (a classic).

Wolfe, A. R. (ed.) *Standardised Questions* (The Market Research Society, 1974).

MacFarlane-Smith, J. *Interviewing in Market and Social Research* (Routledge and Kegan Paul, London, 1972).

Ehrenberg, A. S. C., *A Primer in Data Reduction* (Wiley, Chichester, 1982).

Cox, K. K. and Enis, B. M. *Experimentation for Marketing Decisions* (International Textbooks, London, 1973).

Davis, E. J., *Experimental Marketing* (Nelson, London, 1970).

ON APPLICATIONS OF RESEARCH

Bradley, U. *Applied Marketing and Social Research* (Van

Nostrand Reinhold, Scarborough, CA, 1982).

White, R. *Consumer Product Development* (Pelican, Harmondsworth, 1976).

Broadbent, S. (ed.) *Marketing Researchs Look at Advertising* (Sigma, Albrighton, 1980).

Davis, M. P., *The Effective Use of Advertising Media* (Business Books, London, 1981).

ON MARKETING MANAGEMENT

Willis, G., Cheese, J., Kennedy, S. and Rushton, A. *Introducing Marketing* (Pan Books, London, revised, 1984).

Oliver, G. *Marketing Today* (Prentice Hall International, Hemel Hempstead, 1981).

Chisnall, P. *Effective Industrial Marketing* (Longman, Harlow, 1977).

Index

Peter F. Drucker
Management £3.95

Peter Drucker's aim in this major book is 'to prepare today's and tomorrow's
managers for performance'. He presents his philosophy of management,
refined as a craft with specific skills: decision making, communication, control
and measurement, analysis – skills essential for effective and responsible
management in the late twentieth century.

'Crisp, often arresting . . . A host of stories and case histories from Sears
Roebuck, Marks and Spencer, IBM, Siemens, Mitsubishi and other modern
giants lend colour and credibility to the points he makes' ECONOMIST

Managing in Turbulent Times £1.95

This is Peter Drucker's latest and probably most searching analysis of the
problems and opportunities facing us as managers and individuals. This timely
and important book considers how to manage the fundamentals of business –
inflation, liquidity, productivity and profit – going on to demonstrate how
tomorrow's manager must concentrate his skills on managing innovation and
change – production sharing, new markets, redundancy planning, the
developing countries, transforming businesses to take account of changes in
the world economy.

The Effective Executive £1.95

'A specific and practical book about how to be an executive who *contributes* . . .
The purpose of this book is to induce the executive to concentrate on his own
contribution and performance, with his attention directed to improving the
organization by serving outsiders better. I believe Mr Drucker achieves this
purpose simply and brilliantly – and in the course of doing so offers many
insights into executive work and suggestions for improving executive
performance. I can conscientiously recommend that this book be given the very
highest priority for executive reading and even rereading' DIRECTOR

John Fenton
The A–Z of Sales Management £2.50

A book for the sales manager determined to succeed. This humorous yet highly practical book covers the ins and outs of managing a sales force from Advertising to Zest, taking in all the vital aspects: credit control, meetings and conferences, decision-making, sales forecasting, remuneration schemes, job specifications, motivation, planning and control, leadership, expense accounts and – last but not least – how to achieve consistently good sales results.

How to Double Your Profits Within the Year £2.50

A programme of improvements, applicable to all types of business, to help you at least double your profits within twelve months. Fictional but highly practical, the book is an extended memorandum, an action plan, written by the MD of an imaginary company to his top managers. It shows, for example, how you can choose which customers contribute most to your profitablity; recruit the right people; improve production efficiency; price for maximum profit; control your sales force. In the few hours it takes to read the book, you will be convinced that the title's claim is a modest understatement.

James Lynch
Making Manpower More Effective £2.50
a systematic approach to personnel planning

Few organizations prosper without competent staff, yet many businesses attach little importance to personnel strategy. They pay the penalties of unsuitable employees, inefficiency and loss of markets. James Lynch emphasizes the value of careful manpower planning in this practical, jargon-free guide, showing how to build a workforce geared to company needs through selection, training and performance appraisal. No aspirant to business success can ignore this book's message.

Rosemary Stewart
The Reality of Organizations £1.95

'Addressed to managers whether in industry, commerce, hospitals, public administration or elsewhere and includes examples from these latter fields . . . its style is excellent, concise and free of jargon' PUBLIC ADMINISTRATION

The Reality of Management £1.95

'Not just another manual for executives, it is rather more like a set of compass bearings to help the manager plot his course in his career and his social life' NEW SOCIETY

David Floyd
Making Numbers Work £2.95
an introduction to business numeracy

A book to introduce the basic skills of business numeracy and explain how to apply them. An ideal text for the BEC General Module on Business Calculations, it also meets requirements of BEC National Module on Numeracy and Accounting, RSA Arithmetic Stages I, II and III and relevant parts of RSA Stage I Mathematics.

A Pan Breakthrough book, published in collaboration with the National Extension College.

David Field
Inside Employment Law: A Guide for Managers 2.50

A succinct guide to all the principle areas of employment law: the legal framework; contracts of employment; payment of wages; health and safety; trade unions and more. *Inside Employment Law* will provide the manager, as well as trade unionists and students, with a comprehensive knowledge of the complexities of the laws governing modern employment. This book will help today's manager avoid the pitfalls of ill-informed action.

Inside Business Law £2.50
a guide for managers

If you are a manager, you cannot hope to become a legal expert in a short time. Nor would you probably wish to be. This book gives a clear explanation in simple language of how the law affects a manager's work and how you can avoid the thousands of legal pitfalls waiting if you are not prepared for them. It explains basic legal principles affecting such areas as making a contract, industrial tribunals, competition law, consumer protection, sex discrimination, health and safety.

Terry Rowan
Managing with Computers £2.95

A book to dispel the myth that computers are special and that they deserve special treatment. *Managing with Computers* helps managers recognize the powerful capabilities of computers and how they can be usefully exploited; what systems are available and the tasks they can perform; how managers can select the source of computing power most suitable for their needs; the essential steps in implementing and developing a computer system; and how a business may need to adapt itself to the presence of a new computer. An invaluable guide to an indispensable management skill.

John Winkler
Bargaining for Results £2.50

Skilful bargaining is crucial to business success, especially when money is tight. John Winkler, one of Britain's leading marketing experts, presents the key to effective negotiation – the methods to adopt and when to employ them. The approach is highly practical, using case histories, illustrations and helpful maxims in a book specially designed for business managers.

Pricing for Results £2.95

Bad pricing decisions ruin the sales prospects of any product. The author's unique appreciation of the price mechanism has served him to win many commercial battles. Here he passes on his expertise, in an approach recommended for all finance and sales directors/managers, key account negotiators, general managers and marketing students. How to set prices; how to present prices; how to discount prices; how to negotiate prices. The concluding Free Chapter shows how to organise for pricing decisions once the Winkler techniques are mastered.

John Etor and Mike Muspratt
Keep Account £2.95
a guide to profitable bookkeeping

Introduces and explains the basic principles of profitable bookkeeping. An ideal text for BEC General level Accounting GCE O level Accounts and RSA Stage 1 Bookkeeping syllabuses, it will also serve students on foundation courses for professional accounting qualifications.

A Pan Breakthrough book, published in collaboration with the National Extension College.

Peter Clark
Using Statistics in Business 1 £2.95

Volume *1* shows how to acquire, judge and apply statistical information.
Especially suitable for statistics courses at BEC National level in Numeracy and
Accounting, RSA Stage II and LCCI Intermediate, it will also serve students of
professional syllabuses: Institute of Chartered Accountants, Institute of Cost
and Management Accountants, Institute of Chartered Secretaries, and
Association of Certified Accountants.

A Pan Breakthrough book, published in collaboration with the National Extension
College.

Using Statistics in Business 2 £2.95

Volume *2* shows how to present and draw conclusions from statistical
information. It develops the ideas explained in volume *1*, and is especially
suitable for statistics courses at BEC National level in Numeracy and
Accounting, RSA Stage II and LCCI Intermediate. It will also serve students of
professional syllabuses: Institute of Marketing, Institute of Personnel
Management, Institute of Chartered Accountants, Institute of Cost and
Management Accountants, Institute of Chartered Secretaries and Association
of Certified Accountants.

A Pan Breakthrough book, published in collaboration with the National Extension
College.

Martin Christopher *et al*
Effective Distribution Management £1.95

Reliable and efficient distribution is crucial to business success – products must
reach their markets on time and in good condition. Efficient distribution brings
the opportunity of increased sales and lower costs. *Effective Distribution
Management* pinpoints difficulties and provides solutions in this key area of
business planning. A thoroughly practical guide, it is geared to the needs both of
managers and of students on management courses. A concise question-and-
answer format is adopted in the text, backed up by case studies which illustrate
common distribution problems.

Roger Carter
The Business of Data Processing £2.95

A comprehensive guide for managers, small businesses and students. It explains data processing systems and computer applications, with exercises for practical illustration. The book covers syllabus requirements of BEC National level Data Processing, BTEC Computer Studies, SCOTBEC Computer Studies, RSA Computers in Data Processing, LCCI Business Computing, also the data processing elements of Institute of Cost and Management Accountants, Association of Certified Accountants and Institute of Administrative Management courses.

A Pan Breakthrough book, published in collaboration with the National Extension College.

W. J. Brown
Practical Company Law £2.95

A complete guide to the moden law, incorporating key statutory provisions and leading cases. Ideal for use as a reference handbook by company secretaries, businesses and financial advisers, the book is geared to the major college and professional courses: Institute of Chartered Secretaries and Administrators, Institute of Chartered Accountants, Association of Certified Accountants, Institute of Cost and Management Accountants, Association of Accounting Technicians.

A Pan Breakthrough book, published in collaboration with the National Extension College.

John Adair
Effective Leadership £2.50
a modern guide to developing leadership skills

The art of leadership demands a keen ability to appraise, understand and inspire both colleagues and subordinates. In this unique guide, John Adair, Britain's foremost expert on leadership training, shows how every manager can learn to lead. He draws upon numerous illustrations of leadership in action – commercial, historical and military – to pinpoint the essential requirements.

Graham Mott
Accounting for Non-Accountants £2.95

A concise practical guide that provides salvation to non-accountant managers baffled by the specialist terminology and complex figures of financial statements and accounting practices. The logical coverage is backed up by numerous examples and a detailed glossary of key words. *Accounting for Non-Accountants* explains the major financial topics necessary for effective business management.

Chris Brewster
Understanding Industrial Relations £2.95

Emphasizes the importance of management's role before explaining the involvement of unions and the state. The legal framework is shown in detail and later chapters examine industrial relations in practice, at the workplace and during negotiations. Ideal for use on Institute of Industrial Management, Institute of Personnel Management and NEBSS courses and for practising managers.

A Pan Breakthrough Book, published in collaboration with the National Extension College.

All these books are available at your local bookshop or newsagent, or can be ordered direct from the publisher. Indicate the number of copies required and fill in the form below
. . . .

Name _____
(Block letters please)

Address _____

_____

Send to CS Department, Pan Books Ltd, PO Box 40, Basingstoke, Hants
Please enclose remittance to the value of the cover price plus:
35p for the first book plus 15p per copy for each additional book ordered
to a maximum charge of £1.25 to cover postage and packing
Applicable only in the UK

While every effort is made to keep prices low, it is sometimes
necessary to increase prices at short notice. Pan Books reserve
the right to show on covers and charge new retail prices which may differ from those
advertised in the text or elsewhere